The
Master
Game

The Master Game

PATHWAYS TO
HIGHER CONSCIOUSNESS
BEYOND THE DRUG EXPERIENCE

by

ROBERT S. DE ROPP

A DELTA BOOK

A DELTA BOOK

Published by Dell Publishing Co., Inc.
750 Third Avenue, New York, N.Y. 10017
Delta ® TM 755118
Reprinted by arrangement with Delacorte Press
A Seymour Lawrence Book
New York, New York
Manufactured in the United States of America
Fourth Printing

CONTENTS

The
Master
Game

I. Games
and Aims

A Game Worth Playing

THIS BOOK IS CONCERNED with games and aims.

It has been stated by Thomas Szasz that what people really need and demand from life is not wealth, comfort or esteem but *games worth playing.*[1] He who cannot find a game worth playing is apt to fall prey to *accidie,* defined by the Fathers of the Church as one of the Deadly Sins, but now regarded as a symptom of sickness. Accidie is a paralysis of the will, a failure of the appetite, a condition of generalized boredom, total disenchantment—"God, oh God, how weary, stale, flat and unprofitable seem to me all the uses of this world!" Such a state of mind, Szasz tells us, is a prelude to what is loosely called "mental illness," which, though Szasz defines this illness as a myth, nevertheless fills half the beds in hospitals and makes multitudes of people a burden to themselves and to society.

Seek, above all, for a game worth playing. Such is the advice of the oracle to modern man. Having found the game, play it with intensity—play as if your life and sanity depended on it. (They *do* depend on it.) Follow the example of the French existentialists and flourish a banner bearing the word "engagement." Though nothing means anything and all roads are marked "NO EXIT," yet move as if your movements had some purpose. If life does not seem to offer a game worth playing, then *invent one.*[2] For it must be clear, even to the most clouded intelligence, that any game is better than no game.

What sort of games does life offer? We can study Stephen Potter for tips on "gamesmanship." We can (and should) read Eric Berne on *Games People Play.*[3] If we have mathematical inclinations we can look into the work of John von Neumann or Norbert Wiener, who devoted some of their best thinking to the elaboration of a theory of games.[4] From the Hindu scriptures we can learn of the cosmic game, the alternation of *lila* and *nitya,* the Dance of Shiva, in which primordial unity is transformed into multiplicity through the constant interplay of the three *gunas.* In the works of the mystic novelist, Hermann Hesse, we can read of the Magic Theater in which all life games are possible[5] or of the game of games (*Glassperlenspiel*) in which all elements of human experience are brought together in a single synthesis.[6]

What is a game? An interaction between people involving ulterior motives? Berne uses the word in this sense in *Games People Play.* But a game involves more than this. It is essentially a trial of strength or a trial of wits played within a matrix which is defined by rules.[7] Rules are essential. If the rules are not observed, the game ceases to be a game at all. A meaningful game of chess would be impossible if one player insisted on treating all pawns as queens.

Life games reflect life aims. And the games men choose to play indicate not only their type, but also their level of inner development. Following Thomas Szasz (more or less) we can divide life games into object games and meta-games. Object games can be thought of as games played for the attainment of material things, primarily money and the objects which money can buy. Meta-games are played for intangibles such as knowledge or the "salvation of the soul." In our culture object games predominate. In earlier cultures meta-games predominated. To the players of meta-games, object games have always seemed shallow and futile, an attitude summarized in the Gospel saying: "What shall it profit a man if he gain the whole world and lose his own soul?" To the players of object games, meta-games seem fuzzy and ill-defined, involving nebulous concepts like beauty, truth or salvation. The whole human population of the earth can be divided roughly into

TABLE I

Meta-games and Object Games

GAME	AIM
Master Game	awakening
Religion Game	salvation
Science Game	knowledge
Art Game	beauty
Householder Game	raise family
No Game	no aim
Hog in Trough	wealth
Cock on Dunghill	fame
Moloch Game	glory or victory

two groups, meta-game players and object-game players, the Prosperos and the Calibans.[8] The two have never understood one another and it is safe to predict that they never will. They are, psychologically speaking, different species of man and their conflicts throughout the ages have added greatly to the sum of human misery.

All games are played according to rules. In man-made games such as poker the rules are imposed by the laws of probability (odds against a straight are 254 to 1, against a flush, 508 to 1) or they are dependent on special limitations (pawns and other pieces in chess each having its own move). In life games, rules are imposed by natural, economic or social conditions. The player must both remember the aim and know the rules. Apart from this, the quality of his game depends on his own innate characteristics.

Great chess masters are born, not made. Great football players are bound to have certain physical characteristics. The game a man can play is determined by his type (of which more later). He who tries to play a game for which his type does not fit him violates his own essence with consequences that are often disastrous.

The Low Games

The main types of life games are shown in Table I. Hog in Trough is an object game pure and simple. The aim is to get one's nose in the trough as deeply as possible, guzzle as much as possible, elbow the other hogs aside as forcefully as possible. A strong Hog in Trough player has all the qualities with which communist propaganda endows the capitalist, insatiable greed, ruthlessness, cunning, selfishness. Pure Hog in Trough is not considered entirely respectable in the contemporary U.S.A. and is generally played today with a certain moderation that would have seemed sissy to the giants of the game who savagely exploited the resources of the continent a century or so ago. The rules of the game have become more complex and the game itself more subtle.

Cock on Dunghill is played for fame. It is designed primarily to inflate the false ego and to keep it inflated. Players of Cock on Dunghill are hungry to be known and talked about. They want, in a word, to be celebrities, whether or not they have anything worth celebrating. The game is practically forced upon people in some professions (actors, politicians), who are compelled to maintain a "public image" which may have no relationship to the thing they really are. But the real player of Cock on Dunghill, whose happiness depends entirely on the frequency with which he (or she) sees his name in the papers, does not much care about public images. For him any publicity is better than no publicity. He would rather be well known as a scoundrel than not known at all.

The Moloch Game is the deadliest of all games, played for "glory" or for "victory," by various grades of professional mankillers trained to regard such killing as creditable provided those they kill favor a different religion or political system and can thus be collectively referred to as "the enemy." Moloch Game is a purely human game. Other mammals, though they fight with members of their own species, observe a certain decent moderation and rarely fight to the death.[9] But the players of the Moloch Game have no moderation. Lured on by some glittering dream of glory or power, they kill with boundless enthusiasm, destroying whole cities, devastating entire countries. The game is played so passionately and with such abandon that nothing, neither pity, decency, sympathy or even common sense, is allowed to interfere with the destructive orgy. As the devotees of the god Moloch sacrificed their children to the idol, so the players of the Moloch Game sacrifice the lives of thousands of young males in the name of some glittering abstraction (formerly "glory," now more generally "defence") or a silly phrase couched in a dead language: *"Dulce et decorum est pro patria mori."* [10] But so great is the power wielded by the players of this game, exerted through various forms of coercion and blackmail, that the thousands of young men involved make little protest. They "go to their graves like beds," not daring to expose the emptiness of the glittering words on which the Moloch Game is based.

These three games, Hog in Trough, Cock on Dunghill and the Moloch Game, are all more or less pathological activities. The players who "win" win nothing that they can truly call their own. "Hog in Trough" may emerge twice as rich as Croesus only to find himself embittered, empty and unhappy, at a loss to know what to do with the wealth he has amassed. "Cock on Dunghill" may make himself so famous that everyone knows his name only to realize that this fame of his is a mere shadow and a source of inconvenience. Players of the Moloch Game may wade in blood up to the ears only to find that the victory or glory for which they sacrificed a million lives are empty words, like richly bedizened whores who lure men to their destruction. There is a criminal element in all these games because, in every instance, they do harm both to the player and to the society of which he forms a part. So warped, however, are the standards by which men measure criminality that players of these games are more apt to be regarded as "pillars of society" than dangerous lunatics who should be exiled to remote islands where they can do no harm to themselves or others.

Between the higher and the lower games is the neutral game, the Householder Game, the aim of which is simply to raise a family and provide it with the necessities of life. One cannot call it either a meta-game or an object game. It is the basic biological game on which the continuation of the human race depends. It is also possible to find, in every human society, a certain number of nonplayers, people who, due to some constitutional defect, are unable to find any game worth playing, who are, as a result, chronic outsiders, who feel alienated from society and generally become mentally deranged, tend to become antisocial and criminal.

The High Games

The meta-games are rarely played in their pure form. The Art Game ideally is directed toward the expression of an inner awareness loosely defined as beauty. The awareness is purely subjective. One man's beauty can be another man's horror. The beautiful of one age can seem ugly to another. But bad players of the art game have no inner awareness at all. They are technically proficient and imitate those who have awareness, conforming to the fashion whatever that fashion may be. The whole Art Game, as played today, is heavily tainted with commercialism, the greed of the collector pervades it like a bad smell. It is further complicated by the tendency to show off that afflicts almost all contemporary artists, whether they be painters, sculptors, writers or composers. As all traditional concepts of the beautiful have been abandoned, anything goes, just so long as it is new and startling. This makes it almost impossible to tell whether a given work of art corresponds to some inner awareness of the artist or merely shows that he was trying to be clever.[11]

The Science Game is also rarely played in its pure form. Much of it is mere jugglery, a tiresome ringing of changes on a few basic themes by investigators who are little more than technicians with higher degrees. The Science Game has become so complex, so vast and so expensive that more or less routine enterprises are given preference. Anything truly original tends to be excluded by that formidable array of committees that stands between the scientist and the money he needs for research. He must either tailor his research plans to fit the preconceived ideas of the committee or find himself without funds. Moreover, in the Science Game as in the Art Game there is much insincerity and a frenzied quest for status that sparks endless puerile arguments over priority of publication. The game is played not so much for knowledge as to bolster the scientist's ego.

To the Art Game and the Science Game we must add the Religion Game, a meta-game played for an aim loosely defined as the attainment of salvation. The Religion Game, as played in the past, had a fairly well-defined set of rules. It was essentially a game played by paid priests of one sort or another for their personal benefit. To compel their fellowmen to play the game, the priests invented various gods, with whom they alone could communicate, whose wrath they alone could assuage, whose cooperation they alone could enlist. He who wanted help from the gods or who wished to avert their wrath had to pay the priests to obtain his ends. The game was further enlivened, and the hold of the priests on the minds of their victims further strengthened, by the invention of two after-death states, a blissful heaven and a terrible hell. To stay out of the hell and get into the heaven, the player of the Religion Game had to pay the priests, or his relatives had to pay them after his death. This "pay the priest" aspect of the Religion Game has caused several cynics to define it as the world's oldest confidence trick designed to enable certain unscrupulous individuals to make a profit out of the credulity and suggestibility of their fellowmen by interceding on their behalf with some nebulous god or ensuring their entry into an equally nebulous heaven. It was this aspect of the Religion Game that caused Sigmund Freud to exclaim, more in sorrow than anger: "The whole thing is so patently infantile, so incongruous with reality, that for one whose attitude to humanity is friendly it is painful to think that the great majority of mortals will never be able to rise above this view of life." [12]

A particularly hideous aspect of the Religion Game resulted from the insistence by certain priests that their brand of god was the only god, that their form of the game was the only permissible form. So eager were these priests to keep the game entirely in their own hands that they did not hesitate to persecute, torture or kill any who happened to wish to play the game by other rules. This practice was started by the Jews, whose enthusiasm for their one and only and very jealous father-god justified those slaughterings the accounts of which constitute so much of the bulk of the Old Testament. The practice was eagerly adopted by so-called Christians, who, not satisfied with slaughtering Moslems and Jews, turned like rabid dogs on one another in a series of ghastly religious wars, Protestant *versus* Catholic. The Moslems, who borrowed the rules of their Religion Game from Jews and Christians alike, did not fail to copy the bad habits of both. Believers were exhorted in the Koran to wage war on the infidel, the slaughter of unbelievers being defined as one sure way of gaining entry into the Moslem heaven (a much lusher paradise than the rather insipid affair offered by their priests to conforming Christians).

It would simplify our account of the games if we could offer the above description of the Religion Game without further comment. Unfortunately, this is impossible. Simply to define the Religion Game as the world's oldest con game is as "patently infantile" (to borrow Freud's words) as it is to take seriously the anthropomorphic father-god floating in his bed sheet somewhere in the stratosphere surrounded by cherubs and seraphs and other improbable species of celestial fauna (the "gaseous vertebrate" so derided by Ernst Haeckel). For it must be obvious to any fair-minded observer that there is another element in the Religion Game besides that of playing on the credulity of believers and selling them entry permits into a phoney heaven. All the great religions offer examples of saints and mystics who obviously did not play the game for material gain, whose indifference to personal comfort, to wealth and to fame was so complete as to arouse our wonder and admiration. It is equally obvious from the writings and sayings of these mystics that they were not so naïve as to take seriously either the gaseous vertebrate or heaven with its golden harps or hell with its ovens. Obviously they played the game by entirely different rules and for entirely different aims from those of the priestly con men, who sold trips to heaven for hard cash and insisted on payment in advance (no refund if not fully satisfied, either).

What game did these mystics play? Within the matrix imposed by their religion, these players were attempting the most difficult game of all, the Master Game, the aim of which is the attainment of full consciousness or real awakening. It was natural for these players to play their game within a religious matrix. The basic idea underlying all the great religions is that man is asleep, that he lives amid dreams and delusions, that he cuts himself off from the universal consciousness (the only meaningful definition of God) to crawl into the narrow shell of a personal ego. To emerge from this narrow shell, to regain union with the universal consciousness, to pass from the darkness of the ego-centered illusion into the light of the non-ego, this was the real aim of the Religion Game as defined by the great teachers, Jesus, Gautama, Krishna, Mahavira, Lao-tze and the Platonic Socrates. Among the Moslems this teaching was promulgated by the Sufis, who praised in their poems the delights of reunion with the Friend. To all these players, it was obvious that the Religion Game as played by the paid priests, with its shabby confidence tricks, promises, threats, persecutions and killings, was merely a hideous travesty of the real game, a terrible confirmation of the truth of the statement: "This people praise me with their lips but their hearts are far from me. . . . They have eyes but see not, ears and hear not, neither do they understand."

So little did they understand that, at least within the matrix of the "Christian" religion, it actually became physically dangerous during several centuries to try to play the Master Game at all. Serious players found themselves accused of heresy, imprisoned by the Inquisitors, tortured, burned alive. It became impossible to play the game openly. To survive at all, one had to adopt a disguise, pretend that one's real interest was alchemy or magic, both of which were permitted by the priests, who did not understand the real significance of either.

Alchemy was particularly safe as its stated aim, the transmutation of base metals into gold, posed no challenge whatever to the authority of the priests. Therefore it was behind the mask of alchemy that many players of the Master Game concealed their real aims, formulating the rules of the game in an elaborate secret code in which the transmutations of substances within the body were expressed in terms of mercury, sulfur, salt and other elements. There were, of course, numerous alchemists who took the whole science at its face value, who believed that the Great Work referred to the production of metallic gold, who impoverished and frequently poisoned themselves in the quest for the great secret, and incidentally laid the foundations of modern chemistry. But for the serious alchemist the transmutation involved the formation of *aurum non vulgi,* or the genesis of the homunculus, both of which symbolized the creation of fully conscious, cosmically oriented man out of the ego-centered puppet that goes by the name of man but is really only a pathetic caricature of what man could be. So well did the alchemists conceal their secrets that it took all the intuitive genius of Carl Gustav Jung (perhaps the leading authority on the subject) a large part of his life to unravel this mystery.[13]

Today no danger is involved in playing or attempting to play the Master Game. The tyranny of the priests has more or less ended. The Religion Game, though often as much of a con game as ever, is played without threats of torture and death. A good deal of the old venom has gone out of the game; in fact, it is even possible for priests who wear round their necks the label "Catholic" to be moderately polite to those who wear the once hated label "Protestant." So the game is now played with a certain amount of restraint not because men have become more tolerant, but because the whole issue of heaven *versus* hell, salvation *versus* damnation, is no longer taken very seriously. Even the theologians admit that the old father-god (Haeckel's "gaseous vertebrate") is dead as far as anyone above the Jehovah's Witness level is concerned. The fight today is between rival political systems rather than rival theologies.

But although it is safe to play the Master Game, this has not served to make it popular. It still remains the most demanding and difficult of games and, in our society, there are few who play. Contemporary man, hypnotized by the glitter of his own gadgets, has little contact with his inner world, concerns himself with outer, not inner space. But the Master Game is played entirely in the inner world, a vast and complex territory about which men know very little. The aim of the game is true awakening, full development of the powers latent in man. The game can be played only by people whose observations of themselves and others have led them to a certain conclusion, namely, *that man's ordinary state of consciousness, his so-called waking state, is not the highest level of consciousness of which he is capable.* In fact, this state is so far from real awakening that it could appropriately be called a form of somnambulism, a condition of "waking sleep." [14]

Once a person has reached this conclusion, he is no longer able to sleep comfortably. A new appetite develops within him, the hunger for real awakening, for full consciousness. He realizes that he sees, hears, knows only a tiny fraction of what he could see, hear and know, that he lives in the poorest, shabbiest of the rooms in his inner dwelling, but that he could enter other rooms, beautiful and filled with treasures, the windows of which look out on eternity and infinity. In these rooms he would transcend his petty personal self and undergo spiritual rebirth, "the rising from the tomb" which is the theme of so many myths and the basis of all the mystery religions, including Christianity.

He who arrives at this conclusion is ready to play the Master Game. But though he may be ready, he does not necessarily know how to play. He cannot draw upon instinctive knowledge, for nature has not endowed men with such instincts. She provides for man's development up to the age of puberty, she endows him with the instinct to propagate his kind, but after this she leaves him to his own devices. Far from helping man to develop further into the harmonious and enlightened being he might become, the blind force of evolution has actually put obstacles in his way.[15]

One who would play the Master Game is therefore compelled to seek a teacher, a skilled player who knows the rules. But where will he find such a teacher? A materialistic, spiritually impoverished culture can offer no instructions to the aspirant. The huge, highly specialized training centers that call themselves universities are obviously lacking in universality. They do not put the emphasis on expansion of consciousness first and acquisition of specialized knowledge second. They educate only a small part of man's totality. They cram the intellectual brain with facts, pay some lip service to the education of the physical body by encouraging idiotic competitive sports. But true education, in the sense of expansion of consciousness and the harmonious development of man's latent powers, they do not offer.

Drugs and Delusions

Because teachers are so hard to find in the West, many who wish to play the Master Game try to become their own teachers and invent their own rules. As a result, they play the game in ways which cannot possibly give right results. The commonest example of this attempt to play the Master Game by an unlawful set of rules is provided by the so-called psychedelic movement, of which the high priest, in the U.S.A. at present, is that intrepid psychologist, Dr. Timothy Leary. This particular aspect of the game is played with great enthusiasm by young people who find the accepted brands of religion devoid of nourishment and who seek in "the drug experience" satisfaction of their hunger for higher states of consciousness.

Because this "drug experience" approach to the Master Game is so popular, a good deal of prominence has been given to it in the present book. It is a blind alley, a cul de sac, a dead end, nevertheless its claims must be explored. One cannot appraise realistically any technique of altering consciousness unless one has had an opportunity to test it personally. Nor is it wise to generalize on the basis of one's personal experience, for the saying of Hippocrates applies especially to the psychedelic drugs: one man's meat is another man's poison. The prohibitive legislation now being enacted to prevent people from determining their own reactions to psychedelics strikes at one of the most fundamental of all liberties, the liberty of the individual to explore his own inner world by means of his own choosing. The legislation, moreover, by endowing the psychedelics with an aura of the forbidden, actually encourages many young people to try them, purely as a gesture of rebellion against the tyranny of so-called authorities whom they instinctively suspect to represent an assembly of the spiritually dead.

When this writer states that the taking of psychedelics is not a lawful way to play the Master Game, he speaks from his personal experience. He does not expect anyone to believe him without personally testing the correctness of the statement. An enlightened legislature would make such testing possible for people who feel this need to know more about their inner world. Instead of enacting blanket prohibitions, they would provide proper facilities under which the psychedelic experience could be studied by any who wished to find out what it had to offer in the way of insights and illuminations. Such enlightened legislation would avoid the pitfall of making psychedelics more attractive to the rebellious by endowing them with the aura of the forbidden. It would prevent a lot of dangerous experimentation with inferior black-market materials, taken without proper supervision and under wrong conditions. It would be in keeping with those guarantees of freedom of religion which figure prominently in the Constitution, for it is clear that devotees of the psychedelic cult regard the drugs as pathways to religious experience. Even the poor persecuted American Indian has been allowed by the all-powerful whites to use peyote for religious purposes.[16] If the Indian is allowed to use peyote, why forbid the non-Indian to use LSD or hashish?

None of which alters the fact that the Master Game, which involves the awakening of the powers latent in man, can no more be played by swallowing a pill than can a difficult mountain peak be ascended by sitting in an armchair drinking beer and indulging in daydreams. If the spiritual heights could be ascended by taking psychedelics, then both the Sufis of Islam and the yogis of India would long ago have discovered the fact, for the subtlest and most "spiritual" of all psychedelics (hashish) has been available in the East for centuries. But neither in the works on yoga nor in the writings of the Sufis does one find the taking of hashish described as a pathway to liberation.[17] The Sufis sing the praises of wine (forbidden by the Prophet Mohammed), but the wine to which they refer is a very special brew, the product of an inward ferment, the result of great effort and inner work. As for the yogis, they put their trust in intensive and prolonged practices designed to awaken the latent forces in man.[18]

Of this more later. Here it is sufficient to say that the Master Game can never be made easy to play. It demands *all that a man has,* all his feelings, all his thoughts, his entire resources, physical and spiritual. If he tries to play it in a halfhearted way or tries to get results by unlawful means, he runs the risk of destroying his own potential. For this reason it is better not to embark on the game at all than to play it halfheartedly.

Creative Psychology

The present book offers a synthesis of many methods derived from different sources, all of which are designed to help the practitioner to emerge from the darkness of waking sleep into the light of full consciousness. Purely for convenience, these methods are referred to collectively as Creative Psychology, creative because they bring about a higher synthesis, a new level of order within the psyche. Creative Psychology is based on the idea that man can create by his own efforts a new being within himself (the second birth). As a result, he can enjoy certain experiences, exercise certain powers, attain certain insights that are quite inconceivable to man in his once-born state.

Creative Psychology involves the highest form of creativity of which man is capable, the creation of a truly inner-directed being out of a helpless other-directed slave. This creative work involves every aspect of man's behavior, the instinctive, motor, emotional and intellectual. It involves an understanding of the chemistry of the body and of the mind. It involves a study of type and all that pertains to type, the strengths and weaknesses that type imposes. It involves a study of creative activity, arts, crafts, techniques of various kinds and of the effects these activities produce on levels of consciousness. It involves a study of events on the large scale and on the small, an awareness of the processes taking place in human and nonhuman communities that affect the individual adversely or otherwise. For man cannot be studied apart from his environment and he who would know himself must also know the world in which he lives.

The theory of Creative Psychology can be studied in books.[19] The *practice* is a different matter. For this a teacher is necessary. One who tries to practice the method without a teacher almost inevitably encounters certain difficulties which he cannot surmount. The illusion-creating mechanism in man's psyche does not cease to operate merely because a man decides to practice Creative Psychology. In fact, in such a one, it may operate all the more actively. So he may enjoy all sorts of pseudo-experiences, the result not of an expansion of consciousness but of the workings of his own imagination. A teacher can help him to sort out the true from the false, can warn him about the traps that lie in his path.

Furthermore, the solitary practitioner of Creative Psychology lives today in a culture that is more or less totally opposed to the aims he has set himself, that does not recognize the existence of the Master Game, and regards players of this game as queer or slightly mad. The player thus confronts great opposition from the culture in which he lives and must strive with forces which tend to bring his game to a halt before it has even started. Only by finding a teacher and becoming part of the group of pupils that that teacher has collected about him can the player find encouragement and support. Otherwise he simply forgets his aim, or wanders off down some side road and loses himself. Unfortunately, it

II. The Drug Experience

A Phantom Haunts Us!

THE PSYCHEDELIC DRUGS, substances which alter the individual's awareness of himself and the world about him, have begun to haunt the collective psyche of contemporary America almost as persistently as does that tired old specter, Marxian Communism. Certainly the drugs are more sophisticated phantoms than Marx's old bogey, which has been rattling its chains since the days of crinolines and become a trifle passé in the process. The threat posed by the drugs (if they do pose a threat) is hard to define and "solid citizens" who routinely oppose the taking of any drugs save aspirin or alcohol have some difficulty justifying their negative attitude toward the psychedelics. When informed that strange mystical experience can be had by the taking of some pill or concoction, they automatically assume that *something must be wrong.* Even if told that people of other races, including the local American Indians, have for centuries taken such substances to help them communicate with God or the spirit world, they still raise their eyebrows. Compelled by their fear of the unfamiliar to view all such practices as "un-American activities," they enact legislation to make the possession of psychedelics a crime. Where these drugs are concerned, the solid citizen is curiously lacking in that respect for individual liberty which he usually claims to be eager to protect. Frightened by this mysterious, unknown force, he becomes as rabidly intolerant as any Commissar or Inquisitor and deals out jail sentences equal to those imposed for high treason or armed robbery on fellow citizens whose only crime is to have in their possession some relatively harmless substance which happens to exert a certain effect on the psyche.

In spite of the disapproval and the repressive legislation, acres of comments in magazines and newspapers testify to the fact that the psychedelics are the rage of the age:

> Do not be surprised if you see in the streets of Berkeley girls wearing the rapt expressions of Madonnas or sandalled youths with the indrawn air of El Greco saints. Do not assume that the millennium has arrived or that our population is heading *en masse* for Nirvana. It merely means that a shipment of high class "pot" has been brought in from Mexico or some really potent "hash" has come in from Beirut. Or one of the local chemists has successfully synthesized a batch of LSD or extracted some mescaline from peyote. I swear that half the population is high on one drug or another—and I don't refer to "beatniks" either. People smoke "pot" as regularly as they smoke tobacco. There is a general feeling of unreality.

Thus writes a California correspondent. Perhaps the account is a little exaggerated but it contains much that is true. Whence comes this enthusiasm for chemically induced stupors, raptures, transcendental experiences, "trips" and "kicks" in general?

The psychedelic age, foretold by Aldous Huxley in 1931, has dawned far sooner than that prophet expected. It was *soma,* the perfect psychedelic, that solaced the inhabitants of *Brave New World,* resolving tensions and frustrations which might otherwise have disturbed the balance of that harmonious society. "Euphoric, narcotic, pleasantly hallucinant—all the advantages of Christianity and alcohol, none of their drawbacks." Nothing so good has been synthesized by our contemporary chemists. But we do have lysergic acid diethylamide (LSD). It is around LSD that the former Harvard psychologist, Timothy Leary, has constructed a cult, its sacred book an exotic mixture of psychedelics and the *Tibetan Book of the Dead*,[21] its headquarters an ugly mansion in New York State, its title The Castalia Foundation, the name being derived from the sacred order described by Hermann Hesse in *Magister Ludi*.

Over Leary's activities there has been much headshaking on the part of so-called authorities—medical, legal, religious, political—who imagine they have the right to dictate to their fellows just what substances the latter may ingest, have in their possession, cultivate in their back yards and so on. But though legislators growl and members of various "narcotics" bureaus (many of them ignorant of the very meaning of the word "narcotic") descend in slavering packs on their fellow citizens, searching their houses and persons, insulting, bullying, harassing and arresting, they have not been able to halt the psychedelic movement.

Why not?

Because, as the history of mankind clearly shows, there is in some, not all, men, a distinctive hunger for experience in another dimension, for an elevated or expanded state of consciousness, for insights seemingly unattainable by ordinary means. For the sake of these insights, many who suffer from this hunger are willing to risk the sort of penalties imposed recently on Leary by a Texas judge (thirty years in jail, thirty thousand dollars in fines). Said Aldous Huxley: "The urge to transcend self-conscious selfhood is a principal appetite of the soul." Baudelaire, poor haunted Baudelaire, described the hunger in more detail:

> Those who are able to observe themselves and can remember their impressions often have occasion to note in the observatory of their thoughts strange seasons, luxurious afternoons, delicious minutes. There are days when a man awakens with a young and vigorous genius. Hardly have his eyelids cast off sleep which sealed them before the outer world presents itself to him in strong relief, with a clearness of contour and wealth of admirable color. The man gratified with this sense of exquisite loveliness, unfortu-

nately so rare and so transitory, feels himself more than ever the artist, more than ever noble, more than ever just, if one can express so much in so few words. But the most singular thing about this exceptional state of the spirit and of the senses, which without exaggeration can be termed paradisical as compared with the hopeless darkness of ordinary daily existence, is that it has not been created by any visible or easily definable cause.

This acuity of thought, this vigor of sense and spirit, has at all times appeared to man as the highest good. For this reason, purely for his immediate enjoyment, without troubling himself about the limitations imposed by his constitution, he has searched in the world of physical and of pharmaceutical science, among the grossest decoctions and the most subtle perfumes, in all climates and at all times, for the means of leaving, if only for a few moments, his habitation of mud and of transporting himself to paradise in a single swoop.

Alas! Man's vices, horrible as they are supposed to be, contain the positive proof of his taste for the infinite.[22]

The taste for the infinite! How well Baudelaire puts it. But what exactly does this mean? The phrase suggests that within the psyche of man are secret rooms, vast chambers full of treasures with windows looking out on eternity and infinity. Man does not enter these rooms, or does so only rarely. They are locked. He has lost the key. He lives habitually in the lowest, dreariest, darkest part of his inner habitation. Concerning this, the mystics of all times and all religions are agreed. But do psychedelics offer the key to those locked rooms or does their use constitute a form of spiritual burglary which carries its own hazards and penalties? Before we attempt to answer the question, let us try to evaluate the varieties of what is loosely called "the drug experience." [23]

A Note on Depressants

Drugs which affect consciousness can be roughly divided into two groups, depressants and stimulants. The depressants, including ether, alcohol, chloroform, nitrous oxide, the opiates, the barbiturates and the so-called tranquilizers, lower the activity of the brain. They produce, in small doses, a state of mild euphoria, a sense of sinking into an ocean of oblivion. In large doses they engender varying degrees of stupor which, in its extreme form, results in death.

Some depressants have been regarded as gateways to higher consciousness or as means of engendering mystical states. There was, during the nineteenth century, quite an upsurge of interest in the anesthetics—ether, chloroform, nitrous oxide—as a means of engendering mystical experiences. Much of this material was reviewed by William James in *The Varieties of Religious Experience*. Alcohol, which should be included among the anesthetics as it produces insensibility when taken in sufficient amount, was praised by James for its *liberating* power:

> The sway of alcohol over mankind is unquestionably due to its power to stimulate the mystical faculties of human nature, usually crushed to earth by the cold facts and dry criticisms of the sober hour. Sobriety diminishes, discriminates and says no; drunkenness expands, unites, and says yes. It is, in fact, the great exciter of the YES function in man. It brings its votary from the chill periphery of things to the radiant core. It makes him for the moment one with truth. . . . To the poor and the unlettered it stands in the place of symphony concerts and of literature; and it is part of the deeper mystery and tragedy of life that whiffs and gleams of something we immediately recognize as excellent, should be vouchsafed to many of us only in the fleeting earlier phases of what, in its totality, is so degrading a poisoning.

Alcohol acts by *lowering the activity of the brain*, first at its highest levels (controlling thought), next at its motor levels (controlling speech and movement), finally at its basic levels (controlling sensibility, reflexes and respiration). The so-called mystical states produced by alcohol are due to the inhibition of that entity which Freud called the "super-ego," a cold, censorious spoilsport whose favorite phrase is "Thou shalt not." For some people, whose spontaneous awareness is strangled in a network of inhibitions, prohibitions, guilts, fears, repressions and other unlovely products of a puritanical conscience, the weakening of the super-ego generates a certain Dionysian ecstasy, a fuller, richer sense of being, a liberation. This happens only at one stage of intoxication, an early one and a transient. It occurs at the moment when just enough alcohol has been taken to affect the thought-controlling part of the brain. This dose will produce a sense of relaxation, a freedom from tension, a general sense of well-being. The mystical "at-one-ness" may be part of this feeling. Moreover, many barriers in the psyche which prevent a man from manifesting various aspects of the self are removed temporarily by alcohol, as the phrase *in vino veritas* attests.

Alcohol, therefore, can be useful for certain kinds of self-study, provided the student knows exactly what dose to use to attain the desired effect. Alcohol itself is not very toxic and, taken in moderation, is utilized as a source of energy, for the body contains the enzymes needed to consume it. Unfortunately, like all the other drugs, alcohol can only *reveal* certain possibilities; it cannot transform those possibilities into realities. Those who come to rely on it use it merely as a club with which to bludgeon themselves into a state of insensibility. They wreck their body chemistry in the process, not so much by overconsumption of alcohol as by underconsumption of vitamins, lack of which gives rise both to delirium tremens and to Wernicke's syndrome.

William James also commented on the properties of the more powerful anesthetics, nitrous oxide and ether, which, when sufficiently diluted with air,

> stimulate the mystical consciousness in an extraordinary degree. Depth beyond depth of truth seems revealed to the inhaler. The truth fades out, however, or escapes, at the moment of coming to; and if any words remain over in which it seemed to clothe itself, they prove to be the veriest nonsense. Nevertheless, the sense of a profound meaning having been there persists; and I know more than one person who is persuaded that in the nitrous-oxide trance we have a genuine metaphysical revelation.

In a more recent study of the effects of an anesthetic, René Daumal, a daring experimentalist, sought a method of confronting death itself.[24] Assuming an analogy between sleep and death, he first "attempted to enter sleep in a waking state." He did not persist in this technique, commenting that the undertaking is "not so utterly absurd as it sounds, but in certain respects it is perilous." He was evidently not easily deterred by peril for he next decided to put his body into a state approaching as close as possible that of physiological death, while concentrating all his attention on retaining consciousness. To produce this condition, he used carbon tetrachloride, figuring that he could regulate its action very simply, as the handkerchief moistened with the volatile fluid would fall from his nostrils the moment he began to lose consciousness.

A toxicologist must shudder at the thought of so poisonous a substance as carbon tetrachloride being used for this purpose. It inflicts damage on the liver which is not repaired and can adversely affect the working of the physical organism for the duration of a man's life. Was the psychedelic experience worth the damage? Did Daumal gain access to the fourth room or even the fifth, or did he merely descend into the second, "the room of dreams"? These questions are hard to answer for the reason that *words cannot communicate a state of consciousness.*

Verbally Daumal described his experience as follows:

1) Everything that made up "the world" for him in his ordinary state was still there, but it was "nothing more than a phantasmagoria," empty, absurd, clearly outlined and necessary all at once.

2) The ordinary world lost all reality because he had abruptly entered another world, infinitely more real, an instantaneous and intense world of eternity, a concentrated flame of reality and evidence into which he had cast himself like a moth drawn to a candle. At that moment came the *certainty,* and speech had to be content to wheel in circles around the bare fact.

On this *certainty* Daumal commented as follows:

> In my ordinary state of mind, all that remains thinkable and formulable of this experiment reduces to one affirmation on which I would stake my life: I feel the certainty of the existence of *something else,* a beyond, another world, or another form of knowledge. . . . In that new state I perceived and perfectly comprehended the ordinary state of being, the latter being contained

within the former as waking consciousness contains our uncon-
scious dreams and not the reverse. This last irreversible relation
proves the superiority (in the scale of reality or consciousness) of
the first state over the second.

The *substance* of the experience, its visual and auditory elements, was described in some detail by Daumal. The endlessly
dividing circles and triangles inscribed one within the other, combining and moving in harmony, seem typical of the "moving hier-
oglyphs" that express ideas to one in this state of awareness. The
auditory component, a chant or formula having the form "Tem
gwef tem gwef dr rr rr" reminds one of William James's "Higa-
mus, Hogamus." The altered sense of time, the awareness of multiplicity regenerating unity, all fit into a definite pattern of
experiences many times described and always with the same
disclaimer (words cannot do justice, etc.).

Of special interest are Daumal's comments on the *dangers* involved in this kind of experience. He warns the reader that it is
terrifying and insists that he does not refer to physiological dangers, which he admits are very great ("if, in return for accepting
grave illness or infirmity, and for a considerable shortening of
physical life, one could attain a single certainty the price would
not be too high"). He does not even refer to the dangers of insanity or of damage to the brain, which he escaped "by extraordinary
good luck." The greatest danger of all, in his opinion, is a complete loss of belief in what ordinarily passes for reality:

> Everything seemed to me an absurd phantasmagoria, no logic
> would convince me of anything and, like a leaf in the wind, I was
> ready to obey the faintest interior or exterior impulse. This state
> almost involved me in irreparable "actions" (if the word still ap-
> plies), for nothing held any importance for me any longer.

This comment is extremely important and should be borne in
mind by all who feel tempted to dabble with the psychedelic experience without knowing what they are doing or why. He who
enters the fifth state of consciousness without preparation may be
spiritually paralyzed by his experience. He has seen too much too

soon and, as a result, all games become meaningless. He cannot play the life games that satisfy men in the third state of consciousness. He cannot play the Master Game because he knows nothing about it and has no teacher. So he becomes, like Daumal's "leaf in the wind," an even more helpless plaything of external forces than he was before his rash experiment.

A similar warning has been voiced by Dr. Sidney Cohen:

> There are hazards. If a person has seen the glory and goodness of life via psychedelics and then backslides, the guilt of failure is added to the hopelessness of his situation. The depression may be deeper than before the treatment. Others who have been touched by the light may develop so unrealistic a view of themselves and the world that they become most difficult to live with.[25]

The other nervous-system depressants, opium, its derivatives, and the barbiturates are dangerous and, for most people, ineffectual. The barbiturates simply induce stupor and are used for this purpose very extensively. Few claim that they offer a pathway to any sort of mystical experience. They offer sleep of a sort. Their habitual use produces a serious form of physical dependence (addiction) and an overdose is the path to a peaceful death.

Opium and its derivatives, morphine and heroin, produce what might be called "mystical states" in certain people. Coleridge, De Quincey, and Baudelaire all found that opium opened certain depths, "the abyss of divine enjoyment" about which De Quincey grew eloquent in his *Confessions of an English Opium Eater*. For the majority, however, they are merely pain relievers and their effects, in the absence of pain, are generally experienced as being unpleasant.

A Subtle Spirit

Of the drugs that can more properly be called "psychedelics," the substance variously known as *hashish, marihuana, bhang, charas,* etc., which is derived from the resinous flowers of the common hemp (*Cannabis sativa*), is the most subtle, the most harmless and the most interesting. The drug is not a narcotic, is not habit-forming, is mild in its action and nontoxic. Were it not for the barbed-wire entanglement of prohibitive legislation that has been erected around this harmless weed by various busybodies who take a professional pride in curtailing the liberties of their fellow-men, it would certainly be the material of choice for one interested in exploring drug-induced changes in consciousness. The effects of this botanical have been described at some length in a previous book.[23] A few additional observations derived from the author's experiences while working on the chemistry of the drug may be of interest.

Red oil of hemp, a partially purified extract,[26] was used in these experiments. A dose of thirty milligrams taken orally after a fast of twenty-four hours began to produce its effect an hour after ingestion. This first, "induction" phase of the drug's action was experienced as being somewhat unpleasant. There was a reddening of the conjunctivae, a dryness in the mouth, an uneasiness in the stomach. An overdose of the preparation (up to 100 mg) induced vomiting. This vomiting was of an especially disagreeable character because hashish, at this stage, inhibits the secretion of saliva, exerting in this respect an action similar to that of the drugs scopolamine or atropine. Such action is called "anticholinergic" and indicates that the drug is blocking the activity of that part of the autonomic nervous system called "parasympathetic." So far as concerns the stop-start mechanism in the brain, hashish, at this stage, presses the stop button.

The induction period lasted from fifteen minutes to half an hour. During this time the active principle of the drug, a resinous substance quite insoluble in water, was slowly absorbed through the walls of the intestine. (When hashish is smoked, this absorption is far more rapid but the acrid resin may damage the lining of the lungs.) After the induction period, the spirit of the hashish began to play its theme with variations on the organ of the brain, pulling out the stops one after another, sounding great colorful chords, marvels of tonality that blended, in a fashion hitherto never experienced, the ordinarily separated components of sensation. Colors vibrated with sound, sounds evoked colors, at the

same time all sorts of odd sensations, so peculiar as to defy classification, scuttled in and out of consciousness like mice.

The spirit of hashish on one's good days (it should never be
evoked on bad ones) is playful as a kitten, puckish, jocular, a con-
jurer performing quaint tricks that one never would have thought
possible. The tricks are associated with the self-sense, that mixed
bag of awareness, of muscle tone, vision, hearing, touch, taste,
smell that gives us the overall sensation of "I am." All these
familiar landmarks in the map of the self were shuffled around
by the playful spirit of hashish. The "I am" became hazy and dif-
fuse. The face symbol of the ego, its emblem and shield, seemed
to twist and stretch like a Halloween mask, now tragic, now comic,
now grotesque until the astonished experimentalist asked himself
in amazement how he could ever have attributed to this rubbery
object the quality of selfhood.

As with the face, so with the rest of the body. Limbs became
free, independent, disconnected as if they had taken on a life of
their own. A hand was seen from a great distance, the structure of
fingers was much admired. It was an object of art. But not *my*
hand. All the selfhood was drained out of it. It existed in its own
right, floating far from the body like a starfish in the ocean. At
intervals the self-sense left the body entirely, floated off and associated with some other form, a tree, a cloud, even a piano. This
is quite a common feature of the hashish experience. Baudelaire
described it when he wrote: "If you are smoking by some sort of
transposition or intellectual quid pro quo, you will feel yourself
evaporating and will attribute to your pipe, in which you feel
yourself crouching and packed together like tobacco, the strange
power of *smoking yourself.*"

As the spirit of hashish continued its performance, the observer
noticed how cyclic is its action. All the experiences came in waves,
and the different reactions generally followed in the same order
as if one center after another, in definite sequence, were being
activated by the drug. A "rapture" began with stimulation of the
respiratory center. The experimenter found himself literally "in-
spired," he gulped down great draughts of air as if to fill his sys-

tem from the inexhaustible reservoir of cosmic *prana*. This air gulping has been observed by many, is an objectively definable effect of the drug. Says Baudelaire: "You have deep raucous sighs, as if your old body could not endure the desires and activity of your new soul." [22] Says Fitz Hugh Ludlow: "Hotter and faster came my breath; I seemed to pant like some tremendous engine." [27]

This stimulation of the respiratory center was accompanied by a strengthening of the action of the heart. Awareness of the action of this vital pump may become acute, even alarming. Ludlow had this experience when he first took hashish and become so frightened that he hastened to consult the nearest physician:

> The beating of my heart was clearly audible. Lo, now that heart became a great fountain, whose jet played upward with loud vibrations, and, striking on the roof of my skull as on a gigantic dome, fell back with a splash and echo into its reservoir. Faster and faster came the pulsations and the stream became one continuously pouring flood, whose roar sounded through all my frame. I gave myself up for lost, since judgement, which still sat unimpaired above my perverted senses, argued that congestion must take place in a few minutes, and close the drama with my death.[27]

Stimulation of the hunger center in the hypothalamus *may* follow this orgy of respiration. More often it is not the hunger center but the sex center that is stimulated. In the male an erection of the penis results from stimulus of the parasympathetic part of the autonomic nervous system. The sympathetic mechanism which results in ejaculation is inhibited. At the same time the intensity of the sexual sensations is enhanced and the duration of the act is prolonged. For this reason hashish is regarded as an aphrodisiac *par excellence* throughout the East, but it cannot be relied on to exert this effect. The spirit of hashish, in its playful performance on the brain centers, may so powerfully stimulate the sex center that the sex act acquires a stupendous Dionysian splendor, or it may miss that center entirely and leave the experimentalist so indifferent that Venus herself could not tempt him into intercourse.

This activation of the centers in the *lower brain* can provide a careful observer with much material. Instinctive functions are illuminated and emphasized, emotional functions are sharpened and given new force. Hashish enhances *all* emotionality, positive and negative. Fear, anxiety, apprehension, distrust can be so augmented by hashish as to make the whole experience a most unpleasant ordeal. But joy or delight are similarly augmented and it is this augmentation of joy to the level of ecstasy that endows the hashish experience with such a powerful appeal. "Over the surface of man's ordinary life the power of hashish spreads a magic glaze, coloring it with solemnity, bringing to light the profoundest aspects of existence." [22] This magic glaze can spread over any form of experience. For many, it exerts its greatest power in connection with music. Patterns entirely unsuspected emerge from the sound. The ear becomes fascinated with a minor theme, follows a single instrument to the exclusion of all the others. Music that seemed clever or even brilliant may, under the hashish influence, stand revealed as phoney and insincere. The merciless spirit of hashish strips from all art forms the overlay of egotism, illuminating with a pitiless radiance the underlying reality. For genuine artistic creation its praise is unqualified; for the contrived, the slick, the merely clever its contempt is biting: "How this fool tries to show off! What a jackdaw in peacock's feathers!"

This clarity of vision, this hard gemlike illumination lit up the experimenter's portrait of himself. The inner contradictions, the multiplicity that tries to pretend it is a unity, showed under hashish as the thing it really was, a patchwork of odds and ends, of dreams and delusions, hopes and fears, held together by the physical continuity of the body. Brought thus face to face with his inner contradictions, he saw himself not as a self at all, but merely as a puppet, helplessly pulled by strings which were manipulated by outside forces. "There is no self!" he exclaimed. "There is no I. There is merely a shifting mosaic of moods and thoughts, changed like a pattern in a kaleidoscope every time circumstances shake the instrument." This realization, depending on his mood, was either terrifying, reassuring or seemed merely comical. "This ridiculous object has been strutting around saying I this and I that and all the while it has no more I than a scarecrow and no more will than a puppet." At this he often laughed most heartily.

At times the spirit of hashish led him further. Penetrating beyond the shadow show of the "I," he contacted an older drama, enacted by awe-inspiring forms, by gods and demons, veritable archetypes. This ancient drama, *The Theater of the Seraphim,* transported him beyond the "I," beyond personal boundaries that define the self as it is usually felt. Here, as in a primeval cosmic dance, he sensed the evolution of the race, the procession of living forms, flowing, changing, perishing, reappearing. He even passed through the process of death and glimpsed the mysteries of the after-death state. He experienced birth (or what appeared to be birth). The details of his life showed as if illuminated, exquisite reproductions from times past, with all their elements supplied, the sounds, sights, smells, the bodily sensations. The drug unlocked the doors of memory, a memory that can be as impersonal as the memory of the race, linking him to the great patterns of living forms, green plants and fungi, invertebrates and vertebrates. Against so expansive a background personal memories appeared trivial. The observer laughed at his most painful recollections which, seen in proportion, perhaps for the first time, astonished him by their insignificance. "How was it possible that I became so upset over such a trifle? How could I allow so minor an incident to poison the springs of my inner life?"

Risks and Revelations

Such are the revelations that hashish can offer. In the writer's opinion, it is the mildest, most benign, least liable to produce a postpsychedelic depression and very nontoxic. It is, however, capricious and quite often produces no effect at all. It's quality is very variable. It also happens to be the victim of a semi-imbecile piece of legislation called the "Marihuana Tax Act" that makes it a criminal offense even to have the hemp plant growing in one's garden unless one has paid for a tax stamp, which the Narcotics Bureau, in most cases, refuses to issue.

Other psychedelics—LSD, mescaline, psilocybin—can produce effects very similar to those of hashish in people with whose personal chemistry they happen to agree, though they may function merely as poisons for those unable to detoxify these substances.[28] Aldous Huxley, for example, was evidently well able to metabolize mescaline. His description of its effects[29] shows that, for him, it had the same consciousness-expanding properties as has hashish. Alan Watts was able to obtain satisfactory results with LSD. His beautifully illustrated book, *The Joyous Cosmology*,[30] reveals insights of the same general type as Aldous Huxley's. Particularly fascinating is his description of the changed sense of self and his resolution of the cosmic drama into two questions of housekeeping: "Where to put it?" and "Who cleans up?" Leary et al. have summarized much of this material in *The Psychedelic Experience*, though their insistence on forcing the insights into a framework which is essentially Tibetan produces a strained, somewhat artificial effect like the efforts of early astronomers to force the movements of planets to fit into the Ptolemaean system. For a more balanced review of the effects of LSD, the reader should consult Sidney Cohen's *The Beyond Within*.[25]

All this evidence leads to the conclusion that these drugs, so different in chemical composition, operate through a common mechanism and bring into action a capacity present in the human psyche but not ordinarily used. This capacity can be defined as the power to transcend temporal limitations, verbal definitions, the limitations of name and form. When P. D. Ouspensky was gathering the material for his chapter "Experimental Mysticism" in *A New Model of the Universe*, he too used psychedelic drugs (mainly opium). He expressed the essence of his experience in a single sentence: "Think in other categories." This is the hallmark of the state of higher consciousness. Somehow these chemicals release the awareness from certain fetters that ordinarily bind it. The doors of perception are cleansed. The taste of the infinite is obtained. The isolated awareness, imprisoned in the illusion of its ego-sense, is suddenly liberated from its fetters. Ecstasy is the result, for ecstasy means nothing more or less than standing outside of oneself. A man dies at one level and is reborn on another.

Now we return to the starting point. If this self-transcendence is in fact the highest prize life has to offer, *if* this jewel can be obtained by the taking of certain drugs, then why should any reasonable person deny himself this experience? The Mystic Way is, by all accounts, hard and long. How much easier it is to break open the locked doors of the secret chambers in the psyche by chemical means. We may suspect that the taking of psychedelic drugs is depraved, realize vaguely that it constitutes a kind of spiritual burglary, a criminal activity on the spiritual level, a stealing of something that one has not earned. So what? A generation reared to rely on labor-saving devices can hardly be blamed for hoping that the insights laboriously earned by saints and mystics may be acquired without effort by the simple process of swallowing a pill. Nor is this attitude confined to contemporary man. There have been members of earlier, more ruggedly reared generations, who showed just as much enthusiasm for the easy rapture afforded by psychedelics. Thomas De Quincey, the English opium eater, was eloquent on this subject.

> Here was a panacea, a *pharmakon nepenthes* for all human woes; here was the secret of happiness, about which philosophers had disputed for so many ages, at once discovered. Happiness might now be bought for a penny, and carried in the waistcoat pocket; portable ecstasies might be corked up in a pint bottle, and peace of mind could be sent down by mail.

De Quincey, of course, was referring to laudanum (tincture of opium), which is a far from ideal drug for inducing changes in levels of consciousness and does not properly belong in the group called "psychedelics," being, for most people, only an *analgesic* (pain reliever). But De Quincey's delight over his discovery of the effects of opium is paralleled by that of contemporary investigators over those of LSD, mescaline or psilocybin. Being familiar with the vocabulary of Oriental mysticism, these explorers sing praises of bottled *samadhis* or encapsulated *satoris* and eagerly spread the word that a short cut exists and that the efforts made by yogis, Sufis, mystics and magi to break into the triple-locked fourth room were needless. All that these seekers had to do was to introduce into their metabolism certain chemicals and all locked doors would open by themselves. Their view is summed up by a saying of the opium smokers of India: "If heaven can be obtained for a *pice* [i.e., a penny], why should you be so envious?"

This may seem a reassuring message but is not a correct one. The high ends of Creative Psychology can no more be attained by taking drugs than the high ends of art can be achieved by slopping paint about at random. There are those who insist that such slopping is art. There are those who insist that pill swallowing can lead to higher consciousness. Both are wrong.

However, this much can be said in favor of the psychedelics. If they are taken under the right conditions, with proper preparation, under the supervision of one who knows how to guide the explorer in the territory he will enter, they can, on occasions at least, be of some value. They can challenge the traveler saying: "These are the mountain peaks. They really exist. Now make up your mind. Are you strong enough, persistent enough to try to climb them?"

When the psychedelics offer this challenge they are performing a valuable function. By awakening the traveler to his own inner potentialities, they provide him with a game worth playing, a task worth undertaking, a pilgrimage on which it is worthwhile to embark. Furthermore, they offer valuable clues to one who wishes to understand his own inner chemistry. They spotlight certain processes and thus make it easier for the experimentalist to recognize the mechanisms involved. When he fully understands how certain effects are produced, he can learn to initiate them at will without the use of drugs.

This is the *lawful* use of the psychedelics. (No reference is intended to *human* laws designed to regulate the use of these substances.) It is *physiologically* lawful to obtain information about the workings of one's own organism by any means that does not damage the organism or render its possessor a slave to the procedure in question (physically dependent on a drug, for example). It is *psychologically* (or spiritually) lawful to obtain such information as part of a life game, the aim of which is realization of

higher states of awareness. It is not spiritually_lawful to take
psychedelics merely for "kicks" or to use them as substitutes for
the special kind of inner work that alone can produce lasting results. Those who use the drugs in this way suffer a penalty imposed not by flat-footed tax collectors disguised as "narcotics
agents," but by the impartial forces that regulate a man's fate. The
penalty takes this form: *he who misuses psychedelics sacrifices his
capacity to develop by persistently squandering those inner resources on which growth depends.* He commits himself to a descending spiral and the further he travels down this path, the
more difficult it becomes for him to reascend. Finally the power
to reascend is lost altogether.

*Moralizing again. Basic
Puritan ethic of "pleasure is evil".*

The Energies of the Psyche

Now consider the psychedelics objectively. How do these substances act? What do they do? We cannot answer this question
without first discussing how the body stores its energies and how
these energies are released. A very large part of the total energy
store is located in the muscles or stored as glycogen in the liver
and is released as muscular work. Another portion of the energy
store is utilized in purely instinctive operations, digestion of food,
storage of products of digestion. The sexual apparatus with its
component urges utilizes a further portion of the total energy.
Emotional functions of various kinds consume their quota and
thought processes consume theirs. There is left over a certain
amount of energy which manifests itself in the level of total
awareness that can range from deep dreamless sleep to the highest state of consciousness possible for man.

All energies in the body are chemically bound. They are locked
up in molecules of one sort or another just as the energy of a log
of firewood is locked in its molecules of cellulose or lignin. To
prevent the depletion of these very specific energy stores, mechanisms exist in the body which lock up the storage sites much as a
careful mother locks up the cookie jar to prevent depredations by
a greedy child. The storage organs correspond roughly to six

glands, the gonads or sex glands, the adrenals (divided into two parts, medulla and cortex), the liver, the pancreas, the thyroid in the throat and pituitary at the base of the brain with its two lobes, anterior and posterior. The pituitary, though a very small gland, about the size of a pea in the adult human being, may be called the master gland of the body because, through its special hormones (the "tropic" hormones), it arouses to activity the other glands. But the pituitary itself is directly linked to that part of the brain known as the hypothalamus, which in turn is linked to the roof brain, the cerebral cortex.

The hypothalamus contains a master switchboard, speeding up or slowing the operation of the glands, regulating the rate of utilization of the body's stores of energy. It is difficult, experimentally, to determine exactly where in this part of man's brain the different switches are located. We are forced to rely for this information mainly on data obtained from monkeys. Such studies show that the instinctive urges—hunger, thirst, the sex urge—are controlled by impulses coming from this part of the brain. They also show that two large switches, which we may call the "start switch" and the "stop switch," are located in this area. The start switch arouses an animal to activity and its operation induces sensations that are largely pleasurable (the "get up and go" sensation); the stop switch inhibits activity and its operation induces sensations that are largely unpleasant ("leave me in peace" sensations, accompanied by general malaise). The first system has been called by the Swiss neurophysiologist, Walter Hess, the "ergotropic system" (inciting to activity), the second the "trophotropic" (inciting to rest).

One who knows this much about the workings of the mental switchboard can accumulate, by direct observation, a great deal of information about the operations of his own brain. He can learn to distinguish one switch from another, to detect the changes in the harmony of the glandular orchestra, to recognize the release of stored energies, to know (more or less, for such observations always lack precision) which systems have been activated, which rendered quiescent.

To one who possesses such knowledge it becomes obvious, as soon as he feels the effects of the so-called psychedelics, that these substances are acting on the hypothalamic switchboard, turning various switches on and off. They exert effects on the centers regulating thirst, hunger, sexual desire, respiration, temperature, sweating, rate of the heartbeat. They may press the stop switch and incite to inaction, inducing feelings of malaise, often accompanied by vomiting. How they do all these things is a biochemical problem of great complexity. We can guess that they alter the balance between excitation and inhibition by exerting a chemical effect at certain strategic junctions in the complex communications network that is man's brain.

Because the psychedelics function by liberating stored energies, their effect will depend on the levels of these energies available. The various tribes of Indians who use peyote understand this well and prepare in advance, fasting and practicing continence, for the level of sexual energy influences powerfully the overall result. "Civilized" Western man, who despises the wisdom of these "poor primitives" and takes his psychedelics without any previous preparation, with all his habitual anxieties gibbering about him like a bevy of ghouls, with his energies scattered, his mind awash in daydreams, may wonder why the experience is unpleasant or downright terrifying. Worse still, he may be inveigled by some asinine experimentalist into being dosed with the drug in a hospital setting, amid sterile, hygienic white walls, starched nurses, syringes and bedpans and all the paraphernalia of sickness and death. Then, while still trembling with the horrors he has experienced, may be thrown out into the street, his psyche still as raw as an open wound, to be set upon by the vampire flock of impressions that suck souls dry in this world's major man swarms.

A quotation from Baudelaire's *Paradis artificiels* seems in order at this point:

> I presume that you have chosen the right moment for this expedition. Every perfect debauch requires perfect leisure. Besides, hashish not only magnifies the individual but also the circumstance and environment. You must have no duties to accomplish

that require punctuality or exactitude, no pangs of love, no domestic preoccupations, griefs, anxieties. The memories of duty will sound a death knell through your intoxication and poison your pleasure. Anxiety will change to anguish, grief to torture. But if the conditions are right and the weather is good, if you are in a favorable environment as in the midst of a picturesque landscape or in a room artistically decorated, if, moreover, you can hope to hear some music, then all's for the best.

This is rule number one for all who wish to experiment with the psychedelics (for what Baudelaire says of hashish is also true of the others). Prepare beforehand. Embark on such a journey only when the energies of the body are at a high level, when that state of inner harmony which the Greeks called *ataraxia* is already the dominant mood. Tranquil, consoling, reassuring surroundings, a soothing pattern of music, perhaps a companion—but this companion must be chosen with the utmost care, for the psychedelics, hashish especially, strip from the everyman his mask (*persona*) and reveal the essence.

However, we must always remember that, no matter what we do, we cannot evade the law which governs the formation and expenditure of certain substances in the body on the supply of which happiness, awareness, tranquility, health and life itself depend. If these substances are destroyed faster than they are made, a condition of depletion results. This depletion is experienced subjectively as depression, a general lowering of the vital flame, a heaviness, gloom, lack of pleasure, weariness, boredom.

Experience suggests that *one* psychedelic "trip" properly prepared for, conducted under the right conditions, will not result in a dangerous state of depletion. But the situation is entirely different when the experience is repeated several times or the session is conducted under unfavorable conditions. Such repeated or ill-regulated use of the drugs can produce a postpsychedelic depression of a most unpleasant kind which can, and in several cases has, resulted in suicide.

There is a second reason why the repeated use of psychedelics fails to produce any permanent alteration in the level of consciousness. In the beginning the drugs, by releasing certain energies in the body, touch off an inner firework display that is often fascinating and very beautiful. But the self-indulgent or lazy investigator who makes a habit of trying to set off such inner pyrotechnics will find that the show becomes less and less rewarding. The body grows accustomed to the drug and ceases to react. This is true of both LSD and hashish. The first few meetings with "My Lady of the Hemp" may produce raptures, ecstasies, give insights never to be forgotten. But continued application for aid to this potent spirit dulls the magic, blunts the effects, evokes misery rather than rapture. As Ludlow put it: "The ecstasy became daily more and more flecked with shadows of an immeasurable pain."

It takes a considerable time (two weeks or even a month) for the body to regenerate the stored energy substances which are casually squandered in one of these psychedelic sprees. If a second explosion is initiated before the body has had time to recover from the first, a point may be reached at which it is actually impossible for the body to regenerate these stores. In this process, as in many others, the old phrase of the alchemists applies: "You must have gold to make gold."

In summary, then, we may state that consciousness-expanding drugs can, if taken in the right doses, after proper preparation, with proper guidance and under the right circumstances, offer glimpses of the contents of both the fourth room and the fifth. They can never, no matter how often they are taken, enable the investigator to change his *level of being*. Their continued use represents a form of spiritual burglary which carries its own penalty, an irreparable depletion of the substances needed for real inner work and a total loss of the individual's capacity to develop. Carefully controlled experiments with the drugs are justified if they lead the experimenter to the conclusion that the fourth and fifth states of consciousness are possible for man. This realization may serve to awaken him to the existence of the Master Game, the only game in life that is truly worth playing. From that point on, he can progress only by combining right knowledge with right effort under the guidance of one who knows the way.

Still moralizing but his phisiology is essentially correct.

III. The Five Rooms

The Myth of the Mad King

IN THE PREVIOUS CHAPTER man was compared to the inhabitant of a house containing locked rooms, "vast chambers full of treasures with windows looking out on eternity and infinity." It was said that man in general does not enter these locked rooms. He has lost the key. Sometimes he suspects that the rooms are there and may try to unlock the doors by the use of drugs. More often he does not even know that the rooms exist.

This concept of man's psyche is very ancient, as old as civilization, probably even older. Like much ancient wisdom, it has come down to us in the form of a myth, which will here be called the "Myth of the Mad King." The myth takes various forms. Some of the better known variations on this theme are the story of Nebuchadnezzar leaving his palace to eat grass with the beasts, Plato's story of the prisoners in the cave, the New Testament story of the Prodigal Son and the related story of the wandering prince contained in the Gnostic allegory called the "Hymn to the Soul." [31]

This old myth, in its essence, compares man to a king with a sumptuous palace at his command. But the king went mad and insisted on living in the cellar surrounded by rags and bones and other worthless objects which he called his possessions. If any of his ministers reproached him for this behavior and tried to remind him of the palace and its splendors, he indignantly replied that he had never left that place. Such was the nature of his illusions that he saw the wretched cellar as a palace and the rags and bones he had collected as precious jewels.

Today we can rephrase this old myth in terms more precise and in more accord with our new knowledge of human nature. We can say that man is a being with great powers at his disposal, which are his by virtue of his large brain and, more specifically, his huge cerebral cortex, an organ he has not yet learned how to use. Because he does not know how to use this powerful machine it tends to operate in ways not beneficial to its possessor, to generate a host of illusions among which he wanders like a babe in the enchanted wood, frightened and confused, a prey to terrors that he himself has created.

In psychological language the myth of the mad king means this: Man's ordinary state of consciousness is not the highest level of consciousness of which he is capable. In fact, it is so defective that the condition has been defined as little better than somnambulism. Man does not really know what he is doing or where he is going. He lives in dreams. He inhabits a world of delusions and, because of these delusions, makes dangers for himself and others. If this is accepted, then we ask the next questions: What can be done about it? Can man really awaken? What other states of consciousness are possible for him and what must he do to attain these states?

Let us repeat an oft-quoted passage from *The Varieties of Religious Experience:*

> One conclusion was forced upon my mind at that time, and my impression of its truth has ever since remained unshaken. It is that our normal waking consciousness, rational consciousness as we call it, is but one special type of consciousness, whilst all about it, parted from it by the filmiest of screens, there lie potential forms of consciousness entirely different. We may go through life with-

This "higher" and "lower" state of consciousness bit is getting ridiculous. Why not just say "different"??

out suspecting their existence, but apply the requisite stimulus, and at a touch they are there in all their completeness. . . . No account of the universe in its totality can be final which leaves these other forms of consciousness quite disregarded.[19]

William James was actually describing effects he obtained while experimenting with nitrous oxide. The statement, however, need not be limited to drug-induced states of altered awareness. One can, in fact, be far more specific than was James in the above passage. One can affirm, on the basis of considerable evidence, that roughly five levels of consciousness are possible for man:

1) Deep sleep without dreams.   The First Level
2) Sleep with dreams.   The Second Level
3) Waking sleep (identification).   The Third Level
4) Self-transcendence   The Fourth Level
   (self-remembering).
5) Objective Consciousness   The Fifth Level
   (cosmic consciousness).

Nature guarantees that man shall experience the first, second and third levels of consciousness. These are necessary for life, for the maintenance of the physical body and for the perpetuation of the species. She does not guarantee that he shall experience the fourth and fifth states. In fact, it appears, owing to an error in the pattern of man's evolution, that mechanisms have developed in him which make it difficult for him to attain the two higher states of consciousness. *Can evolution make "errors"?*

Dreamless Sleep

Let us consider the characteristics of the five states. In the first state man knows nothing. His activity is reduced to a minimum. He breathes, his heart beats, various instinctive processes go on, but he is not aware of himself in any way at all. Dreamless sleep. Oblivion. Death's brother. This is the first room in which man must spend a large fraction of his life because only when he is in this state can certain storage organs in the body (the vital batteries) be recharged. If deprived of the chance to enter the first room, he suffers damage that may prove irreparable. Inability to enter the first room is an early symptom of the approach of schizophrenia, one of the commonest and most disturbing forms of mental illness.

Man does not enter the first room in a single bound. He approaches it gradually as if descending a stairway of steadily diminishing consciousness. Contemporary students of sleep have divided this descent into roughly four stages.[32] During the approach to sleep (drowsiness) a regular rhythm called the "alpha rhythm" appears on the electroencephalogram (EEG), which records the shifts in electrical potential in the brain. The appearance of the alpha rhythm is accompanied, subjectively, by a serene state, similar to that induced by meditation. In fact, that enterprising neurophysiologist, Dr. Joe Kamiya of the Langley Porter Institute, has shown that this rhythm is characteristic of the state induced in Zen Buddhist monks by the practice of *zazen*, in which the mind is emptied of content but alertness remains unimpaired.[32] Into this state there may intrude various, often quite vivid images called "hypnagogic hallucinations." They are not dreams but have certain dreamlike qualities.

The alpha rhythm fades as the descent toward the first room continues. Small uneven waves appear on the EEG, there are more drifting images, floating or sinking sensations, the muscles relax, the body temperature declines, respiration grows more even and the heart rate becomes slower. Persons can be easily awakened at this first stage of sleep, may enter it momentarily as when the head nods at a boring lecture. It is the borderland of sleep, the gate of entry to the first room. It generally lasts only for a few minutes.

Students of sleep distinguish three more stages as the sleeper moves further into the first room. These stages are characterized by changes in the EEG recording. The muscles become steadily more relaxed. The breathing is even, the heart rate continues to slow down, the temperature to decline. Finally the most oblivious sleep (stage 4) is reached. The muscles are very relaxed and the heart rate is slow. We know almost nothing about the subjective sensations of stage-4 sleep because the whole apparatus of consciousness is turned off. <u>Studies of the EEG recordings show a steady train of large, slow waves.</u> They also indicate that every sound, every touch is registered by the brain but the mechanisms that render these stimuli conscious are completely inactive. (Curiously enough it appears that somnambulism—sleep walking—occurs at this stage of sleep. Despite inactivation of the mechanism of consciousness, people rise from their beds, negotiate rooms full of furniture, look at other people with open eyes, return to bed, recall nothing of the incident when awakened.) A normal person will spend a considerable portion of the night in this stage of sleep and, if his night is disturbed, will make up for it by spending proportionately longer time there on the following night. The restorative effects of "a good night's sleep" are probably the result of relatively long periods spent in stage 4.

The Room of Dreams

Man never spends the period of sleep entirely in the first room. Indeed, it seems downright unhealthy for him to do so. He must, in accordance with some little understood law of his being, emerge from time to time into the second room, the room of dreams. When man enters the second room, he apparently "sees" a series of episodes enacted before him as if on a wide screen. We put the word "see" in quotes because obviously, with both eyes closed and the room dark, he cannot receive any image on the retina. The seeing is purely mental and yet, through some curious hook-up between brain and eye, the eyes move rapidly during dream episodes as if they were following a drama. It was these rapid movements that gave to contemporary students of sleep, N. Kleitman and W. Dement, the clue as to when dreaming occurs.[33]

The second state of consciousness, the room of dreams, has from the earliest times fascinated human observers. Here is a mechanism which nightly fills the awareness with a host of dramas, without any prompting from the will, without external stimulation. From what do they come, these astonishing inner performances? Artemidorus, in the second century A.D. collected every known treatise on dreams (the literature was voluminous even in those days) and distilled the essence of the ancient wisdom into a work of four books (with an appendix). He firmly maintained that dreams are never meaningless, nor do they result from natural causes. They are sent directly by some god as a promise or warning of the future. The gods never lie, but they often veil their meaning in order to test men's faith and patience. Hence the need for skilled interpretation.[34]

The dream state was universally regarded by the ancients as the surest and shortest route to health of both body and soul. In the great Aesculapia at Cos and Epidaurus there were special rooms in which patients underwent the temple sleep (incubation), during which the gods of healing (Apollo, Serapis, Aesculapius) visited them and revealed the causes of their ailments. Aristides, also of the second century, has left us a detailed account of his long quest for health in all the great shrines of healing of the ancient world. His dreams were alarming and his faith extraordinary. He once dreamed that all his bones and sinews must be excised and stubbornly demanded that the attendant physicians perform this incredible operation. They finally managed to persuade him that, in this instance, literal interpretation of the dream was not demanded.

Freud and Jung, dream doctors of the twentieth century, seem at times to place almost as much reliance on dreams as did Aristides in the second. Their theories of repressed material symbolically represented in the dream state demand more faith than some skeptical investigatiors are willing to permit themselves. It is, however, firmly established that the dream state is not at all the same as deep sleep. Dreaming, in the words of a contemporary investigator (Dr. Frederick Snyder, Chief of the Section on Psychophysiology of Sleep, National Institute of Health), "is the subjective concomitant of a pervasive and distinctive physiological state, a third basic biological mode of existence, of the same order yet different from sleep or waking." Dr. Snyder calls the state "REMS" (Rapid Eye Movement State). The state has other characteristics than dreams and eye movements. The muscles twitch, the breathing is shallow, rapid and irregular, pulse rate and blood pressure increase; in the infant there is grimacing, brief vocalization and sucking; in the male there is often penile erection not necessarily accompanied by erotic dreams.[32]

The Half-dream State

The direct observation of dreams is made difficult by the sequence of stages in sleep. Normally, people first enter stage 4 of sleep, remain there for awhile, then emerge from it and reenter stage 1. After reentering stage 1 they begin to dream. If awakened artificially while dreaming, they may recollect a good deal of the dream but, if they awaken naturally, the dream recollection is rapidly erased, often in a matter of minutes, by the stream of daydreams that begins as soon as the third state of consciousness is re-established.

The normal course of sleep, with its initial descent into oblivion, makes it impossible for the student of dreams to carry over a thread of awareness from the waking state which would enable him to bring to his dreams an attitude of impartial self-observation. The descent into the first room severs the thread and the student, however hard he tries, cannot pick up the thread again as he passes from stage-4 sleep to stage 1. So dreams are almost always remembered from the end backwards and the beginning of the dream may be completely out of reach.

The intentional study of the dream state would be made easier if it could be entered directly without the preliminary descent into stage 4 sleep. Can this be accomplished? The student must answer this question for himself, but material from two completely different sources can throw light on this problem. Among the writings assembled by Evans-Wentz in *Tibetan Yoga and Secret Doctrines*[19] is a scripture entitled "The Doctrine of the Dream State." It is part of *The Path of Knowledge,* a group of six doctrines all bearing on the development of higher levels of consciousness. This Tibetan teaching declares that the practitioner can and should firmly resolve to maintain unbroken continuity of consciousness throughout both waking state and dream state. In order to do so, he must learn to focus awareness in a psychic center (*chakra*) located in the throat, visualizing in that *chakra* the syllable AH, red in color and vividly radiant. This concentration on the throat psychic center will, if correctly performed, enable the student to enter the dream world while keeping hold of a certain thread of awareness. The Tibetan yogis know nothing of the reticular system at the base of the brain which is so directly involved in sleeping and waking, but they state, from direct observation, that a tubelike psychic organ exists between the heart center and the throat center. If the vital force is quiescent in this organ, there is dreamless sleep. If the vital force is in motion, dreams occur. In *Tibetan Yoga and Secret Doctrines*[19] we find:

> By mentally concentrating on the AH and recognizing every phenomenal thing to be in essence like forms reflected in a mirror, which though apparent, have no real existence of themselves, one comprehends the dream.

In the further development of this exercise, the AH in the throat is reduced to a red dot holding the awareness in such a way that the dream process can be observed as if through a lens. To the Tibetan yogi, all forms are the expressions of the play of *māyā* (the manifest world seen as illusion because of its transitory nature) and dream forms are neither more nor less "real" than the forms seen in the waking state. Concentrating his awareness in the manner described, he is able to "see" whatever aspect of the cosmic process he desires, from the very small to the very great, from the atomic to the galactic, from the hells to the Buddha realms. The gods in their various heavens, the sufferers in their various hells, all sorts of sentient beings in all kinds of situations become visible in the dream state. To the enlightened mind, all these are the stuff that dreams are made of. Thus, the phenomenal things of Sangsara, the cosmic dance in which the three forces interact to weave the web of events on the loom of time, have all a dreamlike quality, are all products of *māyā*. For, waking or sleeping, we do not see things as they are but watch, in both cases, a sort of shadow show projected within the brain either by senses stimulated from outside (when we are in the waking state) or by inner events, spontaneous activities of the brain, experienced as dreams (when we are in the dream state).

Much can be learned from the Tibetan doctrine of the dream state, but the teaching is an integral part of the *Yoga of the Six Doctrines* and has to be studied in conjunction with the other five. All these Tibetan techniques call for a good deal of help from one who understands the methods and they have to be practiced under special conditions. They are suited to the last phase of life, when, putting aside all material entanglements, dwelling in solitude and with singleminded devotion, the practitioner sets out to reach those high levels of the Way, in which he can leave the physical body, shedding it as one would shed an outworn garment.

A similar approach to the experimental study of dreams is the one described by P. D. Ouspensky, who devoted a whole chapter to the subject in a *New Model of the Universe*.[19] Ouspensky discovered his own method of retaining awareness during the dream state. To do this, he found it necessary to enter the *half-dream state*, a condition which could be induced by holding in the mind some definite image or thought while gradually allowing oneself to sink into sleep. The half-dream state would not come without such definite effort. This is in line with the Tibetan practice that emphasizes concentration either on the AH in the throat or on the red dot in that region.

Ouspensky was very impressed by the half-dream state. He concluded that *"without these half-dream states no study of dreams is possible."* But though the states offered him what appeared to be a reliable key by means of which he could enter the room of dreams, he was also suspicious of this power and somewhat afraid of it. His fear arose out of the observation that, if he allowed the half-dream states to take their course, they tended to encroach both upon sleep and upon the waking state.

It is up to the student himself, by using the above techniques, to decide whether or not it is possible *for him* to obtain a key to the world of dreams. He must also decide whether, for him, the practice is worthwhile or beneficial. In this writer's opinion, much can be learned in the second state of consciousness, but in order to learn it one must not only master some rather difficult inner exercises having to do with the placing of awareness, but also liberate oneself from a host of preconceived ideas about the significance of dreams imposed on one's consciousness by the speculations of psychoanalysts.

Dream Categories

To avoid influencing the dream content all theorizing about the meaning of dreams must be avoided. Only the simplest classification should be used. Ouspensky, in the course of his studies, divided dreams into three categories. These do not impose any structure on dreams, merely make it easier to recognize them, for most dreams recur with minor or major variations:

Category 1: Nonsense or chaos dreams. These dreams may be very terrifying or very comical but in all cases have a lack of structure that makes them seem peculiarly senseless. They result from some physical condition. A dream of snow or ice may signify simply that the bed clothes have fallen off. Horrendous dreams of witch burnings and conflagrations may accompany overheating of the body by too many coverings. Panic dreams (one is stuck in a quicksand, one is entangled in ropes, snakes, tropical creepers, etc.) can result from nothing more than getting one's feet entangled in the sheets. Dreams of flying, of sudden infinite vistas, vaguely disquieting because of their fluctuating perspective, may be produced by moments of dizziness as can the dream sensation of falling. Choking dreams, dreams in which one tries to cry out but cannot, often result from a blockage of the breathing tube with phlegm or saliva.

Category 2: Dream dramas. Dramatic dreams, in which the dreamer takes part in a series of escapades in a more or less orderly sequence, are far more coherent than the nonsense dreams. These dreams are apparently a manifestation of the work of a creative artist that exists in many, perhaps in most, people but who may not, for various reasons, be able to manifest in the waking state. Artists, writers, scientists have all experienced the working of this element of their totality. A picture, a story, a solution to a scientific problem springs suddenly, fully formed, into the mind. *Something* has evidently been at work on the project but that something is not an element of the ordinary (third) state of consciousness.

This creative faculty, encountered in the second state of consciousness, may impart in symbolical form an important piece of information, like Kekule's dream of the snake with its tail in its mouth that gave him the clue to the cyclic structure of benzene. More often it tells a story of some kind in which the dreamer performs some role that may be very different from the roles he plays in life.

Ouspensky, discussing this type of dream, commented on the skill of the dream agent. It possessed, or appeared to possess, capacities that he was not able to use in the waking state. It was an artist "extraordinarily versatile in his knowledge, capacities and talents." It was not only a playwright, producer and scene painter but also an actor-impersonator. The latter quality impressed Ouspensky because he had very little of that capacity when awake. He had never been able to imitate people, reproduce their voices, intonations, gestures, movements. Yet the dream agent could do all these things.

Ouspensky made the further observation that this actor-impersonator can, at times, so realistically present the being of a dead person that the dreamer becomes convinced he is receiving a communication from the dead. This forms the basis of many so-called spiritualistic phenomena. There is, in such a phenomenon, an element of "magic" and the dreamer can hardly be blamed if he accepts somewhat questionable theories to account for his experience. Perfect impersonation of another being involves the projection of consciousness into that being (as in the Tibetan art of *tron-jug*). It tells the one who thus projects his awareness many things about that being which he could not normally know. It appears that this projection may, at times, occur when a person is in the dream state. The projection is involuntary and the information fragmentary; the dream may be remembered only dimly but carries with it an almost overwhelming impression that something has been communicated from "the other side."

An aspect of the dream state that has impressed several observers is the *déjà vu* phenomenon: "I have been here before." This feeling may come to a person in the waking state or in the dream state. Sometimes the sensation takes the form: "I have been here before, but in a dream." For some, this experience is so impressive that they have made it the basis of an entire theory of time. Ouspensky, commenting on this experience, stated that it was characteristic of dreams *observable in the waking state*. He went on to say that the machinery which generates dreams operates in the waking state but is obscured by the workings of the roof brain and the streams of thought that it pours into the awareness. To become aware of the dream world, it is necessary to achieve the state of consciousness without thoughts. In this state, dream images emerge and the experimenter finds himself "surrounded by a strange world of shadows, moods, conversations, sounds, pictures."

The *déjà vu* sensation, that elusive feeling "I have been here before" appears, from this observation, to result from the *superimposing of a dream on the waking state*. There are, of course, other possible explanations, as for instance Ouspensky's own favorite, "Eternal Recurrence," which gives to time a three-dimensional structure and thus ensures that every event is repeated. It is also possible that the *déjà vu* sensation is purely subjective and has no significance whatever. The neurophysiologist, Wilder Penfield, has been able to evoke the sensation by stimulating electrically a part of the cerebral cortex called the "temporal lobe."

Category 3: Revelation dreams. These dreams are quite rare but very impressive. They give to the dreamer a powerful impression that *something*, a god, an angel, a "higher power," is trying to reveal something to him or communicate with him in some way.

A characteristic of these dreams is the tremendous emotion which they generate, an emotion that can only be described as "religious awe." People of the ancient world attributed enormous importance to such dreams, were willing to rearrange their whole lives as a result of such an experience. Even a modern man, armored against superstition by the prevailing skepticism of a scientific era, may be much impressed by revelation dreams and may, on occasion, change his way of life as a result.

Dreams of this kind, either expressed in sleep or evoked by hypnosis, are often so dramatic that they are accepted as evidence of a previous incarnation. A whole class of literature has grown up around such dreams. A recent example of such literature, M. Bernstein's *The Search for Bridey Murphy* (New York: Doubleday), was a very modest affair compared with such effusions as *The Third Eye* (New York: Ballantine Books) by T. Lobsang Rampa, a catalog of marvels reputed to be Tibetan, recorded by a man whose proper British soul was displaced by that of a Tibetan lama without the usual formality of death!

Experiences of this kind may occur not only in the dream state but also during certain forms of meditation. Ouspensky recorded them during the experiments described in his chapter "Experimental Mysticism." With characteristic good sense, he refused to take the "revelations" seriously. The same cannot be said of such "clairvoyants" as Charles W. Leadbeater and Rudolf Steiner, who constructed, on the basis of revelation dreams, an entire pseudohistory of things past derived, as they expressed it, from the "Akashic records" (supposed "cosmic records" of all that has occurred) with which they firmly believed they had made contact.[35]

The feeling (common to all revelation dreams) that *some stupendous secret is about to be revealed* is also often experienced by people who have taken psychedelic drugs. They stand trembling on the threshold scarcely daring to look lest the revelation overwhelm them entirely. "I looked up," wrote Fitz Hugh Ludlow of one of his hashish experiences, "but my eyes, unopposed, every moment penetrated further and further into the immensity, and I turned them down, lest they should presently intrude into the fatal splendors of the Great Presence." [27] Such is the emotional tone that fills the sleeper who experiences a revelation dream, and it often compels him to endow the revelation with supernatural significance. Actually, it may not be significant at all. William James thought he had recorded the ultimate mystery under the influence of nitrous oxide. On returning to his normal state, he eagerly consulted the paper on which he had scrawled the great message. It read:

> Hogamus, Higamous,
> Man is polygamous.
> Higamous, Hogamous,
> Woman is monagamous.

Does this mean that revelation dreams are always deceptive, that despite their grandeur and the sense of awe they inspire they are actually never more than empty fantasies? No general answer can be given to this question. It is permissible only to warn the traveler that he who enters and explores the *second room* must interpret his experiences with caution. In the second room nothing can be trusted. The light is dim, the place is full of shadows, reverberates with echoes, is haunted by phantoms, filled with whispers and rumors. By all means, explore it but treat with caution what you find there.

Waking Sleep

The third state of consciousness is experienced when man awakens from physical sleep and plunges at once into the condition called "identification." Identification is the essence of the third state of consciousness. In this state, man has no separate awareness. He is lost in whatever he happens to be doing, feeling, thinking. Because he is lost, immersed, not present in himself, this condition, the third state of consciousness, is referred to in the Gurdjieffian system as the state of "waking sleep." Man in this state is described not as the real man but as a machine, without inner unity, real will or permanent I, acted upon and manipulated by external forces as a puppet is activated by the puppeteer.

For many people, this concept of waking sleep makes no sense at all. They firmly maintain that, once they "wake up," they are responsible beings, masters of themselves, fully conscious, and that anyone who tells them that they are not is a fool or a liar. It is almost impossible to convince such people that they are deceiving themselves because, when a man is told that he is not really conscious, a mechanism is activated within him which awakens him for a moment. He replies, indignantly, "But I *am* fully conscious," and because of this "trick of Nature" as Ouspensky used to call it, he does become conscious for a moment. He moves from the third room to the threshold of the fourth room, answers the challenge, and at once goes to sleep again, firmly convinced that he is a fully awakened being.

So, in the Myth of the Mad King, it makes no difference how often the king's ministers tell him that he is living in the cellar instead of his palace. He will reply, and really believe his reply, that the cellar is his palace and that they are the mad ones for suggesting that it is not.

It was exactly this reaction that Plato described in his account of the prisoners in the cave (which is actually a variant of the Myth of the Mad King). Suppose, says Plato in his *Republic* (Loeb edition), that one of the prisoners in the cave, whose only impression of reality is derived from watching shadows on the walls, escapes into the world outside. Suppose he is of an altruistic disposition and returns to tell the other prisoners of the bright and varied world that lies beyond their prison. Suppose he announces that all things they have ever seen are merely shadows. Will they welcome that message? Not likely!

> There will certainly be laughter at his expense and it will be said that the only result of his escapade up there is that he has come back with his eyesight ruined. Moral: it's a fool's game even to make the attempt to go up aloft; and as for the busybody who goes in for all the liberating and translating to higher spheres, if ever we have a chance to catch and kill him we will certainly take it.

The fact is that man in the third state of consciousness is in a situation from which it is hard to escape. He does not recognize the state as waking sleep, does not understand the meaning of identification. If anyone tells him that he is not fully conscious, he replies that he *is* conscious and, by the "trick of Nature," becomes conscious for a moment. He is like a man surrounded by distorting mirrors which offer him an image of himself that in no way corresponds to reality. If he is fat, they tell him he is slender. If he is old, they tell him he is young. He is very happy to believe the mirrors for they save him from that hardest of all tasks, the struggle to know himself as he really is.

Furthermore, this sleeping man is surrounded by other sleeping people and the whole culture in which he lives serves to perpetuate that state of sleep. Its ethics, morality, value systems are all based on the idea that it is lawful and desirable for man to spend his life in the third room rather than in a struggle to enter the fourth. Teachings that exhort men to awaken, to adopt a system of values based on *levels of being* rather than material possessions are distrusted. *Theoretically,* in the United States at least, what are loosely called "spiritual values" are accepted as valid, but practically they do not carry much weight.

Self-transcendence

A man's chance of attaining the fourth state of consciousness depends on whether or not he has experienced this state. If he does not even know it exists, he will not long for it any more than a bird born and raised in captivity can know what freedom is like or long for freedom. Man can, and from time to time does, experience the fourth state as a result of some religious emotion, under the influence of a work of art, in the rapture of sexual love or in situations of great danger and difficulty. In these circumstances it is said that he "remembers himself." This term is not entirely descriptive of the fourth state but it is the best available. Self-remembering is a certain separation of awareness from whatever a man happens to be doing, thinking, feeling. It is symbolized by a two-headed arrow suggesting double awareness. There is actor and observer, there is an objective awareness of self. There is a feeling of being outside of, separated from, the confines of the physical body; there is a sense of detachment, a state of nonidentification. For identification and self-remembering can no more exist together than a room can simultaneously be illuminated and dark. One excludes the other.

Several characteristics of the fourth state of consciousness have been described by A. Maslow in a chapter entitled "Peak Experiences as Acute Identity Experiences." He emphasizes the paradoxical quality of this state: "The greatest attainment of identity, autonomy or selfhood is itself simultaneously a transcending of itself, a going beyond and above selfhood. The person can then become relatively egoless." [36]

One statement in this chapter by Maslow calls for some elaboration: "Peaks are not planned or brought about by design; they happen." This may be perfectly true, but does not have to be. The whole practice of Creative Psychology is based on the hypothesis that man *can* change his level of being through intentional effort properly guided and persistently exerted. As a result of this effort, he will attain the fourth state of consciousness (roughly corresponding to Maslow's peak experience) with increasing frequency. He will also get glimpses of the fifth state of consciousness. The difference between experiencing these states by accident and inducing them deliberately is like that between finding money in the street and earning it by the sweat of one's brow. One may find money now and then, but it is not an event to be relied upon. In the same way, some drug experiences may produce a state akin to self-remembering and generate what Baudelaire called "The Taste of the Infinite." There are several ways of getting glimpses of the interior of the fourth room or even the fifth which a person may stumble upon more or less accidentally. This is not at all the same thing as finding the key and unlocking these chambers. For this, both effort and knowledge are required.

Once a man knows that the fourth room exists, he reaches a parting of ways so far as his life is concerned. He can either try to forget all about the fourth room, behave as if it does not exist, lapse again into the state of total identification, or he can decide to play the Master Game and set about looking for someone to teach him the technique. Two factors will influence his decision: the intensity of his dislike of sleep and the intensity of his longing for real awakening. These are the stick and the carrot which between them get the donkey moving. The struggle to unlock and enter the fourth room and, having entered it, to remain there, is a task so difficult under the conditions of modern life that few undertake it and even fewer succeed. It may well be that even the appetite for this adventure is gradually disappearing from the psyche of man. In this respect, the words of Nietzsche in *Thus Spake Zarathustra* may be relevant:

> Alas! there comes the time when man will no longer launch the arrow of his longing beyond man. . . .
> Lo! I show you the last man.
> The earth has become small and on it hops the last man who makes everything small. His species is ineradicable like the ground flea; the last man lives longest.

It may be asked at this point why should one make great efforts to enter the fourth room when things have been made so easy and pleasant in the third room. For there is no doubt about it; we of the so-called advanced nations live, on the whole, like kings. Better than kings. Not all the wealth of Croesus could have brought him even so commonplace an experience as a flight through the air, nor did all the riches of Egypt suffice to give Cleopatra freedom from the pangs of childbirth. The great ones of antiquity were as prone to pestilence as the meanest of their slaves. Even for the rich, life was dangerous and uncomfortable. For the poor, it was one long struggle to keep body and soul together.

Things are very different now. Watched over from cradle to grave by a paternalistic government, protected from overwork by unions, from hunger by the bounty of a scientific agriculture, from pestilence by an art of medicine so advanced that all the great plagues of antiquity have been conquered, soothed by tranquilizers or stimulated by antidepressants, perpetually hypnotized by the unending circuses offered by television, radio, the movies, why should we ask for more? When the third room is comfortable, safe and full of delights, why should we strive to ascend to the fourth? What does it have to offer that the third room does not?

The answer, of course, is freedom. Only when he enters the fourth room does a man become free. Only in the fourth state of consciousness is he liberated from the tyranny of the personal ego and all the fears and miseries that this entity generates. Once he has attained the fourth room and learned to live in it, a man becomes fearless. The words "I" and "mine" have ceased to be meaningful. He does not identify the self with the physical body or attach much importance to the possessions of that body. He feeds it, dresses it, cares for it and regulates its behavior. In due course he leaves it. One of the powers conferred by entry into the fourth room is the capacity to die at will.

Man in the third room may think he is his own master but actually has no control over his actions. He cannot so much as walk down a street without losing his attention in every stray impression that "takes his fancy." Man in the fourth room really is his own master. He knows where he is going, what he is doing, why he is doing it. His secret is that he remains unattached to the results of his activity, measures his success and failure not in terms of outward achievement, but in terms of inner awareness. He is able, as a result of his knowledge of forces at work about him, to know what is possible and what is impossible, what can be achieved and what cannot be achieved.

This may sound like a small accomplishment but it is actually a very large one. Dabblers in various forms of occultism and theosophy, dilettantes who play with what they imagine to be yoga, show a pathetic naïveté when it comes to evaluating what can and what cannot be obtained by these means. All sorts of miraculous achievements are accepted as possible, for man in the third state of consciousness tends to love miracles and to believe all sorts of nonsense that could not possibly happen. In the fourth state of consciousness such naïveté disappears. A man knows what combination of forces can produce what sort of result. He knows that everything happens in accordance with certain laws governing the relations of matter and energy. He knows that there is no miracle and anything that appears to be a miracle is merely a manifestation of some rare combination of forces, like the rare combination of skill and knowledge that enabled the master magician, Houdini, to extricate himself from every form of restraint that was ever applied to him.

Cosmic Consciousness

In addition to the fourth room, there is said by some commentators on this subject to exist a fifth room, corresponding to the fifth level of consciousness. It is related to that condition which R. M. Bucke described in *Cosmic Consciousness*, the "prime characteristic of which" was "a consciousness of the cosmos, that is, of the life and order of the universe." [37] Flashes of this state of consciousness may be experienced by certain people for no apparent reason. They may also be induced by psychedelics. Much of the material described by Alan Watts in *The Joyous Cosmology* could have been obtained as a result of his having entered the fifth room. The cosmic vision offered to Arjuna by Krishna and described in the eleventh chapter of the *Bhagavad Gita* is another example of the working of the fifth state of consciousness.

It must be understood, however, that this state, cosmic consciousness, is impossible for man to sustain without long and special training. The normal course of development demands that man must learn to enter and live in the fourth room before he can safely ascend to the fifth. If he enters the fifth room unlawfully, either by the use of drugs or any other means, he may suffer permanent damage as a result of the force of the impressions poured into his unprepared awareness. His situation is akin to that of an electrical machine suddenly subjected to a current much more powerful than that for which it was designed. The result at best is a blown fuse, at worst a burned out machine. Fortunately the physiological equivalent of a fuse does exist in man. Its operation results in the loss of consciousness when a man accidentally enters the fifth room. He is simply overwhelmed by the terrific rush of awareness and "blacks out," retaining afterwards scarcely a memory of that extraordinary moment.

This concept of the five rooms, or five levels of consciousness, is the theoretical basis of the whole teaching of Creative Psychology. We say "theoretical" because, unless a man has experienced the five states, they must remain for him theoretical possibilities only. No one, no matter how great his skill, can communicate to another the feeling of a different level of consciousness. Man in the fourth room cannot communicate his condition to man in the third room, nor can man in the third room communicate with man in the second.

Samadhi *and* Satori

Those familiar with the terminology of Zen Buddhism and yoga may ask what relationship the states called *satori* and *samadhi* have to the fourth and fifth states of consciousness. The answer is that neither *satori* nor *samadhi* represents one condition. They may range all the way from a brief experience of the fourth state to a profound experience of the fifth. *Satori* is the psychological result of the practice of *zazen* or "wall gazing," which, combined as it is in most Zen monasteries with strenuous physical work and certain types of physical exercises, induces the "objective awareness of the self" characteristic of the fourth state of consciousness. *Satori* is not a trancelike condition but *a new mode of awareness*. It does not, in the early stages at least, occur all the time but only in flashes, induced perhaps by a struggle with some *koan* or by some shock or stimulus supplied by the Zen Master.

Samadhi is a state of consciousness beyond name and form and, for this reason, cannot be described in words. "As salt being dissolved in water becomes one with it, so when *atma* and mind become one, it is called *samadhi*." [38] It is further stated, in this same text:

> The whole of this world and all the schemes of the mind are but the creations of thought. Discarding these thoughts and taking leave of all conjectures, obtain peace. As camphor disappears in

fire, and rock salt in water, so the mind united with the *atma* loses its identity. All that appears is the knowable, the mind is called knowledge. When the knowable and the knowledge are both destroyed equally, then duality is destroyed.

Commenting on these passages, Theos Bernard wrote:

Samadhi cannot be experienced until a condition of mindlessness has been created. All modifications of the thinking principle must cease; all thought forms must be removed, yet some form of awareness must remain. Without yoga experience it is difficult to imagine what is meant; that is why teachers do not even try to explain.[39]

Samadhi, as generally described, involves a trancelike state, in which awareness of the body and its surroundings is lost. Is this an essential accompaniment of the state? Is it possible to "enter *samadhi*" and still maintain some sort of external activity? Is *samadhi* the fifth state of consciousness, the ultimate level above which no man can ascend and still remain linked to the physical body? All these questions can be answered only by experiment and observation. Words, definitions, commentaries merely serve to confuse the issue. If one wants to find out what lies beyond the frontier, the only way to do so is to go beyond it and see. On this journey one will do well to obtain both a map and a guide but he will have to travel every step by his own efforts.

IV. The Silent World

Simple Awareness

THE LEGITIMATE ROAD to the fourth room and the fifth lies through the silent world, the world of simple awareness, beyond words, beyond thoughts. Psychedelic drugs may lead the traveler into the silent world, may give him a taste of the beauties and wonders it contains, but they cannot keep him in this world. Though he takes mescaline by the spoonful, saturates his system with LSD, inhales nitrous oxide till he reels in stupor, he still cannot hope to hold the treasure of silence. Only by work, by a steady, unremitting effort can he learn to stop the wheel of the imagination, to halt that flood of inner conversations, arguments, mere chatter, with which the roof brain, by its useless overactivity, floods the awareness from dawn to dusk. ?????

While this noise persists, no deep awareness is possible. So for one who really wishes to *practice* Creative Psychology, the first rule is very simple: *enter the silence as often as possible; remain there for as long as possible.*

Stop thoughts!

In the quiet which follows, like the healing silence after a long political speech, permit the impressions brought by each separate sense to float on the surface of a calm awareness. The eye rests on the objects of sight, not naming them, not desiring, passing no judgments. The shapes of buildings, the texture of trees and grass, of clouds and earth, take on a meaning so new, so fresh and so exciting that they seem on the point of relating their innermost secrets. A horse, a cow, a stray dog, a skinny cat furtively snatching a morsel from an overturned garbage can, all speak in a wordless language of their innermost condition. Nor is there a danger, where these dumb beasts are concerned, of committing the pathetic fallacy of transforming the creatures into "woolly men" like the panthers, bears and wolves in Kipling's *Jungle Books*. To the silent awareness, the skinny cat is all cat, the very essence of cat. Its sneaky feline motions are all of a piece, speaking directly to the consciousness in soundless tones of all that cat means, of cat in past, present, future. The eternal cat.

And even buildings . . .

They have less to say than cats but they communicate. They almost turn themselves inside out in their eagerness to share their secrets. They tell of the men that made them, the beings that dwell in them; indeed, they portray a whole history of architecture but again without words, without discourse, all in an instant, for time itself, in this silent world, attains a new dimension—the eternal Now—in which millennia can be experienced as instants.

As with sights, so with sounds. In the healing silence that follows the stopping of thoughts, all sounds take on a new significance. Nature echoes, reverberates through a rich spectrum of tonalities formerly unperceived. The breath of wind in the trees, the patter of raindrops falling on autumn leaves, the roar of a rain-swollen brook, the rumble and restless tooting of traffic in city streets offer to the inward ear their vibrant essences. All cries resound with new significance, bird-cries and beast-cries, man-cries and child-cries, the buzz of a fly, the moo of a cow, the slurp of soup, the smack of a kiss, of a hand on flesh, a foot on concrete. There are inward sounds also. Not merely the squirt and gurgle of toiling guts passing their products from pouch to pouch in a soft succession of peristaltic waves; not only the almost imperceptible throb of the heart squeezing or sucking its blood surge from lungs to aorta, but subtler sounds, scarcely sounds at all, originating from who knows what interactions. (The yogis have known them for centuries and call them *nadas.*) There are vibrations almost cosmic in their immensity; the Music of the Spheres, perhaps, or terrestrial shivers as old earth stirs in its sleep.

As with sights and sounds, so with odors. How rich a world, how subtle, how unexplored! Man's olfactory sense is a poor and shadowy affair lacking sensitivity, little more than a rudiment, but is still an extraordinary and subtle instrument. Its range is enormous. No classification has been devised which adequately conveys the complexity of the odor spectrum. Acrid, putrid, fragrant, appetizing, sickening, stupefying, ethereal—all these adjectives may be applied without precisely defining the sensation. Whole ranges, octaves of smells overlap in the awareness of one who has trained this neglected sense, who is able, by virtue of his inner silence, to receive these elusive messages, made doubly transient by the fact that the sense of smell is so rapidly fatigued.

Intertwined among the odors are memories, for odors have the wonderful power of evoking recollection. The balsamic odor of clove oil transports the writer to the old botanical laboratory where his first crude sections, cut from plant stems with a razor and stained with safranine and haematoxylin, attained translucence in this clarifying agent. The no less potent but very different smell of decaying fish transports him to the beach of Positano, where, in sea-washed windrows, deposited by the high tide, thousands of rotting squid lay decomposing under a shimmering mantle of iridescent flies. The odor of drying seaweed hauntingly evokes childhood vacations with painted buckets, wooden spades, sand castles transient as children's dreams.

Then there is the sense of touch, the sense of the muscles, awareness of physical posture, of heat and cold, of various forms and intensities of pain, the subtleties of taste, sexual sensations in all their variety, sensations of vigor and of fatigue, of health and sickness. All, without a single exception, take a new meaning when the doors of perception are cleansed, when the wandering thoughts are silenced, when simple direct awareness takes the place of daydreams and our "thought-ridden nature" (T. E. Lawrence's phrase) throws off the burden of a useless cerebration leaving consciousness open to receive the sensory messages derived from physical realities.

Stopping thoughts, the practice of simple awareness, these are the keys with which a man can unlock the fourth room. To one who has never tried to use this method, it might appear almost too easy. What could be simpler than to impose silence on the gibbering roof brain, which, like a badly designed radio, generates so much noise (using this term in the electronic sense) that every message is distorted? So obviously salutary is the method that one psychiatrist (Roger Vittoz) made it the root of his therapeutic techniques.[40] A pity that more of them did not follow his example! The enormous volume of words which these healers of minds evoke in the course of their ministrations are more apt to confuse than help the patient, entangling him in a veritable labyrinth of verbiage, further stirring up the already too noisy roof brain.

Few disciplines, however, are more uncongenial to contemporary man than the intentional silencing of the noise machine. This gibbering mechanism ceaselessly pouring out its flood of inner conversations, arguments, schemes and aimless chatter, has come to occupy so large a place in man's awareness that he often regards it as his very self. If this noise is switched off accidentally or if he switches it off intentionally, he has an uneasy feeling of nonexistence. Contemporary man, using this term somewhat loosely to describe the mass produced semi-automata that make up the bulk of the world's large man-swarms, fears inner silence and avoids places that induce inner silence, be they deserts or mountains or empty stretches of ocean. In case their inner noisemaker ever fails them and by some accident falls silent, they carry with them portable radios, drowning any awareness they might happen to develop in a wash of senseless sound. Should this recourse fail, they hasten to some party where, in an atmosphere poisoned by the fumes of alcohol or tobacco, they exchange at the tops of their voices a stream of inanities concerning their own or other people's lives.

All inner work involves the imposing of inner silence. To enter the silence as often as possible and to remain there for as long as possible is the goal of all followers of the Way, be they yogis, Sufis, Zen Buddhists or Christian mystics. But, as John Cassian complained to the Abbot Serenius, whenever the mind is brought under control, it slips away "like an eel out of my hand," [41] (Appendix D) or as Arjuna said to Krishna: "The mind is restless, turbulent, powerful and obstinate. I deem it as difficult to control as the wind." [42]

There is nothing dramatic or heroic about the struggle with the noise machine. Results are obtained by the repetition of small efforts, like drops of water wearing away stone. Before these efforts can be made, the student must have an inner conviction that the daydreams and imaginary conversations really are useless, unprofitable, and, at times, downright dangerous. Only when he has acquired a taste for the inner silence and a corresponding distaste for the inner noise can his efforts attain a level of intensity that produces a real change. He must realize, not just intellectually but also emotionally, that the stream of daydreams occupying his mind is a symptom of the state of waking sleep, of existence in the third room, a world of unreality and illusion. If he wishes to emerge from the third room, he must *sacrifice his daydreams* however attractive or harmless these dreams may appear.

Awareness and Attention

The practice of simple awareness is impossible without control of attention. Attention is to awareness as the oil in a lamp is to its flame. While there is oil in the lamp, the flame persists. Once the oil is exhausted, the flame goes out. Control of attention is the one function that man possesses which may be said to confer on him a certain amount of free will. He can "direct his attention." But his power to do this depends upon his possessing a certain kind of energy the supply of which is limited. Each day, on awakening, he has just so much of this energy, as a battery, after being charged, contains just so much electrical potential. His inner work each day depends on the conservation of this energy. Once it has been squandered, it is hard to replace.

A man's level of consciousness can be measured by the freedom of his attention. In the state of identification he has no "freedom to attend." He *thinks he has,* but this is one of the illusions which this state imposes. Actually, he is a slave to whatever stimulus happens to have taken his fancy. "I could not put the book down." "I could not take my eyes off the game." "I was absolutely *immersed* in what I was doing." In these and countless other phrases people describe the condition of identification and the loss of freedom to attend which it imposes. A sight thrilling or spectacular, a story real or imaginary, has taken our fancy and swallowed us in the process. Our inner space is totally occupied with the subject matter about which we are reading, the spectacle we are watching. There is nothing in the least bit voluntary about this form of attention. We are caught up like flies in a spider's web, manipulated, directed, enchained. Look at the faces of people at the race track, a baseball game, a bullfight, a prizefight, any spectacle of a flamboyant or brutal kind. There is nothing behind the face. It is empty, a mask. The house is vacant.

This is *enslaved attention.* In this condition, inner silence and simple awareness are lost and the whole field of consciousness is "occupied" by a victorious enemy. In the state of enslaved attention, the vital force is squandered. The whole day's supply can be lost in a few moments.

No less costly in terms of energy is *dispersed attention,* attention which wanders all over the field of awareness, dragged now here, now there, "a feather for every wind that blows." Fickle, feeble, ungoverned, it flits about, changes color like a chameleon, changes shape like Proteus. The eyes rove aimlessly, the ears flap like shirts on a clothesline. Scattered impressions pull the attention about like dogs fighting over a bone. There is a total absence of inner stability. This state drains the organism of its strength insofar as the power to maintain awareness is concerned. There results a trancelike condition, a state of semi-hypnosis that borders on the pathological but is not recognized as such by psychiatrists because a large majority of the "well" population pass their lives in this state, including the psychiatrists.

"Waking sleep," "hypnotized sleep," "walking sleep," "identification" are different names for the same thing. In this state man does not really know who he is, where he is, why he is or even whether he is—a sleep walker. . . . If man could be aware of his state of sleep, how eagerly, how urgently he would struggle to awaken! For waking sleep is dangerous and dismal. Waking sleep is inner slavery and inner unrest. Endlessly men prate about freedom, and shout and demonstrate and riot and demand Congressional legislation and civil rights. All in vain. The fetters are inward, the bondage is spiritual. The name of the great enslaver is "Identification" and the result of his domination is "Waking Sleep."

We have spoken of "enslaved attention and dispersed attention." But what is the function of directed attention? A medical student pores over his anatomy text. Every bone, every muscle, every vein, nerve, artery, ligament, tendon must be fixed in the memory with its name, function, location all held in place, at least long enough to enable him to spill the information in answer to an examiner's question. No one would accuse this poor fellow of being so lost in the story that he cannot put the text down. Tangles of terminology writhe in his brain. He himself writhes in his chair. Again and again his attention wanders, again and again he drags it back. He would like nothing better than to hurl the text into the wastebasket, turn on the television, "lose himself" in some tale of violence or fraud or the antics of a funny man with synthetic laughs dubbed in ready-made. But exams are near. Fear of failure cracks the whip behind him, ambition dangles its carrot before his nose. So back he goes to the text and focuses his tired attention on that maze of pipes and pulleys that is the human frame.

That is work, not play. That is directed attention, not attracted attention.

Is he, therefore, less identified because he is working? Is his state of consciousness higher than that of the viewer, the listener, the reader lost in his hypnotized trance before the magician who weaves his spell and fashions his illusions on a screen or off it? Alas, no law operates to ensure that he who works attains inner freedom thereby. Would that it did! Were work itself the liberator, all men would long ago have attained the status of Christs or Bodhisattvas. Our medical student is making use of a different mechanism from that used by the merely passive viewer or listener. He is, however, every bit as identified, every bit as lost in the task. He lacks the separated awareness, the sense of two, of observer and observed. He is *immersed* in his text or *immersed* in his boredom with the text, or *immersed* in his craving for alternative, easier activity, like turning on the television and being "entertained."

Directed attention does not hypnotize or stupefy in the same way as does enslaved or dispersed attention. But it does not induce full awakening either. A person using directed attention can still be deeply identified with the task in hand. His inner space is still completely occupied with whatever he happens to be doing. He has no existence apart, no real being.

Only when he learns to withdraw from the task in hand, to maintain a certain thread of awareness which remains apart from thinking, feeling, sensing, does he begin to get the taste of the fourth state of consciousness. In this state he *is*, he exists objectively for himself as a tree exists, a table exists, a book exists. He is aware of the room in which he is sitting, of himself as one of the objects in that room, of his "inner space" and of his outer space, room, house, surroundings, planets, suns, not in specific details but as a totality, as a presence. In this state, the self is not separate and the attention, though directed to whatever the task in hand, is at the same time flexible and open, not rigid and narrow.

This sensing of the self as not self but merely as one of the objects of the environment removes at one stroke all fears, all tensions, all anxieties. A condition of buoyancy and ease, a delightful *ataraxia*, falls to the lot of one in whom such a condition has been induced. He is in harmony with *Tao* (the unconditioned, unnamable source of all reality). His work, like that of Prince Hui's admirable cook, perfectly accords with eternal principles and accordingly shows a rhythm, an inner balance. Nowhere is there impatience or disharmony. The face which, in a state of identification, is either tense or stupid, now wears the calm, withdrawn air that one observes in the features of meditating Bodhisattvas. In such a one is embodied that condition so aptly described by the Zen patriarch:

> What life can compare with this! Sitting alone at the window I watch the flowers bloom, the leaves fall, the seasons come and go.[43]

In art this condition is depicted in certain landscapes by the Chinese masters, especially Ma Yuan. Among towering peaks and misty valleys the tiny traveler wends his way, insignificant as a gnat. But he does not bother about significance or insignificance. He does not say, "How tiny am I, how great is the world." Such statements merely entangle him in the web of dualism. His inner space and outer space are harmonized. Rocks, trees, mist are not separate from "I." There is, instead, a unity, a "suchness" which goes beyond "I" and not "I."

This living in harmony with *Tao*, this inner freedom, is not attained without long and careful training. It is a state of physiological and psychological equipoise, seemingly effortless, but maintained by a watchfulness as real as that which enables the tightrope walker to maintain his balance high above the heads of the crowd. There is no tension in this watchfulness. It is flexible, pervasive, an invisible shield, an instrument that *catches and holds* impressions before these impressions can set the inner machinery in motion.

Awareness and Impressions

Generalized attention separated from the ego offers to one who employs it the power of choice of impressions. He who has a watchman at the gate can scrutinize all who try to enter, can receive the impressions he chooses and reject the rest. There is no other art more important than the art of receiving impressions, for a man's impressions are as much a food as his daily bread. Deprived of impressions, a person soon becomes deranged, his mental world becomes disorganized, he suffers from delusions and hallucinations, as the work of Donald O. Hebb[44] and of John Lilly has clearly proved. Less well understood is the effect of the "malabsorption" of impressions, the effect on the "digestion" of impressions of different levels of attention, the poisonous action of certain types of impressions and the nourishing effect of others.

As far as impressions are concerned, man's instincts seem to give him little guidance. A cow or a horse grazing in a meadow is generally warned by instinct to avoid poisonous plants, but a man, whose impressions are just as much a food as his bread, shows no such discrimination. On the contrary, he will often *deliberately* *seek* poisonous impressions, compelled by some perverse impulse to degrade his own inner life, already sufficiently polluted without that. A degenerate "entertainment" industry does not hesitate to take advantage of this perverse taste, pouring out through all its various channels a stream of more or less pathological material which readers, viewers, listeners eagerly absorb into their psyches.

Poise, balance, inner harmony, the "creation of an island that no flood can immerse" [45]—all this can be achieved by one who has learned to handle his impressions. Between the moment when an impression strikes and the reaction to that impression, elapses a time so short it can hardly be measured by man's ordinary awareness. Yet much may depend on what happens in that brief interval. If the watchman is awake, the impression can at once be arrested as a burglar is arrested by an alert policeman before he can enter the house and steal the silver.[46] The blow is taken on the shield, the shock is absorbed. There is no mechanical reaction which will later be regretted.

Accept or reject—this is the basis of the inner work that leads to the genesis of a truly free being. A man's health, as well as his inner development and level of being, depends just as much on how his impressions are metabolized as on how his food is metabolized. The way in which impressions are metabolized depends on the level of attention and on the *quality* of that attention.

There occurs, in the Gurdjieffian system, a series of very interesting and provocative diagrams which are collectively known as the "Food Tables." [47] These are provocative, at least to a chemist, because they take liberties with the names of four chemical elements, carbon, oxygen, nitrogen and hydrogen, using them to designate any substance through which a "force" is acting (active force in oxygen, passive force in nitrogen, neutralizing force in carbon, no force in hydrogen). This is apt to stick in a chemist's craw if he jealously insists that the names of elements must refer to forms of matter with specific atomic configurations.[48]

What makes the Food Table interesting is the idea that impressions require for their full development a certain chemical catalyst. This catalyst is present in the body but, in the third state of consciousness (identification), is neither present in the right place nor in sufficient amount to make possible the full digestion of impressions. For this reason man in the third state of consciousness suffers from a state of chronic malnutrition in one part of his being not because he is deprived of impressions, like the subjects in Hebb's and Lilly's experiments, but because he does not properly metabolize the impressions he receives.

This digesting of impressions depends on the quality of attention in the person who receives the impression. The special kind of effort involved in self-remembering brings to the appropriate place and in sufficient amount that catalyst on which the transformation of impressions depends. This is why, in the fourth state of consciousness, impressions take on such extraordinary richness, as if seen for the first time. The simplest objects become enhaloed with all sorts of hidden meanings which were previously not noticed. In certain mystics, such as William Blake and Jakob Boehme, this full development of impressions seemed to take place without their having to make this special kind of effort. It may occur often in children and cease to happen later. (Wordsworth's *Intimations of Immortality* laments this fact.) It may be brought about by certain psychedelics. (Aldous Huxley precisely describes the mescaline-induced transformation of impressions in *The Doors of Perception.*) But for the majority of people, no other way is available but to begin work on the control of attention, preventing it from wandering, holding it as one holds water in a brimming bowl, using it to "capture" impresssions, to accept and digest those that nourish, reject those that poison.

Skeptics will probably complain that the above account of the digestion of impressions is highly subjective, that there is no chemical evidence of the existence of the catalyst here described. The criticism is pointless. We can never hope to enter the brain and snatch from the midst of its seething myriad neurons the exact material involved in the transmutation of impressions. The only way to check the validity of the above statement is to induce, by suitable exercises, that condition which here is loosely called "self-remembering." One who does this will find that his impressions *do* change. There is nothing imaginary about it. He is not suffering from hallucinations. He has simply, for the time being, *woken up* and is enjoying those insights into the cosmic drama which are man's birthright, but which, like the mad king in the cellar, he cannot experience because he refuses to emerge from the confines of the personal ego.

Conservation of Awareness

Nothing that man possesses is more precious than his awareness. It is a material entity, like muscular energy, and its level fluctuates during the day. It lies within a man's power to squander the vital resource or to conserve it. It is lost every time a mechanical happening, wandering thought, a casual glance, or any trivial event or accidental impression causes the student to lose his sense of objective awareness, to plunge into a state of identification as a fly into a honey pot. Each of these plunges involves loss of the energy of awareness and the lost energy cannot easily be regained for the body has only so much at its disposal. The vital energy-substances are manufactured during the hours of sleep and used up during the day. They *can* be used creatively but rarely are, because impressions, instead of being digested in the way they should be through the application of objective awareness, function merely as distractions, pulling the attention this way and that, wasting energy instead of creating it.

Choice of Activities

"Surely you are demanding the impossible. Every force in our culture serves to distract the attention. The incessant turmoil in our cities, the endless advertisements, the clang of telephones, the clatter of subways, the shrieking headlines of newspapers, the curves of women and their painted faces, the exciting shop windows, not to mention a thousand incidents in daily life are all specifically designed to cause the greatest possible degree of identification. No matter how hard I try to remain inwardly silent, these distractions dissipate my awareness. How am I to avoid being trapped by the hypnotizing effect of my own activity? Short of entering a monastery or retreating into the desert, I do not see how I can protect my awareness from being squandered on ten thousand distractions."

These are valid objections and they need to be answered.

"Short of entering a monastery or retreating into the desert . . ."

This is an ancient stratagem and many have used it. The way of the monk, the way of the hermit or the recluse is the way of one who tries to obtain victory by avoiding the battle. He makes a fortified position in a remote place and hopes that the enemy will not find him. There were days when men and women in thousands flocked to the desert, lived in caves, remote hermitages, perched like storks on the tops of tall columns. Does such a retreat ensure victory? Not necessarily. It simplifies the struggle but the hermit, too, has his problems. There are devils in the desert, as St. Anthony discovered. Besides, as a permanent way of life, it is sterile. A year's retreat into the desert may be profitable but a lifetime in the wilderness—that is another matter. A man owes something to the society that produced him even though he may dislike that society and reject its values.

What then? Shall he fight an unequal battle and waste his life opposing forces stronger than himself? Is this the action of a hero or a fool?

Neither or both. The question needs rephrasing. He must seek a means of making his livelihood that will not entangle him too inextricably in mechanical activities. There are creative activities and destructive activities. There are activities that enrich the doer. There are activities that serve to inflate the false ego, that involve falsehoods and depend on the propagation of big or little lies. There are activities (they constitute a huge and hideous industry) that prostitute the fruits of scientific discovery for purposes of mass destruction. There are activities that funnel funds and resources into semi-imbecile projects and feats of stratospheric jugglery only fit to arouse the wonder of children and fools.

All such activities the discerning student of Creative Psychology will avoid, as a wise old fox avoids traps even though these traps are baited with very tempting morsels. He will do well to stay as close as possible to simple realities, shunning the poisonous exhalations of the man-swarm, unless he has reached that stage of inner development at which a man can live *anywhere*. ("By skilfull means [*upaya*] one can live comfortably even in hell.") He who has not reached this stage (and it is a very advanced one) should be guided in his choice of occupation by the saying: "You will never smell like a rose if you roll in a dunghill." He will not despise activities that involve manual as well as mental skills, even though these manual skills seem rather humble, for he will recall the example of Prince Hui's wonderful cook and the fact that Jakob Boehme was a shoemaker, Paul of Tarsus a tentmaker, Peter a fisherman and Jesus himself a carpenter. He will be careful to plan his activities in such a way that they leave him ample leisure for meditation, contemplation and the psychophysiological exercises necessary for the generation of high energy-substances. In this connection he will do well to bear in mind a saying of G. Gurdjieff's: "He who would progress in the Work must learn to earn his living with his left foot."

Intentional Doing and Mechanical Happening

"How am I to avoid being trapped by the hypnotizing effect of my own activity?"

This is a good question. Activity, even quite simple activity, *does* have a hypnotizing effect on the one who acts, tends to generate the state of identification that the seeker of inner freedom strives to avoid. The student begins an activity with every intention of retaining double awareness, of maintaining the sense of two, doer and observer. All goes smoothly for awhile, then a slip occurs; he loses focus, loses his attention in some daydream, becomes totally immersed in what he is doing. In short, he falls asleep and remains asleep until, quite by accident, something happens to arouse him and he suddenly recalls his original aim, like a sleepwalker awakening to find himself in another room.

Two forms of activity must be clearly distinguished: *intentional doing; mechanical happening.*

What is *intentional doing?*

> Moreover, brethren, a brother whether he departs or returns, whether he looks at or away from, whether he has drawn in or stretched out his limbs, whether he has donned under-robe, over-robe, or bowl, whether he is eating, drinking, chewing, reposing, or whether he is obeying the calls of nature is aware of what he is about. In going, standing, sitting, sleeping, watching, talking or keeping silence, he knows what he is doing.[48a]

Such is intentional doing. It begins with awareness of aim. At the beginning of an activity he must know— "I am about to do this." It may be a totally minor thing. He is about to go into the house and get his hat. So he goes, he gets the hat, he puts it on. Mission accomplished.

But suppose as he enters the house he notices dust on the furniture, finds fault with his wife on this score, gets into an argument: "Why is the house dirty? Why do I live in a pigsty?" The hat is forgotten. Instead, he is quarreling with his wife. Later, when he has stopped quarreling, he cannot remember why he came into the house in the first place. He must go back into the garden, where the impact of the hot sun on his bald pate reminds him of his first intention—to get his hat. So he must make a second trip into the house to perform what he intended to do in the first place. This is *mechanical happening.* An accidental impression, in this case dust on the furniture, counteracted the intentionality with which the action was begun. The man lost his awareness, plunged into a state of complete identification, arguments, recriminations, all on account of one stray impression.

Know what you are doing and why.

In large activities, in small activities, set definite limits. I have such a thing to do. I will allow myself so much time in which to do it. Clearly visualize the process, the tools involved, the materials involved, the forces involved. Such preparation may make all the difference between accidental happening and intentional doing. To keep the watchman awake work as quickly as possible. If the watchman is awake, stray impressions will be excluded as well as wandering thoughts. If the activity does not go as planned, if an error is made, if some persistent daydream distracts awareness—

STOP!

Stop all activity. Return to the starting point. Redefine the intention. Start again. Strive all the while to keep the inner silence, to practice simple awareness, to receive impressions simply and directly. Every activity offers profound insights concerning the interplay of forces, the qualities of materials, the triads and octaves needed to produce the desired result. Similarly the activity, performed with the right degree of double awareness, illuminates the inner workings of the organism, revealing to the objective observer those subtle rhythms of tension and relaxation that give to the simplest act a smoothness and flow reminiscent of musical harmony or the gestures of a dancer. To this Chuang-tze referred when describing the movements of Prince Hui's cook:

> Every blow of his hand, every heave of his shoulders, every tread of his foot, every thrust of his knee, every *whish* of rent flesh, every *chhk* of the chopper was in perfect harmony, rhythmi-

cal like the dance of the Mulberry Grove, simultaneous like the chords of the Ching Shou.[49]

There was nothing lofty or romantic about the task which the cook was performing (cutting up a bullock). In fact, from a Buddhist standpoint, it was a degrading activity. But so obviously was it an example of intentional doing, so perfect was the inner poise of the man performing the task, that it moved the Prince to exclaim: "From the words of this cook I have learned how to take care of my life."

Anyone who wants a brief sentence to sum up the "essence difference" between intentional doing and mechanical happening need remember only a beautiful saying of Yun-men as recorded by Alan Watts in *The Way of Zen:* "In walking, just walk, in sitting, just sit. Above all, don't wobble." Watts, elaborating on this theme, has introduced the idea of feedback and of the "chatter" which results when a feedback mechanism (thermostat, for instance) is set to operate between too narrow limits and so switches the power off almost as soon as it has switched it on.[50] This is a very fruitful line of thought as many servomechanisms operate in the human body and may at times become set too finely and respond too readily for the welfare of the organism.

Restoring Lost Balance

The above procedures all relate to maintaining the state of simple awareness, of inner silence. The state can be compared to balance, the "vital balance" [51] that enables a man to control his reactions to impressions instead of being blown about like a feather in the wind. But the reader will rightly insist that maintaining this balance is a difficult art, one learned only by long practice. So what is one to do who has lost his balance? The watchman (to use another simile) has fallen asleep. An undesirable impression has intruded and is creating havoc. Now the man is "upset." His thoughts and feelings are in turmoil. "I was wronged, insulted, underrated, maligned, slandered." In this state, no matter how often he tries to silence the "noise machine" and concentrate on simple awareness of sounds, sights, sensations, he cannot do so. His noise machine is agitated to the point of frenzy by impulses coming from the lower brain (thalamus or hypothalamus), which is the seat of man's emotional life. His entire awareness is occupied with stormy thoughts, accusations of others, justification of himself, expostulations and recriminations. These go on and on with maddening persistence, like a phrase repeated by a phonograph with its needle caught in a groove. With a storm raging in the mind, he can no more engage in the practice of simple awareness than can the captain of a ship being battered by a hurricane engage in writing sonnets.

Transfer the energy from the destructive process into a creative process.

This is most readily accomplished by undertaking some physical task, the more vigorous the better. Chop firewood, dig the garden, dance the *gopak*, climb the Sierras. But the physical outlet is often not available. This leaves two other procedures either of which can serve to drain the energy from its destructive cycle. The first of these is *repetition*, the second *visualization*. Both practices serve the same end; they provide the agitated mind with a firm support to which it can cling as a shipwrecked sailor clings to a floating spar. It is not a *substitute* for the practice of simple awareness. It is a temporary expedient, to be used in emergencies.

Repetition involves some phrase or a series of sentences which is placed so forcibly in the focus of attention that it drives out all other material. In the Judeo-Christian tradition, repetition centers around a *prayer*. In the Hindu-Buddhist tradition it centers around a *mantra*. A mantra differs from a prayer in being often only a sound, perhaps a single syllable, like the syllables "AUM" or "HUM." A prayer consists of a sentence or several sentences. There are very few real prayers. Most so-called prayers, especially those which involve demands on the deity (God give us rain, sun, health, a bigger salary, victory over our enemies, etc.) are merely examples of a pathetic type of wishful thinking and are not really prayers at all. Real prayers always have the same aim: to lead the one who prays out of the third room into the fourth, to bring the lower into contact with the higher.

The simplest of prayers, and from the standpoint of repetition the most effective, consists of three words: "GOD HELP ME." This is a simplified form of the Pilgrim's Prayer: "Lord Jesus Christ, Son of David, have mercy on me." The prayer, as readers of *The Way of a Pilgrim*[52] will remember, formed the basis of a special inner practice, "The Prayer of the Heart," which was actually a form of *mantra yoga* handed down by special teachers in the Greek Orthodox Church (see Appendix C of this book). In its trisyllabic, mantric form, the prayer evokes the three components of a triad: the higher consciousness above and beyond the ego (GOD), the lower separated individualized consciousness (ME), and the striving of the second to draw strength from the first (HELP). It makes no difference actually whether the person using this prayer "believes in God," whatever this hackneyed phrase may mean. The important thing is that, by relating the petty ego struggling in its morass of self-pity, indignation, injured dignity, etc., to another entity far greater than itself, a sense of proportion is restored. Furthermore, by concentrating the attention on the repetition of the syllables, accompanied by rhythmic and directed breathing, he who repeats the prayer drains away energy from the destructive, repetitive inner noise. Thus, the useless drain of vital energy is halted, the vicious circle is broken and the awareness shifted from a very narrow preoccupation to a wider horizon.

All prayers, to be of any value, must have this horizon-widening effect. The Lord's Prayer, for instance, is a series of mantras all of which, properly expressed, would be trisyllables, the triads intepenetrating to form a design relating the microcosm to the macrocosm. The first triad, "Father in Heaven," establishes this relationship, stating, in effect, that man's consciousness is linked to the universal consciousness (the Father in Heaven). The second, "Hallowed be Thy Name," introduces the *wish* that the goal of attainment of higher consciousness might be regarded by men as a lofty and holy one. The third and fourth are further developments of this wish. The fifth, "Give us bread," relates to the generation in the body of the high energy-substances on which the development of higher levels of consciousness depends. It is "daily bread" because it must be renewed daily. The sixth and seventh triads, "Lead us not into Temptation," and "Deliver us from Evil," have so many meanings that it would be out of place to go into them here. They refer to certain traps or catches which divert the inner work from its proper ends.

So the Lord's Prayer, correctly uttered and understood, is a mantra of great power and can be used as such for the purposes of quietening destructive thought processes that have taken hold of the mind. It will be effective only if the significance of each of its component triads is borne in mind so that energies employed in negative imagination, self-pity, self-reproach or self-justification are diverted from these useless activities into creative channels.

The Buddhist mantra, "AUM MANE PADME HUM," can also be used as a basis for repetition by those who prefer "Buddhist" forms to "Christian" ones. (These religious tags are meaningless to one who thinks in terms of Creative Psychology.) The mantra is harmonized with the breathing, the outbreath corresponding to the "AUM," the inbreath to the "HUM." The significance of the mantric syllables is held in the mind. The "AUM," on the cosmic scale, symbolizes the process of outflowing, differentiation, the octave of becoming, progress from one to many, the Dancing Shiva, the Day of Brahma. The "HUM" on the cosmic scale stands for the octave of reunification, the indrawing, progress from many to one, the Meditating Shiva, the "Night of Brahma." The two words, "MANE" and "PADME" (generally translated as "the jewel in the lotus"), symbolize two states of being, *nirvana* and *samsara*, and enshrine the principle that, to the fourth state of consciousness, which is beyond dualism and the pairs of opposites, *nirvana* and *samsara* are one.

In a more simplified form, this mantra has only three sounds, "AUM, AH, HUM," the symbols visualized as white, red, blue respectively. This mantra is the basis of mantric breathing described in Tibetan literature, the "HUM" corresponding to the in breath, the "AH" to the suspension when breath is held locked in the body, the "AUM" to the out breath. The three sounds symbolize the three aspects of nature, the passive, active and neutralizing, which, in their various combinations, underly the play of phenomena.

Visualization, the second method of silencing the restless mind, is based on various symbols or diagrams which, in the Western tradition, are called *arcana* and in the Hindu tradition *yantra.* *Arcana* of various kinds have long been associated in the West with magic, the "calling up of spirits" and the release of "higher forces" (whatever this may mean). About this, a good deal of nonsense has been spoken and written. Actually, the sign of the microcosm and macrocosm, the twenty-two *arcana* of the Tarot cards, the pentagram and hexagram, the Adam Kadmon of the Cabala, are merely symbolical representations of forces working in man and in nature. By holding them in the mind, the student learns to "think in other categories," above all to think without words. This type of effort brings a certain degree of awakening, a glimpse of the contents of the fourth room or even the fifth. The transformation only occurs after long practice, when the *arcana* come to life and begin to move and interact. Until they do so, they remain merely pictures and diagrams.

Exactly the same thing is true of the Eastern *yantra.* A *yantra* may be a picture of some god or a diagram such as a *mandala.* It expresses in symbolical form the interplay of forces between microcosm and macrocosm, between man and the world in which he lives. The Buddhist "Wheel of Life," for example, summarizes in one picture the whole concept of *karma,* the interplay of forces that shape man's fate. The *mandala* in its various forms symbolizes the different levels of energy locked in the human organism, the forces needed to release those energies (the four circles), the ways of approach (the four gates), and the energies themselves (the four triangles). A properly drawn *mandala* is a book in itself containing a great deal of information but he who would read the symbols must learn the language.[53]

Arcana or *yantra* can be used to provide a fixed point for the disturbed mind, the diagram or picture being visualized and held in the field of awareness. The effort of holding it little by little drains energy from the destructive mental process and attaches it to a creative process, reestablishing the sense of proportion and enabling the student to laugh at his egotistical preoccupations which, in the presence of the larger concepts, appear trivial in-

V. The Theater of Selves

We Are Many

"I do not have much success in my inner work. No sooner do I step out of the door, or arrive at the office, or have a difficult interview or some crisis to cope with than all my inner resolves are forgotten. I lose my way. I react mechanically. I become a slave. I am pushed around by my impressions. Events take charge and my inner aim disappears. Some external aim takes its place. I become a different person."

Sincere observation soon brings the student face to face with this fact. There is no single self. A man is one self at home and another at the office; one self at work, another when on vacation; one self with his wife, another with his secretary. Now and then, after some lapse of behavior, he may express astonishment or regret: "I don't know what possessed me. That is not the real me, I forgot myself." To which the careful investigator will reply, "Forgot which self?" For it should be fairly obvious from the above that *multiplicity of selves is the common condition.* Existence of a single "I" corresponding to a single aim and a single will is the exception rather than the rule.

The sense of self depends on man's level of consciousness, the room in which he happens to be at a given moment. In the first room, dreamless sleep, there can be no self-sense. Man is totally unaware of his own existence. In the second room, the dream state, man has a self-sense that is full of contradictions and absurdities, a vague, fragmentary, confused affair. In the third room, identification or waking sleep, the self-sense is narrow, limited and strictly personal. It is subject to change without notice. Every thought, emotion, sensation can wear the mantle of the self, call itself "I" and dominate behavior, only to be pushed aside by some other "I" which is equally mechanical, equally accidentally evoked. In the fourth room, the room of self-transcendence, self is no longer personal; it transcends the limitations of time and of space, is not altered from moment to moment by changing circumstances. In the fifth room, the separate self is transcended completely. In the words of the *Bhagavad Gita:* "He sees the self [*atman*] in all things and all things in the self."

In order to pass from the third room into the fourth, a man must die at one level and be reborn at another. This was the secret which underlay all the mystery religions, including *true* Christianity (there are so many false Christianities that this qualification is essential). In practical terms a man must be ready to sacrifice everything he calls "I," to regard all the manifestations of his being as objectively as if they were part of a theatrical performance, to *hold on nowhere,* neither to body nor to possessions nor to wife, children or home, to become, inwardly in any case, a nonpossessor.

The Five Wills

The Theater of the Selves portrays the interplay of five wills which lead men to act (Table II). They work within man, creating a ferment of one sort or another, compelling him to perform the role they select. Does man control the wills? Do the wills control man? The question is oversimplified. Man without inner unity has no true will. He changes from moment to moment. He says, "I want this, I want that," but he has no permanent "I" and his wants can be completely contradictory. The "I's" or selves change like characters on a stage and each "I" suffers from the delusion that it has a will of its own.

Only in the fourth state of consciousness does man possess will, but by that time he has stopped thinking in terms of "I." "All action is the product of the three forces of nature. Only he who is blinded by egotism thinks 'I am the doer.'" [54]

So we think of the five wills as forces of nature. They work in man with varying intensities and are embodied in men's various selves. The role a man plays in life depends on the relative power of the five wills. First and most primitive of the wills is the "will to pleasure." This is the pleasure principle of Freud, the lusty Eros, striving for the satisfaction of desires, goading man into activity through the primitive biological hungers, the need for food and the need for sex. Man can, and frequently does, perform no other role than that forced upon him by the will to pleasure. If of a philosophical turn of mind, he calls himself a "conscious hedonist" or an "epicurean." If less prone to philosophize, he merely plays his role, plunging his nose as deeply as he can into the trough, exerting as much force as possible to elbow the other pigs out of the way. His performance is simple—that of the Hog in Trough.

The second will we may call (again following Freud) the "will to death," the joy-destroying, life-negating Thanatos. Is this a universal urge? Or is it simply a disease of the mind confined to man,

TABLE II
The Five Wills

| Will to Self-transcendence |
| Will to Meaning |

| Will to Power |

Will to Pleasure	Will to Death
(activity)	(inertia)
Eros	Thanatos

whose hopelessly conflicting aims have entangled him in such a web of contradictions that death seems the only way out? Perhaps the will to death shows in nonhuman forms. One thinks of migrating lemmings hurling themselves in thousands over the precipitous cliffs of Norwegian fiords. But really this will to death is merely an extreme form of universal biological urge, the will to inaction, the great inertia, the will to rest. It counter balances the will to action, the will to pleasure. It involves activation of a part of the nervous system, the *trophotropic,* as opposed to the *ergotropic,* activated by the will to pleasure. It could more correctly be called "will to inertia" than "will to death."

The third will we define as the "will to power." This will is not confined to man. Hierarchies have been observed among birds and mammals in which one individual is dominant over the others. One thinks of the pecking order among chickens, struggles over territory seen among such animals as the Kob.[55] This is surely the will to power and its effect on the Kob in particular is to compel the dominant male to make extraordinary exertions, first to defend his territory, second to satisfy the sexual demands of a host of adoring females which his position as dominant male has attracted to him.

In man the will to power has operated at various times as a destructive force, activating certain individuals to become "conquerors" and to destroy vast numbers of their fellowmen in the process. It is certainly a dangerous will and badly needs restraining and directing, especially in the contemporary period of "megadeath" and "overkill." The will, however, has creative as well as destructive aspects. The quest for excellence (the urge to excel) is a product of this will. When coupled with the two higher wills, it becomes the fire which generates pressure in the boiler, a main source of the high energies by means of which man penetrates the locked rooms of the psyche.

The two higher wills are the "will to meaning" [56] and the "will to self-transcendence." These wills work only in man, and only in a very limited proportion of the human race. The lack of development of these wills prevents man from enjoying the two higher states of consciousness that are possible for him and might even be considered his birthright. It is useless to ask why these wills operate powerfully in a few people, feebly in a larger number and hardly at all in the majority. This is the nature of man, his chief tragedy, for certainly if these wills operated more strongly, he would make more effort to awaken and strive to correct the glaring errors in thinking and acting that make him a menace to himself and to the other creatures with which he shares the surface of the planet. Much might be done, in a properly organized society, to strengthen these wills in children. But our gadget-intoxicated culture has little use for the higher wills, encourages instead a fatuous race for possessions and prestige combining the silliest elements of the Hog-in-Trough game and the Moloch Game. The resultant hubris must surely be followed by nemesis.

The two higher wills are essential for the development of those aspects of the self that can lead man out of the third state of consciousness and into the fourth and fifth. Without these wills, nothing can be achieved. It is possible that the drug experience, by momentarily opening the doors of the locked rooms, may awaken these wills. But drugs cannot strengthen the higher wills. They work in the opposite direction, weakening the wills by dissipating vital energies. The wills are strengthened only by effort against resistance, as muscles are strengthened by persistent and vigorous exercise. To think otherwise is to indulge in the silliest form of self-delusion, as if one were to insist, contrary to all the evidence, that muscular strength can be generated by lying in bed.

The Seeker

The transformation of an ego-centered being to a free being does not take place either easily or quickly. One is converted into the other gradually, by a series of stages, and each stage carries with it its own dangers and difficulties (Table III). The transformation begins when one of the selves in a man's personality (the Seeker) develops an *awareness of the state of sleep*, or, alternatively, a *hunger for the fourth state of consciousness* (Baudelaire's "Taste of the Infinite"). The Seeker forms as a result of the working in man of the will to meaning and the will to self-transcendence.

The self or group of selves that comprise the Seeker form a definite force in the personality, creating a ferment, a restlessness, a dissatisfaction with all the games that have previously proved satisfying. The effect of this force is often disruptive and may produce great misery. The old games no longer satisfy but a new game has not been found. Much of the material which William James incorporated in the chapter "The Sick Soul" [19] described the grief experienced by one in whom the Seeker is beginning to develop. Leo Tolstoy, John Bunyan, William James himself and his father, Henry James, Sr., all suffered greatly during this phase of their inner development. William James wrote: "In Tolstoy's case the sense that life had any meaning whatever was for a time wholly withdrawn. . . . At about the age of fifty he began to have moments of perplexity, of what he calls arrest, as if he knew not how to live or what to do." [19] John Bunyan found himself in a similar condition, also recorded by James. "I was both a burthen and a terror to myself; nor did I ever so know, as now what it was to be weary of my life; and yet afraid to die. How gladly would I have been anything but myself! Anything but a man! and in any condition but my own." [19]

TABLE III
Stages in Work

STAGE	CHARACTERISTIC
4 MASTER	Body of consciousness or "soul" is formed. Inner-directed, cosmically oriented man.
3 OBSERVER	Prospero dominates Caliban.
2 MAGNETIC CENTER	Active quest for teacher.
1 SEEKER	First realization of sleep.
0 SLEEPING MAN	Outer-directed puppet. No inner aim or real will.

These examples could readily be multiplied. They illustrate the fearful ferment which the genesis of the Seeker may produce, at least in the early stages. Selves that were once believed in and trusted now seem as lifeless as rag dolls. Aspects of the *persona* that once appeared admirable show themselves as grotesque masks, grinning and silly. The artist becomes disenchanted with his art, the scientist with his research, the preacher with his sermons and with his whole religion, the businessman with his business. There is an awful awareness of the limitations of life, of an imperative need to set up new values, new aims, to start a new game, before death sweeps all the pieces from the board. Unless the sense of total futility has completely paralyzed his will, a person in whom the Seeker has developed is bound to search diligently for some way out, for the Master Game, which he feels almost instinctively must exist and be worth playing. To find this game he will read everything available that might possibly provide a clue to the mystery and enable him to emerge from the prison of total disenchantment. He will study works on psychology, religion, yoga, occultism, theosophy, magic. He will seek out others whose interests are similar to his own. What is the way out? What is the great secret? What is the Master Game and from whom does one learn how to play?

All this activity results in the transformation of the Seeker into a new and more powerful entity within the personality, an entity called, in the Gurdjieffian system, the "Magnetic Center." The Magnetic Center feeds on all those materials that the Seeker has culled from his readings and researches, his conversations with fellow seekers and so on. The *magnetic* quality of this element in the personality consists in its power, *if it is rightly formed,* to draw its possessor in the direction of a teacher from whom he can learn the things he needs to know.

A person's success in this respect depends on the strength and quality of his Magnetic Center. A defective center leads its possessor into the swamps of phoney mysticism or occultism, brings him to a teacher who is either a fool or a fraud, exposes him to the breed of spiritual vampires which prey on the credulous. A weak

Magnetic Center does not lead its possessor anywhere. It leaves him comfortably sitting in his armchair dreaming about the marvelous powers that will be his when he attains higher consciousness.

To find a teacher appropriate for his needs, the student needs much discernment. Even a genuine teacher (as opposed to a fool or a fraud) has limitations imposed on him by his type which are difficult or impossible for him to transcend. Thus, a man who is an adequate teacher for one person may be unsuitable for another. The main function of the teacher, besides instructing in physiological and psychological techniques, is to hold up for the pupil a mirror, helping him thereby to look objectively and impartially at the selves in his own makeup, without trying to hide from the unpleasant manifestations or overemphasize the pleasant ones. To do this, a teacher needs profound insight into types and the limitations which type imposes. It is hard for him, unless he has reached a very high level in his own development, to understand types very different from his own. Much of the difficulty encountered by members of the psychoanalytical cult (it is really more of a religion than a branch of medicine) results from too great a difference in type between patient and analyst. An encounter, for instance, between a highly somatotonic analyst and a highly cerebrotonic patient is likely to produce nothing but a series of misunderstandings.

The actual work of observing the selves involves watchfulness on the part of the pupil, an ability to catch manifestations, ability to remember gestures, tones of voice, reactions to impressions. This takes time. There are barriers between the different selves. They live in the same house but do not know each other. They are often elusive. The observing self, the self that wishes to awaken, may be far from popular with the other selves, who resent this lofty talk about higher states of consciousness and only want to be left in peace to go on with the life games that please them.

A wise teacher will encourage his pupil to step carefully in this area. The selves have to be accepted in all their variety. Nothing is gained by repression or inner tyranny. The curse of the Judeo-Christian tradition has been its excessive preoccupation with sin and its unwillingness to accept the Dionysian aspects of the self. By ceaselessly harping on the "lusts of the flesh," "mortification of the flesh," and kindred topics, it increases men's bondage to the very forces from which it exhorts men to escape. Indeed, this "struggle with the flesh" became so malignant a force that, for several centuries, it reduced the population of large areas of Europe to a condition verging on mass insanity.

The Observer

For an enlightened study of the selves, two attitudes are necessary: acceptance of their multiplicity and acceptance of their mechanicalness. The selves are like a box of clockwork dolls, some dressed one way, some another, some pleasant, some unpleasant, some clever, some stupid. The dolls have no free will. They are wound up and activated by circumstances. Under a given set of conditions, one of the dolls will leave the box, go through its performance, lapse back into quiescence. In the third state of consciousness all these dolls call themselves "I," but to the Observer,[57] who takes over from the Magnetic Center when the inner work has begun, they are merely puppets. In calling themselves "I," they attribute to themselves a quality they do not really possess.

It is the task of the Observer, that element of man's being which carries within it the seed of higher consciousness, to watch the puppets, learn how they behave, gradually accumulate material concerning their roles. To do this he must learn to be impartial. He will never obtain an understanding of the contents of his box of dolls if he refuses to look at *all of them,* the ugly, misshapen, villainous ones as well as those which seem pretty. This calls for effort and honesty as well as accurate observation.

Impartial self-observation is not easy. How can a man learn to regard his own manifestations with the detachment of a naturalist observing the behavior of an insect? There are tiresome, degrading, foolish, destructive manifestations of the self that can hardly be accepted without comment. And what of those embarrassing memories which, coming suddenly into the conscious mind, hit the ego with such force that one literally squirms with anguish?

How can one learn to accept impartially this material which is so unflattering to one's picture of oneself as a rational and more or less civilized being?

A little self-study soon reveals that observations which are painful and almost unbearable in one state of awareness are not painful at all in another state. What determines whether an observation is painful or not? First, the degree of muscular relaxation; second, the degree of steadiness of the awareness. Muscular relaxation is of the utmost importance. That discerning psychiatrist, Joseph Wolpe,[58] whose methods deserve to be more widely used, induces muscular relaxation in his patients by the methods of Edmund Jacobson,[59] then cautiously brings them face to face with the traumatic experience that has been causing their neurosis. The technique works almost infallibly and is a fine example of the results obtained by therapeutic application of the methods of Creative Psychology. Muscular tension, apprehension, and emotional pain are associated with one another. A fully relaxed person will not be apprehensive and does not react with pain to memories that may be almost unbearable when recollected unexpectedly in a state of tension. Wolpe correctly maintains that neurotic behavior results from an error in learning and that the cure for such behavior is unlearning and then relearning, replacing negative painful associations with positive pleasant ones.

The student of Creative Psychology uses a similar method to that advocated by Wolpe. He has, however, a somewhat different aim. He is not primarily concerned with liberating himself from the bondage imposed by patterns of neurotic behavior. His aim is to know the self in all its manifestations, pleasant or unpleasant, creative or destructive. To do this, he uses a meditative technique that involves preliminary exercises designed to bring the body into a state of complete relaxation (see Appendixes A and B); when the state of relaxation has been induced, the practitioner "enters the silence," thinking of nothing, holding the mind empty, like a cinema screen before the show begins. Then, exactly as if he were watching some private movie, he projects onto the screen incidents from his own life. These incidents may appear spontaneously or he may select them intentionally. Painful incidents as well as pleasant ones must be projected if a balanced representation of the self is to be obtained. In the state of meditative calm in which this exercise is conducted, these painful incidents will not trouble the observer. Seen objectively, without comment and without identification, the figure going through its antics on the screen of the mind will not even be regarded as "I" but rather as "it." The essence of its mechanicalness will be perceived. The comment will be: "This ridiculous, pompous, frightened or angry creature is not a self-directed being at all, but simply a puppet reacting to external forces." This is a very valuable realization. The only way to escape from the fetters of one's own mechanicalness is to recognize that mechanicalness. Only in this way does one learn to be on one's guard against mechanical reactions.

Those who are psychoanalytically oriented may object at this point. No matter how hard he tries, they may protest, a person with traumatic material heavily repressed will not, by merely sitting relaxed in meditation, be able to bring this material into the conscious mind. It is difficult to give a general answer to this objection. Anyone who is honest enough, resolute enough and observant enough can probably find all the monsters in his personal labyrinth *if he goes on looking for them long enough.* He may get some help in this from the psychedelic drugs, some of which bring to light repressed material. But far more helpful are those sensitized reactions which, like twinges of toothache, occur when the mind, in its random wanderings, approaches repressed material. These reactions provide the clues that, in the period of meditation, can bring to light the incident involved. Such clues have to be noted and acted upon. If it is objected that people rarely observe themselves closely enough to pick up such clues, we can only reply that the practice of Creative Psychology calls for a certain level of inner awareness and that the work cannot begin until that awareness is attained.

Inner Theater

The practice of projecting the self in its various aspects and watching its behavior as if it were somebody else forms part of a technique called "Inner Theater." This practice, rightly used, can give very valuable results; wrongly used, it can give very bad ones. The technique has been widely employed. It plays an important part in several practices, ranging from techniques described in the books on Tibetan yoga to the spiritual exercises of Ignatius Loyola.

The essence of Inner Theater is the intentional creation of visualizations, sensations, forms, situations, experiences within the theater of the mind. Every creative artist, be he novelist, playwright, painter or sculptor, makes use of Inner Theater to some extent. Mystics such as William Blake were almost continuously immersed in this inner performance, which went on more or less independently of their conscious will. The process, when it happens spontaneously, may generate visions, which can, if the visionary keeps his hold on reality, add an extra dimension to his existence. To Blake, for instance, this new dimension seemed one of his most precious possessions. "May God us keep from single vision and Newton's sleep." But this vision-generating power is not always so benign. When it operates without control, it can impose such a veil between the psyche and the outer world that it makes normal life almost impossible. Certain states diagnosed as schizophrenia are in fact due to this hyperactivity of the vision-generating power. It is a useful servant but a bad master.

In the East, in Tibet especially, Inner Theater may be used to bring the practitioner face to face with the illusory nature of the self. It plays an important part in that practice loosely defined as the "Yoga of the Non-Ego," of which the Chod Rite is an interesting if somewhat bizarre manifestation. In connection with this rite, Evans-Wentz makes the following observation in *Tibetan Yoga and Secret Doctrines:*

> The master of yoga, consciously and at will, can create any number of equally unreal bodies, of human and non-human shape, and give to them illusive separate existence. He may even make them physically as "real" as his own body, and, infusing into them a portion of his animal vitality, direct them as though they were living creatures.[19]

The Chod represents the practice of Inner Theater in an extreme form and is spiritually a somewhat hazardous undertaking, being conducted at night in a graveyard in the presence of corpses, which, in Tibet, are not buried but simply dismembered and left strewn on the earth to be devoured by beasts and birds of prey. In these surroundings the practitioner, seated on the skin of a beast of prey, with a drum made from two human skulls and a trumpet made of a human thigh bone, calls up the flesh-eating and blood-drinking demons and symbolically offers them his body to devour.

The experienced yogi can perform this rite without danger. Firmly holding to the state of inner detachment, he evokes the terrifying forms, puts them through their cannibalistic feast, never forgetting for an instant that the whole performance is *māyā*, that the flesh-eating demons along with the flesh they devour are but symbols of the transitory nature of the self. At the end of the rite he simply draws the manifestations back into himself, deprives them of form, remains quietly in contemplation of the uncreated.

"Apart from one's own hallucinations," says *The Tibetan Book of the Dead*,[19] "in reality there are no such things existing outside oneself as Lord of Death, or god, or demon."

A more credulous practitioner, however, may not manage so well when confronted with the powerful images evoked by the Chod ritual. Madame Alexandra David-Neel was so distressed to observe the obvious mental imbalance of one Tibetan novice that she even went to his teacher and asked him to inform the youth that the demons were all illusory. She was soundly reprimanded by the *guru* for her sentimentality, informed that followers of the Short Path undertook the rites with full knowledge of the hazards involved, deliberately risking madness, sickness and death in the hope of attaining liberation in one lifetime.[60]

Outer Theater

Inner Theater will not give the student a full understanding of the different selves unless it is linked to the practice of Outer Theater.

Outer Theater takes many forms. Its most practical and valuable form involves the attempt to play, in the daily affairs of life, some role that is slightly different from that which one plays mechanically. There is nothing esoteric about this. People attempt to use the technique every time they make a resolution to change their behavior patterns. A person who habitually loses his temper resolves to "play it cool" in a situation which he knows will be likely to provoke wrath. A timid person resolves to "play it strong" in a situation in which he is likely to be overruled and passive. A lazy person resolves on an active role, etc. These resolutions arise, not out of any desire to fulfil the Delphic commandment, "Know Thyself," but rather to obtain something, avoid something, put oneself in a good light, gain respect, gain friends.

The resolutions are almost invariably broken because man in the third state of consciousness (waking sleep) does not have enough inner unity to play any unfamiliar role consistently. Thus the habitually irascible man begins with every intention of being meek as a lamb but, as the action progresses, an entirely different "doll" is wound up by external stimuli. This doll has not heard about the good resolution and could not change its pattern even if it had. So the would-be lamb is soon pounding the table, roaring like a lion, portraying his habitual angry self. In exactly the same way the timid person who resolved to do some roaring and table pounding for a change slips, without even noticing, back into his usual meek performance, betrayed by habitual postures, habitual facial expressions, habitual tones of voice which he does not recognize or have enough power to change. For his repertoire of gestures and facial expressions determines the role a man plays and he who would change the second must have enough self-mastery to change the first.

The practical student of Creative Psychology uses Outer Theater not to gain friends and influence people, nor to give what is loosely known as a "good impression." His aim is to gain self-knowledge, to understand the limitations imposed by his type, to determine how far these limitations can be extended. Teachers of Creative Psychology who employ Outer Theater as a means of instruction are themselves generally adepts at this form of intentional manifestation, can create situations that place the student in a position where he must play a role not in his natural repertoire. Or the teacher may ask the pupil to portray some person in a given situation, a fat glutton sitting down before a good meal, a lonely dejected tramp on a rainy night, a boastful muscleman challenging an opponent, an angry housewife arguing with the local butcher.

Such exercises may appear to be nothing more than the kind of practices taught in any school of drama, especially those concentrating on the "method" of Stanislavski and his various imitators. There is a difference, however. The teacher of Creative Psychology uses Outer Theater to help his pupils to understand the difference between other-directed and inner-directed activity. Other-directed activity is typical of man in the state of waking sleep. It consists entirely of mechanical reactions to outside stimuli. This activity has been previously compared to that of a puppet when the puppeteer pulls the strings. An arm goes up, a leg kicks out, but the motive power does not come from the puppet. Similarly, an animal with electrodes implanted in a certain region of the brain can be compelled to manifest quite complex patterns of behavior as soon as the current is applied.[61] So our habitually irascible man, mentioned earlier, is showing other-directed activity as soon as he forgets his resolve to be meek as a lamb and allows himself to be provoked by outer stimuli into pounding the table and shouting at the top of his voice.

Inner-directed activity occurs whenever a person arrests some mechanical reaction and performs in its place an intentional action not provoked by external stimuli. Thus, our irascible character who has resolved to play it meek is giving an inner-directed performance every time he checks his tendency to roar. By the same token, Mr. Meek-as-a-lamb puts on an inner-directed performance whenever he checks his tendency to submit and adopts a firm line. Similarly, the poker player who, having been dealt four aces, portrays just the right degree of nonchalance to convince his fellow players that he is holding nothing better than two of a kind is giving an inner-directed performance. Indeed gamblers, con-men, tricksters, spies, secret agents all have to be capable of inner-directed performances. Their fortunes, their very lives depend on their ability in this respect. Epictetus used an apt simile when he compared the true Stoic philosopher to a "spy of God," capable of adopting all sorts of disguises, beggar or king, slave or free, but always inwardly independent of the role he happened to be playing.

VI. The Mask
and the Essence

Essence, Persona, *False Ego*

THE PRACTICE of Inner and Outer Theater will bring the student to one conclusion. There are some roles he can play well, some he can play indifferently, some he cannot play at all. His expressions, gestures, tones of voice, bodily postures all tend to follow a certain pattern, a pattern established by years of habit and imposed in the first place by the individual's type and his physical and emotional environment.

Type is immutable. Nothing we can do will change it. It is as much a part of us as the color of our eyes, shape of our nose, our blood type, our sex, our pigmentation or our stature. No matter how intensely he practices Creative Psychology it will not change a person's type. The slender, skinny ectomorph will never become a roly-poly endomorph, nor will the high cerebrotonic, with his love of solitude, hatred of noise and crowds, ever acquire the temperament of a high somatotonic, with his indifference to noise, or a high viscerotonic, with his love of company and gluttonous appetite.

To know himself a man must know his type, know the limitations it imposes, the obstacles it places in the way. For every type there is a corresponding set of obstacles, inborn weaknesses of which the student must become aware. Though he cannot change his type, he can *know* his type, know his limitations both psychological and physiological. Many of the difficulties a student encounters result from attempts to perform tasks for which, by type, he is unfitted. But whereas there are certain traits that *cannot* be changed, there are other patterns of behavior which must be changed if one is ever to make any progress. These include various wrong workings of the machine that destroy its energies and exhaust its resources. Some of these are essence-defects, resulting from the structure of the essence and very difficult to change. (The inborn physical craving for alcohol which drives some people to alcoholism may be an example of such an essence-defect). Others are located in the *persona* (they are learned rather than inborn) and are much more easily corrected.

It is necessary, though not always easy, to distinguish between the essence and the *persona*. The *persona* in ancient Greece was a mask, an indispensable part of an actor's equipment. Painted on linen in forms appropriate to comedy or tragedy, the masks covered the heads of the actors, eliminating from their performances the "self element," turning them into prototypes, generalizations without individualized features. By a curious development of semantics, the word "personal," which developed from *persona*, has come to have the meaning of "self" or "that which is intimately associated with the self." "He told me things of a very personal nature." Properly speaking, the words "personal" and "personality" should not have this meaning at all. They should mean "something put on, acquired, something not essentially one's own," as the mask of the actor is not his own face but something he puts on to conceal his own face.

In the Gurdjieffian system, in Carl Jung's teachings and in William Sheldon's classification of temperaments, the word *"persona,"* or "personality," is given the meaning "something not one's own." It is made up of patterns of behavior acquired in the course of life, imposed by education, by the culture in which a man lives, the people he associates with and so on. In the course of growing up, an individual develops several *personae*, masks which he wears and behind which he takes refuge. Sometimes these masks are very grotesque and unsuitable, having no correspondence to the essence or type. Such unsuitable masks are often adopted by adolescents who cannot decide what role they wish to play in life. Indeed, much of the storm and stress to which the adolescent is subjected results from his difficulty in finding a *persona* which he can comfortably wear. (The little child does not have this difficulty because he lives in the essence and has no need of masks. This living in the essence, so typical of the small child, is referred to many times in the gospels: "Except ye be converted and become as little children," etc.)

The view might be taken that, as the *persona* is "not one's own," it is therefore false, whereas essence is one's own and therefore genuine. Such a view is too simple. In the conditions (civilized?) under which we live, a *persona* is necessary. It enables us to play roles, cope with various situations that the essence could not handle. If it is artificial, so is our culture artificial. If we lived close to nature, drew our nourishment direct from sea or soil, we could dispense with the mask. Indeed, the further one goes from city streets and what passes for culture, the less necessary does the *persona* become. Among people transacting their affairs directly with nature—farmers, fishermen, trappers, prospectors—essence commonly dominates and the *persona* is rudimentary. Confronting the land, the sea, the woods or the deserts, these people have dignity and strength, and seem wholly admirable. But the lack of development of the *persona* causes these same "children of nature" to behave quite often like idiots as soon as they are let loose in a town, compelled by some obscure desire to show off, which, for them, generally takes the form of drinking too much and starting a fight.

A third element in man's totality is the false ego. This is an outgrowth of the *persona* which can be separated from the latter on the basis of its uselessness. The *persona*, in any civilized society, is necessary. It is an adaptation that helps a man to fit into his environment, as a leopard's spots help to render him invisible in the jungle. It carries within it much that man has learned, is a vital component in the machinery that enables him to earn his living. False ego, on the other hand, is in no way necessary. It is made up entirely of egotistical illusions, negative emotions, lies, delusions of grandeur, self-pity or arrogance. It is essentially a malignant entity, a sort of spiritual cancer and, where it becomes the dominant component, destroys its possessor's capacity for growth just as physical cancer destroys the body.

The three components of man's totality—his essence, *persona* and false ego—cannot be separated and placed in watertight compartments. They are closely interrelated and one affects the other. The structure of the personality is dependent on that of the essence, but in one individual there are commonly several personalities (the dolls in the box alluded to previously) which are wound up and set in motion by different circumstances. The "hunger for consciousness" is in essence, but the Seeker who results from this hunger develops in the *persona;* so does the Magnetic Center to which it gives rise. Even the Observer is at first predominantly in the *persona* and only after many years of work does it begin to affect the essence.

Although it has been stated that essence is what one is born with, "the totality of inborn characteristics biochemical and physiological," it has also been stated that essence can grow. This "growth of essence" results from actual biochemical changes produced in the body by intensive inner work. Actually, a man is only said to have "entered the work" or "embarked on the Way" when these biochemical changes have started. Up to that point his inner work consists only of an accumulation of ideas located in the *persona.* Qualities in the *persona* are easily gained, easily lost, like words written in the sand. But those that have been graven in the essence are not easily erased, like a message carved on a rock.

Physical Type

The study of essence characteristics involves an understanding of physical type and of the traits which tend to go with that physical type (Table IV). Ever since the days of Hippocrates the existence

TABLE IV

Components of Type

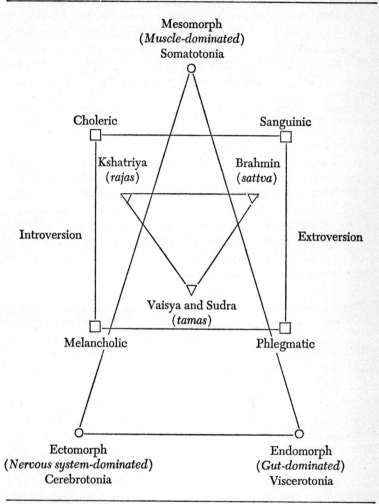

NOTE: The three *gunas*—*sattva*, *rajas* and *tamas*—correspond on the cosmic level to intelligence, energy, mass. In man they correspond to three components of being—intelligence, energy, inertia. They are elements of the essence. (See *Bhagavad Gita*, Discourses 14 and 17.)

of varieties of types and temperaments has been recognized. Hippocrates himself, a careful observer, noted that certain physiques carry with them certain weaknesses, a proneness to certain diseases. Dominated as he was by the theory of the four humors, he classified his types accordingly, designating them choleric, melancholic, phlegmatic and sanguinic. It was not a bad classification as far as it went and remained in use for more than two thousand years.

Recent, more sophisticated classifications (Ernst Kretchmer's, Carl Jung's, W. H. Sheldon's, H. J. Eysenck's, R. B. Cattel's)[62, 63] bring to the science of typology a wealth of biochemical and morphological data which may, at times, seem embarrassing in its abundance. For practical purposes it seems difficult to improve upon the system offered by Sheldon in his two books, *The Varieties of Human Physique* and *The Varieties of Temperament*. Only the barest outline of the system is offered here, designed to familiarize the student with Sheldon's terminology and to indicate the *kind of obstacles* that people of different types are liable to encounter when they begin to make intentional efforts to attain higher states of consciousness.

Sheldon's basic theory (supported by an abundance of evidence) is that temperament is related to physique. This is intuitively understood by every experienced novelist and playwright. Shakespeare's three prototypes, Falstaff, Hotspur and Hamlet, correspond both physically and temperamentally to Sheldon's three physical *morphs* and three temperamental *tonias*. Falstaff is the extreme *endomorph*. He is shaped like a barrel ("this tun of a man"), typically oval in outline. Hotspur, the fiery fighter, is the extreme *mesomorph*, muscular, broad-shouldered, narrow-hipped, triangular in outline. Hamlet, the irresolute thinker, is lean and angular, linear in outline, the typical *ectomorph*. Their temperaments correspond to their physiques. Falstaff, with his passion for eating, is *viscerotonic;* Hotspur, with his passion for action and risk, is *somatotonic;* Hamlet, entangled in endless cerebration, is *cerebrotonic*.

By Sheldon's system both the somatotype (variety of physique) and the variety of temperament can be quantitatively expressed.

The "index of physique" has three figures, the first measuring *endomorphy,* the second *mesomorphy,* the third *ectomorphy.* They range from 1 to 7. Thus an index of physique reading 7-1-1 informs us that this is a body having the highest possible level of endomorphy unbalanced by any strength in the other components (a comical fat man, Kretschmer's "pyknic practical joke"). But a 3-4-3 index would indicate a balanced physique with a slight preponderance in mesomorphy. Similarly, the index of temperament has three figures, measuring viscerotonia, somatatonia and cerebrotonia in that order. They, too, range from 1 to 7. An index of temperament 7-1-1 indicates extreme viscerotonia with no compensating strength in the other components. But a 4-4-4 index suggests a richly endowed temperament in which all three components are well developed.

He who would know his own essence should evaluate both his somatotype and his temperament and learn to estimate these quantities in others. This is an elegant art, analogous to the "feeling for form" developed by an expert judge of livestock. The practice encourages the development of objectivity and sharpens observation. Somatotype and temperament are both essence qualities, but the *persona,* in most cases, is determined by the essence, as the form of a building is influenced by the outline of its foundations. Occasionally one encounters an individual who tries to adopt a *persona* quite at variance with his essence. The result, unless the individual is a born actor (an essence quality), is generally ludicrous.

The following outline of Sheldon's system is offered only to give the student a framework within which to fit his observations. For a full understanding of the method, he should consult the original texts.

VISCEROTONIA—GUT DOMINANCE

Endomorphy is that component of the physique which gives the body an oval outline. The index of physique highest in endomorphy (7-1-1) indicates a body having a massive, protuberant abdo-

men housing a highly developed gut. The midsection (hip measurement) is broader than the chest; there is fullness in belly and
buttock but relatively weak development of the limbs.

Viscerotonia is that variety of temperament which tends to
occur in people of predominantly endomorphic physique. It is
characterized by twenty traits. Taken generally, the traits depict a
temperament in which love of physical comfort, eating, polite ceremony, company and sleep are prominent characteristics. Viscerotonia endows its possessor with softness of body and of mind. The
face is soft and almost babyish, the lips flabby and fond of sucking
and kissing, the whole body is relaxed, the movements are soft
and easy. Emotionally, the viscerotonic shows what he feels.
When troubled, he turns to others for consolation. He readily
weeps and his weeping is unrestrained, a primordial upwelling
from the depth of the belly. Viscerotonia makes interpersonal re-
lationships easy, for these somewhat fat and flabby individuals are
generally ready to give consolation to others, to embrace the
world, to comfort, to console.

One who detects in his makeup a strong component of viscerotonia (he can measure this as well as the other components by
rating himself on the scales given in Sheldon's book) will inevitably encounter certain "essence weaknesses" which are as much
an expression of his type as is the outline of his body. For the
viscerotonic, these essence weaknesses are likely to include the
following tendencies: excessive food intake, excessive relaxation,
excessive complacency, excessive amiability. A more detailed examination of these tendencies will reveal their origins and indicate
what steps can be taken to correct them.

Excessive intake of food. Because he loves to eat, the high viscerotonic tends to eat more than he needs. If cultured and well
educated, he tends to be fascinated by culinary art, is a connois-
seur of food and wine. If uncultured, he tends to be merely a
glutton. From the standpoint of Creative Psychology, there is
nothing wrong with developing an interest in cuisine. The complex patterns of aromas and tastes and textures which together
constitute the flavors of food are fine subjects for study. Much can

also be learned from careful observation of the process of digestion, an awareness of which can teach us many things about the inner working of the machine. But excessive food intake is always harmful and may, for some people, be positively disastrous. People of predominantly endomorphic physique tend to convert their surplus nutrients into fat. By persistently overeating they readily transform themselves into quivering masses of jelly, so grossly overweight that much of their energy is uselessly consumed in merely moving the physical body from one place to another.

Excessive food intake overloads all those organs of the body the task of which is to process nutrients. The liver becomes overloaded and swollen. The kidneys are overstrained by the labor of eliminating excessive amounts of breakdown products. High levels of uric acid enhance the tendency to gout. High levels of blood cholesterol increase the danger of arteriosclerosis. Large amounts of semi-digested waste in the lower gut encourage the growth of putrefactive organisms and lead to autointoxication through the absorption of by-products. There is also an abundance of evidence to indicate that overeating shortens the life-span both of mice and men. The lean of almost all species tend to outlive the fat.

So his love of eating presents a challenge to any person whose temperament is high in viscerotonia. Such a one must learn to hear the voice of the *appestat* and impose on himself the task of obeying that voice. The appestat is a very delicate mechanism in the base of the brain that tells us both when to eat and, to some extent, what to eat. It is one of the most easily heard of the body's instinctive voices because it speaks in a fairly simple language of hunger and satiety. In our civilization, however, an abundance of food is usually available and our ideas about food intake are governed largely by habit. We eat what we vaguely call "three square meals a day" without so much as a reference to the appestat, merely because this is what we are accustomed to do. But three square meals represent, under some circumstances, too much food and, under others, not enough. There are days when, owing to accumulation of certain toxic materials, no food at all should be taken into the body. There are other days when, owing to some unusual exertion, large amounts of food must be absorbed to replace not only depleted stores of energy but also to repair the actual substance of the body. There are also occasions when certain mineral elements, especially salt, are required in unusual amounts and other times when certain vitamins may be needed, particularly ascorbic acid (vitamin C), which the body cannot store and needs in fairly large amounts.

About all these needs the appestat speaks to the conscious mind if this mind is alert enough to hear its voice. All food intake and choice of food ought to be based on what it says. Those who are on speaking terms with their appestats have no use for the various diets which people impose on themselves with or without medical advice. These diets are merely examples of the intellectual brain interfering in matters that are none of its concern. There is no such thing as a perfect diet. Requirements vary from day to day, from person to person. Only the appestat can tell one whether a given day calls for high food intake, whether one should eat mainly protein, take in a large amount of salt, consume quantities of fruit and vegetables or eat nothing at all.

The practice of fasting can be salutary if the fast is imposed for physiological rather than penitential reasons. Man is a creature whose ancestors fasted often, not because they wanted to but because they had to. A lucky day's hunting or fishing gave the tribe a feast but that feast, as often as not, was followed by days of famine. It is clear from Frederick Hoelzel's experiments[64] that a thirty- or even a forty-day fast does not actually damage the organism and fasting one day in three certainly increased the life-span of the rats with which he and A. J. Carlson had experimented.[65] But the indication when to fast has to come from the appestat, the muted voice of which its possessor must learn to hear and to interpret correctly. An initial fast of a day or two days, during which fluids are taken but no solid food, generally suffices to cleanse the system of some of its toxic overload, to empty the gut and evoke from the appestat a genuine hunger signal, the quality of which can be noted and "listened for" in future. If the viscerotonic individual hears the voice, eats only when it tells him to eat and refuses to eat at other times, he will avoid that overloading of the gut which so often occurs in one of his temperament. Viscerotonics often do well on two meals a day and may do even better on one. Their large gut has a great capacity and digests its contents efficiently. In this respect they are the opposite of cerebrotonics, who need to eat little and often.

Excessive relaxation. Viscerotonics are naturally relaxed people. They love to subside into well-padded armchairs, they like soft beds, they are extremely fond of sleep. Left to itself their machinery is apt to press the stop button, to allow trophotropic, vegetative mechanisms to predominate. Indeed, in extreme cases, the viscerotonic tends to become purely vegetative, rooted in the earth like a cabbage, serenely digesting his food in his large, efficient gut.

This capacity to relax, to fall asleep readily and sleep deeply may be envied by cerebrotonic people, who lack this ability. Taken to excess, however, the relaxing tendency produces a being so torpid and so muscularly weak that he has a hard time making efforts of any kind. One high in viscerotonia has, for this reason, to learn the secret of pressing the start button, of getting his machinery moving and active again. To do this, he must know how to increase the tone of his muscles.

Muscular tone is a measurement of alertness, of readiness for action. It is not the same thing as muscular tension, though it quickly turns into tension under conditions of stress. Muscular exercises shown in Appendix A are especially valuable for those high in viscerotonia because they compel the start mechanism to operate. They involve an outpouring of nervous impulses powerful enough to overcome torpor. The hatha yoga exercises called *uddiyana* and *nauli* are especially important as they strengthen the musculature of the abdomen, prevent that sag of the belly to which the viscerotonic is all too prone.[66] Exercises of the isometric type are also of value as they can be used at any time and do not involve special postures.

Excessive complacency. "There is an inclination to an unshakable complacency which approaches or reaches smugness. The individual is placidly complacent about himself and his relations to his world, and about the outer affairs of life. He sees no hurry or urgency in any situation, however acute and desperate the matter may appear to others." In these words William Sheldon described what he calls "trait V 14" of viscerotonia. Again a cerebrotonic, who is typically lacking in this quality, may be inclined to say: "How admirable." Up to a point it is admirable. It endows the individual with a capacity to remain calm and collected in a crisis, to avoid hasty, ill-considered decisions, to avoid "losing his head." But that which is a virtue in moderation becomes a vice when taken to excess. The viscerotonic's complacency is similar in its psychological effect to his fondness for sinking into padded armchairs. It reduces him to a state of vegetative immobility. His defense against it lies in remembering his aim, and the limited time he has in which to attain it. This reflection tends to banish complacency as surely as the *asanas* (yogic body positions or postures), briskly performed, banish muscular flabbiness. It is especially necessary for a viscerotonic to remind himself, from time to time, of the inevitability of his death. Viscerotonics do not like the idea of death. "They typically have a devil of a time of it, dying with great protest, as if they were being torn from life untimely by the roots." [62] For this reason the thought of death can provide a valuable corrective for viscerotonic complacency.

Indiscriminate amiability. Here again is a viscerotonic trait which constitutes a virtue in moderation but becomes a vice when taken to excess. In its extreme form this quality reminds the observer of a wet-mouthed puppy which indiscriminately slobbers over everyone it meets. The trait tends to cloud awareness and weaken judgment. It produces a soft, overly tolerant attitude in which all distinctions become fuzzy. One who has failed to control this tendency does not make an effective teacher though he is often an extremely popular one. His approach is sentimental and "grandmotherly" [67] and he tends to foster the very weaknesses that his pupils most need to overcome. The error lies not in amiability but in lack of discrimination. A viscerotonic who has mastered this weakness can be stern enough when the occasion demands, as indicated by Marpa's treatment of Milarepa.[68] (Marpa, if the traditional descriptions are accurate, was a very viscerotonic Tibetan lama and his rough treatment of his disciple, Milarepa, as described in the latter's biography, must have involved great intentional effort on Marpa's part—Outer Theater of the highest quality.)

Summarizing, viscerotonia is a quality tending to generate a condition of inertia in which the vegetative function of digestion becomes the central theme of existence. One in whom this quality predominates is liable to sink into a state of torpor and must learn by experience and experiment how to press the start button and thus reactivate his inner machinery.

SOMATOTONIA—MUSCLE DOMINANCE

Mesomorphy is that component which gives to the body a hard, firm, upright quality and a relatively triangular outline. A physique high in mesomorphy shows broad shoulders superimposed on relatively narrow hips. Extreme mesomorphy can be seen in such cartoon characters as "Superman" and "Li'l Abner." All the various Tarzans who have cavorted through the treetops have been high mesomorphs. This is the hero type, the "he-man."

Somatotonia is Sheldon's term for a variety of temperament that generally goes with the predominantly mesomorphic physique. This is the temperament of action and its focal point is the musculature (as opposed to viscerotonia, with its focal point in the gut). High somatotonics are doers and conquerors. They conquer mountains, forests, other races, and, of late, have been busily (as they put it) conquering space. Their delight is vigorous action, the overcoming of external obstacles. They have powers which less rugged individuals may envy, have a high capacity for physical endurance, a low sleep requirement; they are relatively insensitive to pain, noise, distraction, and the feelings of others.

The following essence obstacles are commonly encountered by types high in somatotonia:

Horizontal mental cleavage. This is a trait which cuts people off from their own inner life. Those in whom it is strongly developed become totally preoccupied with externals. They are free of doubts, have little or no awareness of the voices of other weaker components within them, their decks are cleared for action and their decisions are swift. Had Hamlet been predominantly somatotonic, there would have been none of that painful hesitation which gives the play its suspense. "To be or not to be, that is the question" is a thought that hardly occurs to one high in somatotonia. So lacking is such a one in inner awareness that he may not even be conscious of internal pain, and serious inner conditions (ulcers, tumors, heart disease) can progress within such people to the stage of being untreatable before they become aware of anything amiss.

This horizontal cleavage that cuts off the somatotonic from deeper levels of inner awareness generally prevents him from feeling that "hunger for consciousness" without which the inner work cannot even begin. He is too identified with external conquests to take much interest in inner ones. If he does happen to develop a Magnetic Center, he is likely to plunge into the work with a vigor that is the hallmark of his type. He is apt to undergo the sudden change in orientation that, in religious language, is called "conversion." Once converted, he will hurl himself (somatotonics characteristically hurl themselves at everything, like bulls charging a matador) into his new activity, with enormous energy, after the manner of Paul of Tarsus, who was, one can guess, fairly high in somatotonia.

In his welter of activity, one high in somatotonia will always be in danger of losing sight of his inner aim, of which he must again and again be reminded by his teacher. He will always tend to put the emphasis on action, on external achievement. He will want to build temples, start crusades, *do* things. Of various forms of yoga, he will be attracted to karma yoga, because of its emphasis on action, and to hatha yoga, because of its emphasis on physical discipline. With his athletic body, he will easily master all the *asanas* which seem almost impossible to the flabby viscerotonic or the overtense cerebrotonic. But he will tend to neglect the inner exercises which are the real essence of yoga and concentrate on the mere gymnastics, which are more or less incidental.

Insensitivity. That same insensitivity which cuts off the somatotonic from the deeper levels within himself also makes him insensitive to the spiritual needs of others. He characteristically marches through life in spiked boots and steps on the toes of others with indifference or even with pleasure. His lack of insight coupled with his natural intolerance causes him, if he becomes a legislator (and high somatotonics often do become legislators because the rough and tumble of politics attracts them), to pass laws prohibiting the use of substances that affect levels of consciousness. Not only does he feel no urge to explore his own depths, but, being afraid of this area of experience, does his best to prevent others from so doing. The horrendous penalties attached to possessing that harmless weed, *Cannabis sativa* (hemp from which hashish is extracted), have all been dreamed up by somatotonic legislators and are enforced by equally somatotonic tax collectors.

The same insensitivity prevents the somatotonic from understanding, in a group, the finer interactions among its members. Surrounded by a mantle of his own obtuseness, he tends to "miss the point" and will often understand only if he is, metaphorically speaking, hit over the head. Because of this obtuseness, people high in somatotonia who become teachers themselves are often very violent in their methods. They assume that, because they themselves never understand anything unless hit over the head, others will necessarily benefit by this treatment. Unfortunately this is by no means true. The rough handling that works wonders with tough somatotonics may do great damage to the more sensitive cerebrotonic. One cannot help but suspect that some of the rougher Zen masters were to some extent led astray by their own somatotonia. The same applies to many Christian "spiritual directors."

Blind obedience. "Somatotonic people tend to lack introspective insight. They are like loaded guns and they want to be pointed somewhere and set off. Hence it is that clever medicine men of all time have made a good living by pointing and exploiting the action-loving somatotonic component in their contemporaries." [62]

So, when the somatotonic becomes convinced that he has found his teacher, he is apt to follow that teacher blindly, to swallow everything he is told, to perform with undiscriminating enthusiasm every task that is demanded of him no matter how ludicrous that task may be. Every phoney Messiah, every founder of a cult, is likely to accumulate a following of somatotonics eager to do his bidding, particularly if this involves risk and an element of violence. It was the collective somatotonia of the German people that caused them so readily to fall for the preaching of Adolf Hitler and the violence, cruelty and general callousness of the Nazi movement expressed this somatotonia in action. The same violence and brutality characterizes the "dedicated Marxist."

Naïveté, an eagerness to follow orders, to be directed rather than to rely on his own judgment renders the somatotonic always liable to be set on false paths by false prophets. It is an essence weakness that is exceedingly hard to correct. If a man does not possess inner discrimination, how can it be given to him? Furthermore, that comfortable conviction of his own rightness and the rightness of the creed in which he happens to have faith, coupled with his insensitivity and passion for action, make the somatotonic the natural crusader. Not only does he adhere to his own beliefs with fanatical intensity, but he also tends to force them down the throats of others. He will quite willingly undergo great hardship and face great danger to "convert the heathen," as he puts it. But if the "heathen" happens not to appreciate his brand of religion, he will have little hesitation in speeding that conversion with fire and the sword. Most of history's great persecutors, as well as its great conquerors, have been individuals high in somatotonia.

His self-righteousness, freedom from doubt and love of action may also lure the somatotonic into the delusion that he himself is a prophet, a seer, a Messiah. This happens when, due to some crack in the inner barrier which normally imposes what Sheldon calls "horizontal mental cleavage," voices from the subconsciousness reach the conscious level and are interpreted as divine messages or divine commands. When such messages and commands reach cerebrotonic individuals, who are much more conscious of their inner world, they are inhibited, when it comes to action, by myriad doubts and conflicts that are the hallmark of this type. The somatotonic does not have these doubts. He plunges in and follows his "inner voice" with singleminded intensity and, even though the message he offers may appear incredible nonsense to intelligent hearers, he offers it with such vigor and conviction that he rarely lacks followers. The most dangerous false prophets, whose teachings, political or religious, have brought death or misery to millions of people have generally belonged to this category of "inner-voice-directed somatotonics."

Will to dominate. Just as, at one level of his development, the somatotonic has a weakness for blind obedience so, at another level, he has a craving to dominate. This craving is an exceedingly difficult quality to evaluate. It is an essence weakness only insofar as it is egotistical. It gives to its possessor the power of leadership, the power to take responsibility, yet at the same time it constantly threatens to destroy him, to turn all the fruits of his inner work to ashes, by causing him to fall victim to delusions of grandeur, by trapping him in his own ego at the very time when he should have transcended that ego.

Teachers high in somatotonia are always in danger of slipping when they have reached a high level, have acquired great powers and come to wield great influence. They are always in danger of "entering the Left Hand Path" and frequently do, leading many astray in the process and creating a disastrous pattern of behavior for themselves. Of all the essence obstacles that confront the somatotonic, the Will to Power is the most subtle, a two-edged sword which he can use either to cut down his inner enemies or to sever his own spiritual lifeline.

Indeed, it can be said of somatotonics that most of their essence weaknesses are examples of virtues which become vices when taken to excess. The more richly endowed a man is in the second component (somatotonia), the more physical force he has at his disposal. He can ride farther, climb higher, make do on less sleep and less food, endure more pain than his more viscerotonic or cerebrotonic comrades. But the dangers he confronts are proportionate to his power. His chariot is yoked to violent and mettlesome steeds and its headlong course often demands more skill from the charioteer than he possesses. For such people, much depends on their finding a teacher powerful enough to lead these energies into the proper path.

Summarizing, the person high in somatotonia has to be on his guard against the Will to Power that leads him, in any situation, to attempt to dominate, to play the leading role ("He that would be greatest, let him be as a servant among you," is a precept specifically directed at the power-hungry somatotonic). On the other hand, he must guard against the tendency to perform blindly whatever his chosen teacher tells him to do. His tendency, unlike the viscerotonic, is to rush about in all directions and squander his energies in excessive activity. He has to train himself to sit still, to relax, to contemplate, to listen. He will tend, because of his passion for physical action, to identify the self with the physical body, to be overattached to that body and, as he grows older, to spend much emotional energy lamenting over the passing of his youth. The struggle of the high somatotonic against the aging process is often a pathetic phenomenon.

"Somatotonics tend to enter upon the most tragic of human quests, the quest for lost youth. One of the cardinal indicators of somatotonia is a horror of growing old. Many such people turn from sport to sport, only at last to settle pitifully upon tennis, like late butterflies in the autumn alighting upon fallen apples." [62] As the viscerotonic fears death, so the somatotonic fears loss of youth. To accept the inevitable decline of his physical power is for him a hard task.

CEREBROTONIA—NERVOUS
SYSTEM DOMINANCE

Ectomorphy is that quality which gives to the physique fragility, linearity, flatness of chest, delicacy in general. The body of the high endormorph is oval, with the greatest mass in the midsection; that of the high mesomorph, triangular, with the greatest breadth across the shoulders; that of the high ectomorph, linear, with not much breadth anywhere. Such people have slender, poorly muscled limbs and delicate, pipestem bones. They lack padding and their nervous systems are overexposed.

Cerebrotonia is that quality of temperament which usually goes with a physique high in ectomorphy. In viscerotonia the temperament centers in the gut; in somatotonia, in the muscles; in cerebrotonia, in the nervous system. Cerebrotonia is a major characteristic of what Carl Jung called "introversion" just as somatotonia and viscerotonia are characteristics of "extroversion." "The cerebrotonic finds both his delights and his defenses in the system and detail of his own consciousness." [62]

Because the high cerebrotonic is so preoccupied with his own consciousness it might be thought that he, more than most people, would show an interest in the theory and the practice of Creative Psychology. As far as *theory* is concerned, this is quite true. People high in cerebrotonia are often "seekers," and have a tendency to read numerous books on occultism, mysticism, theosophy and the like. But the high cerebrotonic has a tendency always to "mentalize" this material. More than any other type, he tends to lose himself in dreams. "The major cerebrotonic danger is dissociation from reality. The freedom of the forebrain is likely to be purchased at the price of a biological losing of the way, and hence at an apparent end-cost of suicide." [62]

High cerebrotonia confronts its possessor with a formidable array of essence obstacles and essence limitations which he must somehow learn to overcome or to live with. These arise out of the following cerebrotonic traits:

Physiological overresponsiveness. This trait is undoubtedly the curse of cerebrotonia. The high cerebrotonic overreacts to practically everything. Both his central nervous system, over which he has direct control, and his autonomic nervous system, over which he has none, are set too finely, on hair triggers so to speak. The digestive tract in such people is thrown into turmoil by even slight emotional stimulation. Nausea, indigestion, migraine headaches, heart palpitations can all be induced by situations which would leave the more placid viscerotonic unperturbed. The skin is frequently sensitive and responds with inflammation to nervous as well as physical irritation.

Whereas the viscerotonic must learn to press the start button to prevent himself from lapsing into a state of vegetative torpor, the cerebrotonic must learn to press the stop button, to slow his jumpy reactions, to calm down his too active digestive system, to relax his tense muscles, especially those of the face. Such people live at all times dangerously near to the point of exhaustion. They lose energy through excessive muscular tension. Their too finely set start system presses the panic button when there is no need for such emergency measures, flooding their systems with adrenalin and leaving them subsequently exhausted.

For this reason the high cerebrotonic, if he wishes to obtain results from the practice of Creative Psychology, may be compelled to select a relatively isolated environment in which to live or work. The hermit who flees to a cave or a desert is often driven to do so not to escape what are loosely called "the lusts of the flesh," but to protect himself from overstimulation and the fearful wastage of energy this involves.

Love of privacy and sociophobia. These two cerebrotonic traits fit logically into the pattern shown above. The high cerebrotonic is not at ease with people. He avoids and dislikes social gatherings, shrinks away from social contacts, particularly new ones. When thrown into a social situation, he becomes tense, awkward and confused. The insatiable appetite for people and company that forms a part of the viscerotonic temperament is lacking in his makeup. When troubled he seeks solitude. His friends are few.

This trait is undoubtedly an essence obstacle to one who desires to attain the state of self-transcendence, "seeing the self in all things and all things in the self." The shrinking, the embarrassment in company are reactions that both can and must be overcome by one who desires to attain the fourth state of consciousness. It can be overcome because all these reactions result from identification with the *persona,* which, in cerebrotonic people, is apt to be socially inept. When identification with the *persona* is broken, the embarrassment disappears. The student no longer cares whether he is liked or disliked, admired or despised. Cerebrotonics who reach this stage discover that their difficulty in social gatherings has disappeared. They no longer fear such gatherings though they will probably continue to avoid them, which, as such gatherings are for the most part a complete waste of time, would seem to be an intelligent decision.

Poor sleep habits, chronic fatigue. This trait of cerebrotonia is an essence limitation that can, under some circumstances, be very damaging. Indeed, there is much evidence to suggest that the "schizophrenic breaks" to which cerebrotonics are particularly prone are brought on or usually preceded by spells of sleeplessness. The cerebrotonic simply cannot fall asleep in the easy, relaxed manner of the viscerotonic nor can he learn to do with very little sleep, as can the somatotonic. His need for sleep is all the greater because he "sleeps badly," which means that, even when asleep, his overalert, overactive roof brain is not really switched off and his muscles are not really relaxed. The slightest noise tends to wake him, especially snoring. Snoring is fatal to the sleep of cerebrotonics and marriages between cerebrotonics and somatotonics are likely to be jeopardized by the former's intolerance of the latter's tendency to snore.

Like most of his essence defects, the cerebrotonic's bad sleep habits result from the overactivity of the start system. And again like most essence defects, this one is difficult to correct. There are a number of techniques which give to the student an insight into the mechanisms involved in falling asleep, entering and exploring the dream state. These have been described in a previous chapter.

Indiscriminate hostility. The undiscriminating amiability of the viscerotonic may, in cerebrotonics, be replaced with an equally undiscriminating hostility. His own excessively quick reactions make him intolerant toward the slow reactions of the viscerotonics. He despises the latter's love of polite ceremony, his love of food, his flabbiness, his complacency. He may envy or even admire some of the qualities possessed by high somatotonics (their Spartan indifference to pain, physical endurance, "cast-iron" digestions), but he abhors their noisiness, their insensitivity, their lack of insight into their own world. This hostility, combined with his love of privacy and his sociophobia, can easily turn the high cerebrotonic into an embittered recluse, who renounces the world in a spirit of savage contempt and pours scorn on those who continue to indulge in its pleasures. Though many of the great persecutors were somatotonics, many others were embittered cerebrotonics. Their lean, drawn, angry faces have gazed on many an orgy of judicial murder wherein witches or heretics perished amid the flames.

Distorted sexuality.   Cerebrotonics are intensely, often almost insanely, sexual. The sexual urge which scarcely ruffles the surface of life for the viscerotonic, which the somatotonic accepts easily and fits readily into his life pattern, hits the cerebrotonic like a hurricane, blowing him this way and that, endangering his stability and even his sanity. He is especially threatened during his teens, when, in our culture, outmoded taboos operate to prevent normal gratification and when, in the male, the sex urge is most powerful.

Because the cerebrotonic is so dominated by his intellectual brain, his powerful sexuality often appears to him as an alien force, a sort of demon against which he has to struggle. In the course of this struggle, the whole sexual force becomes distorted, turning in upon itself to generate destructive impulses centering about the idea of "mortification of the flesh." The struggle against sexuality which played and still plays a large part in the so-called morality of the Christian Church has probably caused more human misery than all the great plagues combined. This struggle which, at its height, reduced large segments of the population of

Europe to the status of devil-obsessed homicidal lunatics, had its origin in the cerebrotonic conflict between a strong sexual urge and an interfering roof brain which refused to accept that urge or to permit it to flow in its normal channels.

Highly cerebrotonic people merely put obstacles in the way of their own development if they allow the influence of the Guilt Cult to prevent them from coming to terms with their own sexuality. For such people, the Dionysian release is essential for normal health. They are, at best of times, overtense, overrepressed and overanxious. For them a full, intense sexual relationship offers a way out of the labyrinth of daydreams in which they tend to be immersed. Such people must learn to love and, in the process, learn to accept their own instincts. This is for them a hard task. They do not love easily and their secretive, inhibited pattern of being tends at all times to cut them off from the mainstream of life, converting them either into hermits or cynics.

All this may give the impression that the cerebrotonic has greater obstacles in his way than has the somatotonic or viscerotonic. Perhaps he has. He has strained his biological moorings and is in danger of coming adrift. The viscerotonic, with his splendid gut, has his lips glued firmly to the breast of mother earth, like the herbivores in general. The somatotonic, active, muscular, agressive, has a somewhat weaker hold, analogous to that of the carnivores, the devourers of flesh, the great beasts of prey. The cerebrotonic defies comparison with other animals. With his huge roof brain predominant, he is perhaps the most "human" of humans, but this does not necessarily constitute an advantage either in the crude struggle for existence or in the more subtle struggle for harmonious and full development of consciousness. High cerebrotonia is a questionable asset.

Problems of Balance

This brief review of Sheldon's typology hardly does justice to the system. It has in it several elements which must be separately evaluated to give a full picture of type. The most elusive of these elements, one of great importance to every student of Creative Psychology, is the capacity to harmonize conflicting traits in temperament. The higher the total of the index of temperament and the more equally it is distributed among the three components, the greater is the potential of the individual. Thus a 3-7-2 and a 4-4-4 both have a total of 12, but of the two the 3-7-2, with his predominant somatotonia, may have an easier temperament to integrate than the 4-4-4. The latter may be pulled in so many different directions that he may end by achieving nothing at all. Such types often take refuge from their conflicts by stupefying themselves with alcohol, taking drugs or deliberately adopting a mediocre disguise. T. E. Lawrence ("Lawrence of Arabia") reacted in this way when, rejecting all the roles made available to him by his natural power of leadership and heroic aura, he took refuge in the anonymity of the R.A.F. as "Aircraftsman Shaw," exclaiming: "there is nothing more restful than taking orders from fools."

An exceptionally rich temperamental endowment results in "Promethean" or "Faustian" man, a type perfectly exemplified by Goethe. This complex genius, who played the roles of scientist, administrator, traveler, poet, artist, lover and mystic with equal enthusiasm, whose surging torrential productivity would have sufficed to supply three lesser geniuses, was practically torn to pieces by his own conflicting elements. "Alas, two spirits dwell within my breast, the one forever fighting with the other." Faust is not satisfied with little Gretchen whom he seduces and abandons. He must have Helen herself, he must be master of the Sign of the Macrocosm and of the Microcosm. "From heaven he demands the loveliest stars and from the earth each joy it has to offer, and all that's near and all that's distant won't satisfy his fathomless desires." [69]

Such is Faustian man. Goethe, after several close calls with both madness and suicide, managed to live to the age of eighty-two and leave behind him collected works which fill 150 volumes. The fact that he was able to do this was due, undoubtedly, to an understanding of the principals of Creative Psychology which he obtained early in life and which guided him afterwards. The whole of *Faust* is a treatise on this subject, one of the richest in all literature but, like so many works of this kind, intelligible only to one who "knows the language." Other Faustian men who have not had this guiding light have been less fortunate.

The aim of Creative Psychology is to give the student an understanding of his essence. Once he really knows his type, he can estimate accurately his innate capacities and live within the limitations they impose. A 7-1-1 index of temperament should inform its possessor that his greatest danger lies in his craving to vegetate and that, unless he constantly strives to press his own start button, he is likely to degenerate into a shimmering mass of fat. A 1-1-7 index warns of a different danger. Such excessive cerebrotonia puts the sanity, indeed the very existence, of such a one in danger unless he finds a very sheltered environment and guards himself against over stimulation. One who has a little less strength in cerebrotonia and a little more in somatotonia faces quite a different problem. A 1-3-6, for instance, can be extremely brilliant or an extremely troublesome character, reformer, martyr or conspirator. Savonarola and the Shakespearean Cassius were, Sheldon states, perhaps classical 1-3-6's. But if the secondary strength is in viscerotonia instead of somatotonia, an entirely different situation results. "The 3-1-6 is an excessively weak, soft, effeminate, harmless person with the muscular strength of a girl and the resolution of a rabbit." [62]

Types and Castes

Sheldon's classification of body types and temperaments can be usefully supplemented by that of Manu. Though this system is very ancient and the rigid caste structure it imposed on the social life of India is, to our way of thinking, very repulsive, it does contain elements necessary for an understanding of man's essence. The laws of Manu divided men into four groups, *brahmins, kshatriyas, vaisyas* and *sudras*. The division was based on essence qualities. These essence qualities were designated *svabhava*, which can roughly be translated "self-being," and on a man's self-being depended his self-duty (*svadharma*), the role he was properly fitted to play in life. The importance of *svadharma* is emphasized in this verse from the *Bhagavad Gita:* "Better one's own duty though imperfectly performed than the duty of another well performed. Better is death in the doing of one's own duty: the duty of another is fraught with peril."

The essence nature of the type called *brahmin* is an urge to know the truth. Depending on the strength with which this urge is felt, the man with this kind of self-being will play the Science Game, the Art Game or the Master Game. The true *brahmin* pursues truth at all costs and will not permit considerations of comfort or convenience to stand in his way. His most outstanding characteristic is his objectivity, his ability to rise above the dust of the arena, to resist the hypnotizing effect of words and the blind passions of cults, political or religious.

People of this type have a vital role to play in society. Their objectivity gives them the power to evaluate correctly the forces at work in society at a given moment. They are not executives themselves but are the natural advisers of executives, not kings but the counsellors of kings. Objectivity is a part of their essence. When their essence becomes polluted by the *persona* or false ego, this objectivity is betrayed. They then become guilty of bad faith. Those who play the Science Game hanker for Nobel awards instead of knowledge. Those who play the Art Game employ slick tricks and become mere showoffs. Those who play the Master Game set themselves up as *gurus* and measure their attainments not by inner standards but by the number of their followers.

That phenomenon which Lucien Benda called "The Treason of the Intellectuals" is the result of sacrifice of objectivity by members of the *brahmin* caste. This treason has resulted in the genesis of a number of pathogenic ideas that, in our century, have proved as destructive as any of the great plagues of history. Such ideas as "All is Permitted," "The Master Race," and "Class War" have brought death to millions, misery to millions of others. All these deadly ideas have been brewed in the minds of traitor intellectuals who, having lost their objectivity, have started to play the game of political passions.

In a healthy society the *brahmins* (objective men) are responsible for the formulation of its aims. They are the spiritual descend-

ants of the prophets equipped by their special capacity to function as the conscience of society. In a sick society, in which the
objective men are guilty of bad faith, they not only fail to perform
their function as navigators but become largely responsible for
running the ship on the rocks. Hence Benda's wry comment on
the treason of the intellectuals: "Although Orpheus could not
aspire to charm the wild beasts with his music one could at least
have hoped that Orpheus himself would not become a wild
beast."

The *kshatriya* in ancient India was a warrior, ruler or both. The
essence quality of this type is the will to power as that of the
brahmin is the will to truth. In a healthy society the *kshatriya*,
the man of action, warrior, natural temporal ruler, is guided by
the *brahmin,* the objective man, prophet or seer. Without such
guidance, the *kshatriya* type becomes lost in the maze of his own
activity, loses sight of long-term ends and higher principles, governs on a day-to-day basis in a more or less opportunistic manner.
The *kshatriya* is typically a high mesomorph and his temperament
is correspondingly high in somatotonia. He has strength but lacks
insight. He may rise to a position of great power in the state; but
only when he has standing behind him the impartial observer,
sufficiently removed from immediate problems not to be swayed
by day-to-day emergencies, can the *kshatriya* steer the ship of
state correctly. For the same reason, if he chooses to play the Master Game, he will need as his teacher objective man, the *brahmin.*

The *vaisya,* whose essence fits him to play the role of merchant
or artisan, performs his essence duty by satisfying needs, buying
and selling, manufacturing, undertaking business enterprises of
various kinds. Like the *kshatriya,* he tends to become overim-
mersed in activity but he is dominated by the will to possessions
not by the will to power. Whereas the *kshatriya* tends to set in
motion the Moloch Game and to try to achieve his political ends
by violence, the *vaisya* becomes totally preoccupied with Hog in
Trough and the accumulation of vast quantities of possessions. As
the *kshatriya* is predominantly a mesomorph, the *vaisya* is predominantly an endomorph.

The *sudra,* traditionally lowest of the four castes, is a being of limited outlook, concerned with the satisfaction of his physical needs. Because of his essence limitations, he cannot do much more than work at a physical level. In ancient societies, in which manual work was despised, the *sudra* was also despised, reduced to a condition of slavery or serfdom, robbed, exploited and deceived by members of the other castes. He was looked upon as being incapable of independent thought, suggestible, easily deceived, easily misled. It was regarded as essential that he should submit to the guidance of those above him in the social hierarchy. Should he take power into his hands, it was thought that the collapse of society would follow inevitably, the higher orders would be destroyed, all spiritual values would be lost, the surviving members of the stricken society would be dragged down to the condition of animals.

In recent times the *sudras* have revolted and, in some cases, taken power, often proving the truth of a saying of Solomon's that there are few disasters worse than "the servant when he reigneth." Which does not alter the fact that, when the *sudra* fulfills his essence duty, he is just as capable of playing the Master Game as is the *kshatriya* or *vaisya* because, being more down to earth, he is less apt to be led astray by false theories. The *sudra* is a simple soul, essence dominated. He often knows a great deal but he knows it in essence and therefore is incapable of expressing it in words. This quality of the *sudra* often endears him to the *brahmin*. Hence Tolstoy's passion for the Russian peasant and T. E. Lawrence's romance with the "children of the desert." New religious movements may start with an appeal to the *sudras* because members of this caste are less loaded with possessions and cluttered with preconceived ideas than are their social superiors. It is significant that Jesus preferred the company of fishermen to that of scribes, lawyers or Pharisees.

Persona *and False Ego*

Study of the essence leads to a clearer understanding of the *persona*. The elements of the *persona* are dependent on those of the

essence but are acquired by imitation or imposed by circumstances. Their manifestations can be changed easily whereas those
of the essence can be changed only with very great difficulty. A
student comes to know his various personalities by observing his
behavior under various circumstances. He collects snapshots, as-
sembles them in the album of memory. In due course he makes
the acquaintance of all the selves and learns to produce them at
will. His inner work does not destroy the various selves. This is
not the aim, if it becomes the aim, work is not proceeding
rightly. The change which takes place is a change in perspective.
A new objectivity dawns. The student says not "I" but "it"; he
watches the selves at play, now one, now another. Gradually the
Observer learns to know the servants in the house, finds out which
can be trusted, which cannot, which are helpful, which harmful.

This applies particularly to those manifestations which are collectively referred to as the "false ego." This malignant growth
within the *persona* is neither useful nor decorative but unfortunately, through wrong education, is often regarded as a vital part
of the self. To sacrifice their belief in the false ego can be, for
some people, the most difficult of all undertakings. Despite the
fact that it is the source of most of their sufferings, they cling to it
with stubborn insistence, like a medieval monk to his hair shirt,
using all their energies to protect and enlarge it, inflicting its im-
becilities on others and resenting bitterly the slightest breath of
criticism directed against it. In such people, the false ego grows
and gradually takes over the entire structure of the self, just as a
virus alters the chemistry of the cell and compels it to manufacture more virus instead of performing its rightful function in the
body.

Our highly acquisitive culture with its emphasis on conspicuous
consumption, on "keeping up with the Jones's," on the general
game of ego-centered oneupmanship, encourages the growth of
the false ego. In great cities, amid a profusion of status symbols
ranging from yachts to orchids, this aspect of the psyche may be
seen flowering like a monstrous creeper nourished by false values
and artificial conditions of life. It shows in its phoney glory in high

priced restaurants, where dishes with fancy French names are served by weary waiters to bored patrons who are visiting the establishment not so much to eat as to see and be seen. There its bright brittle face and synthetic smile is as obviously artificial as a plastic orchid.

But no one should suppose that this tinsel-bright, overpainted aspect is the sole manifestation of the false ego. The bearded beatnik with his long-haired "chick," sandaled or barefooted, without a nickel in his ragged pants, may be manifesting his false ego in this eccentric guise just as surely as does the painted lady in the ritzy restaurant. There is no limit to the disguises the false ego can assume. It penetrates everything. An artist under its domination engages in a feverish game of oneupmanship, employing slick tricks to demonstrate his cleverness. A writer is deliberately obscure in the hope that readers may think him "difficult" and therefore profound. In the field of religion, the false ego leads to intolerance and self-satisfaction (the "Lord, I thank thee that I am not as other men" of the Gospel Pharisee). Even the research scientist, who, being concerned with objective reality, might be thought to be free of this plague, is often completely dominated by his false ego, expending vast stores of emotional energy on puerile arguments concerning priority of publication, on proving that some rival was wrong and that he was right, or chasing that supreme will o' the wisp, the Nobel award, arch status symbol and a stumbling block for many.

Only when one moves from city to country and consorts with simpler types—farmers, fishermen, woodsmen—does one escape a little from the miasma of the false ego. The closer one approaches to the breast of mother earth, the less chance does this clown have of manifesting itself. Thoreau alone at Walden, Tolstoi mowing with his peasants, Gauguin with the brown Polynesians in the Marquesas were all, in their way, seeking refuge from their own false egos or from the collective false ego of human society. So no doubt was Simeon Stylites on top of his column, so was Milarepa in his cave in the Himalayas, so were countless other recluses in solitary hermitages, monasteries or retreats of one sort or another.

They were not always successful. So subtle is this manifestation of the psyche of man, so skillful is it in adopting disguises, that the very austerities that are utilized to suppress it can become its ornaments, the objects of its pride. So those stylites of the desert, perched on top of their columns, shelterless, in constant discomfort and danger of breaking their necks, could become more arrogant as a result of their privations than the self-indulgent citizens of Alexandria who came from time to time to gaze on these holy men with mingled feelings of wonder and repulsion.

To the student of Creative Psychology the false ego represents an ever-present obstacle. It can, and frequently does, appropriate for its own purposes all the powers that a person gains by inner discipline and inner work. There is nothing in man's nature to guarantee that the powers he gains will be used for the transcending of the self and the attainment of liberation. At every point on the Way, even up to a very high level, the traveler can make a mistake and choose the Left Hand Path rather than the Right Hand Path. If he makes this mistake, then all the power he has gained is used to reinforce his ego rather than to transcend it. There results what Gurdjieff has called "wrong crystallization." A man becomes unified, has will, has very great power, but all his powers are directed to the wrong ends. Such a one can only re-enter the Way as a result of great suffering in the course of which the whole structure of the ego has to be shattered as a badly set bone must be rebroken before it can unite correctly.

Anatomy of a Dwarf

The false ego is a component of man's psyche which follows him into high places, a clown, buffoon, hunchback, dwarf, a poor companion but one not easy to shake off. To know its aspect, to be able clearly to define its limits, the student must observe and gather material. Nothing is gained by concealment. The false ego derives its power from its capacity for disguise. It shows itself now in one form, now in another, will pick up high-sounding phrases and trot them out like a parrot, will learn the language of the inner work and talk of higher states of consciousness, mystical experience, occult powers and celestial influences. Talk is its milieu. It loves talking. If it cannot find anyone else to talk to, it talks to itself or engages in imaginary conversations with some friend or admirer.

Admiration it loves. To strut and show off like a jackdaw in peacock's feathers is for the false ego the very height of bliss. But if anyone criticizes this performance, if anyone dares to suggest that the plumage is borrowed and the whole display a fake, how bitter the resentment, how anguished the outcries and protests! Not satisfied with weeping on the shoulder of everyone within reach, this tiresome entity will fill the whole psyche with lamentations, airing its grievances in imaginary conversations which, because of the cyclic nature of the mental hookup, repeat themselves interminably. "He wronged me, he insulted me, he damaged my reputation, he made me look foolish." In such phrases as these, with a thousand variations depending on circumstances, does the false ego express its reaction when the praise it so dearly loves is withheld or its antics are treated with disdain.

The counsel of perfection is not to let the false ego take charge, to avoid those situations in which he is likely to play a dominant role. True to the old saying, "Birds of a feather flock together," this aspect of the psyche is automatically drawn into the company of fools who pander to his weaknesses and praise his performance. Certain people, as any careful observer can note, get together for no other reason than to reinforce each others false egos, forming little mutual-admiration societies within which they can display their most artificial aspects without fear of censure.

Friends of the false ego are foes of the essence. An essence friend is no flatterer and does not admire the antics of the inner fool. It was well said by the Sufi poet, Jalaluddin Rumi, that the friendship of a fool is like the friendship of a bear. He added, in another story, that even Jesus fled from the fool, saying: "I can make the blind see, the deaf hear, the lame run and raise the dead, but I cannot turn the fool away from his folly." [70] So the practical student of Creative Psychology learns to avoid those people and circumstances which encourage the manifestations of the false ego. Instead, he seeks essence friends whose aims are similar to his own. This does not mean that he lacks compassion or is excessively critical. He is simply a realist who knows his own limitations and does not propose to make a hard task still harder by deliberately fostering his own delusions.

If a man really wishes to see his false ego, all he need do is to put that entity in a situation in which it looks foolish, contemptible, inept or unsophisticated. To do this deliberately, not as a means of self-punishment or as an excuse for playing the buffoon, requires considerable effort and constitutes an aspect of Outer Theater which is as profitable as it is difficult. The extent to which we identify with the false ego becomes painfully obvious the moment we attempt intentionally to place it in a bad light. The attempt may consist of nothing more than making a naïve remark in a company that considers itself sophisticated or intentionally appearing not to know something one should know and actually does. This trick of playing dumber than one is gives insights not only into the structure of one's own false ego but also into the false ego of others, whose reactions (scorn, condescension, polite contempt or tolerant smiling) give a clear indication of where they stand on the scale of being.

It has been said: "Only a very clever man can intentionally play the role of a fool." Shakespeare knew this. The whole of *King Lear* is a profound representation of the interplay between false ego and essence. The two aspects of man's psyche are dramatically juxtaposed against a background of storm and catastrophe; the conscious element deliberately plays the role of Fool while the false ego, in the role of the Mad King, struts and declaims in the face of the indifferent tempest, putting the blame for his misfortunes on everything except his own stupidity. Again and again King Lear (*King Lear*, IV. i, Laurel edition) confronts his mentor, but every time he fails to hear the message.

> LEAR: Dost thou call me fool boy?
> FOOL: All thy other titles thou hast given away,
>   that thou wast born with.

VII. Education of Psychic Centers

The Four Brains

EDUCATION IS THE ESSENCE of Creative Psychology, but its concept of education is different from that which is generally accepted in our culture. True education involves every aspect of man's being, his instinctive, motor, emotional and intellectual functions. What passes for education in our universities and centers of "advanced learning" is a lopsided affair in which all the emphasis is placed on stuffing the intellectual center with facts, in much the same way as a computer is stuffed with information by feeding it "bits" in the form of punched cards which it duly stores in one form or another and can retrieve on demand.

To treat a human being like a computer is to insult his humanity. This fact is vaguely understood even by those who seem most anxious to "computerize" man. Though they do their best to express all human functions in computer terminology, they still admit, in their more honest moments, that some aspects of human behavior refuse to fit into the computer pattern. A computer can certainly be programmed to play a passable game of chess, to compose a simple tune, to write the kind of word salad that, in some "sophisticated" circles, passes for poetry. But ask it to emulate Michaelangelo (paint the Sistine Chapel), Beethoven (compose the nine symphonies), Shakespeare (write the plays and the sonnets), or to produce the spiritual equivalent of the Katha Upanishad or the Sermon on the Mount and it at once becomes apparent that there exists in man a certain "something" that the gadget is not likely to develop however complex we make its circuits.

So "fact stuffing" is a travesty of education. Even the more rigorous training in observation, experimentation, analysis of results which the contemporary scientist receives in the laboratory still leaves a man stranger to himself. It does not enable him to understand the laws of his own being, the limitations imposed by his type, the nature of the forces and energies at work within him, the possibilities available to him in the form of other modes of consciousness. To realize these things he needs a very different form of education, one designed to develop all the parts of his being, and not merely to increase his store of "bits" (in the information sense) or to strengthen his purely intellectual capacities. William Sheldon, commenting on this subject in *The Varieties of Human Temperament*,[62] observes that there are several kinds of intelligence. He lists symbolic and intellectual intelligence, somatic and manipulative intelligence, imaginative intelligence, affectional intelligence, social and sexual intelligence, economic intelligence, aesthetic intelligence, time orientational or religious intelligence, topographical or spatial intelligence.

The levels of these different kinds of intelligence vary with type and with the way in which the three components of temperament —viscerotonia, somatotonia, cerebrotonia—blend and integrate with one another. "It may be that the most *generally* intelligent person is he who most successfully carries and integrates a heavy endowment in more than one component, possibly in all three. The most supremely intelligent person in the world may then be temperamentally something like a well-integrated 4-4-4. (God is usually pictured as about 7-7-7: all-loving, omnipotent, and omniscient.)"[62]

The four "seats of intelligence" loosely described as the intellectual, emotional, moving and instinctive centers are neither harmoniously nor fully developed in the man who exists only in the third state of consciousness. A person may have a brilliant intellectual center and yet be an emotional moron. Or he may be well developed emotionally and yet have a moving center so inept that he can barely tie his own shoelaces. What Sheldon implies in the above quotation and what G. Gurdjieff taught throughout his colorful career is that man does not and cannot attain his full spiritual stature by developing only one kind of intelligence. He must, if he is to grow harmoniously, develop all four.

It is permissible, on anatomical grounds, to speak of the four centers as "four brains," occupying different regions of the nervous system. Each brain is the seat of a different sort of intelligence and each plays a different role in the maintenance of the body. The study of types, if it is to have practical value, must be linked to a study of these four brains, to an effort to understand their operations, to improve their working, eliminate wrong functions. This involves much work and begins, as all such work must begin, with self-observation.

Self-observation leads to self-knowledge, self-knowledge to self-mastery. This is true of every aspect of Creative Psychology, but the truth is often not understood. So the student tries to run before he can walk, to be master of himself before he knows himself, as if a man who had never touched a piano were to sit down at the instrument and expect at once to perform with the skill of a master player. Obviously this is impossible. It is equally impossible to attain control over the four complex organizations that together make up the being of man without first laboriously collecting, over a period of years, the necessary observation. Only these observations, taken directly from life and not from some textbook, will give to the student the actual *feel* of his own centers, will enable him to understand how these four brains act, both when they are operating well and when they are operating badly. The study is far from simple for these complex organizations interact constantly with one another. Though they can, for convenience, be separated into instinctive, moving, emotional and intellectual brains, it must be realized that their activities overlap. They influence one another, interfere with one another, and may at times seriously damage one another. Indeed, the whole tragic story of "man's inhumanity to man" that makes human history such unpleasant reading, can be represented as a result of the malfunctioning of the four brains, above all of the intellectual and emotional brains, which function so defectively at times that one wonders how the human race has managed to survive.

Education of Instinct

It is logical to study the instinctive center first because, in the order of evolution, it developed first. The instinctive center or instinctive brain operates in all living things, even those which have not localized their "intelligence" in a separate nervous system. It is the essence of what we call "life," which we define as a "self-regulating, self-reproducing chemical system based on a double code (DNA and RNA) with molecular symbols that appear to be the same for all living things." Basically what "living" consists in is the self-translation of this code into an organism which may be one-celled or many-celled or even, in the viruses, nothing more than the code molecule itself with a protein overcoat. This translating is completely beyond the reach of any conscious control. It regulates itself and proceeds at a rate characteristic of the organism. It may continue for millennia in a giant sequoia or last only for a few hours in some microorganisms. In green plants the translation involves energy taken from sunlight; in all other forms chemical energy is derived from the molecules formed in green plants or from bodies of animals that have eaten those plants.

It is humbling and salutary for man's "presumptuous brain" (by which we mean the intellectual center) to realize how small is its contribution to his totality compared with that of the instinctive brain. This brain, "the great translator," started to operate at the fateful moment when the sperm terminated its journey by plunging headlong into the massive ovum, introducing the second half of the vital code and setting the elaborate machinery in motion. Even before there was a nervous system in which it could localize, this brain worked through a mysterious chemical system (the organizer) to block out the ground plan of the organism when it was still nothing more than a hollow ball or cup of cells. Throughout embryogenesis it continued to work, outlining the fate of the organism in accordance with the blueprint in the genetic code, creating not only a being of a certain physical type but stamping that being with a biochemical signature which would make him unique among the millions of others on the earth.

There is no doubt about the uniqueness.[71] It extends to every tissue of the body except the cornea, proclaiming that this tissue belongs to John Jones and no one else. This prevents the aforesaid John Jones, however urgently he may wish to do so, from giving his tissues to another, even his nearest and dearest. For no matter how carefully a graft is made, the instinctive brain recognizes the tissue as "not I" and rejects it, using the same mechanisms as it has for millions of years to repel parasites, also recognized as "not I." This reaction may, in some cases, prove more of a curse than a blessing and certainly increases the surgeon's problems when he attempts to repair a bad burn or replace a ruined kidney. But the instinctive brain is very conservative. It cannot change the practices it has evolved during millenia to accommodate the discoveries of modern medicine.

A man's instinctive brain operates so far out of reach of his ordinary consciousness that most of its workings take place completely unnoticed. The host of processes of which this brain takes care include the transformation and storage of food materials, the neutralization and elimination of poisons formed in the course of the body's functioning, the elaboration of hormones and their balanced release, the defense of the body against invaders, the repair of tissues, the replacement of cells, the regulation of the blood flow, and many other functions. All these are concerned in one way or another with the maintenance of the internal balance of the body (homeostasis). So numerous and complex are the processes involved that, if a man had to attend to them with his conscious mind, he would have no time for anything else. The whole operation is therefore automated, depends on a series of interconnected feedback mechanisms, all of which, for the most part, take good care of themselves. Only now and then, in a healthy man, does some upset in this inner harmony attract the attention of the intellectual brain and remind that somewhat conceited entity of its utter dependence on the wisdom of another brain to the workings of which it normally gives no thought.

Despite its remoteness from the ordinary consciousness, the instinctive brain constantly affects the workings of the other brains —the intellectual and emotional—which normally regard themselves as the seats of consciousness and of the ego. This influence shows itself in the "mood of the moment," in fluctuations of energy level, in cycles of uplift and depression, joy and gloom, purposive activity and helpless drifting, sexual urgency and sexual indifference, mental brilliance and mental dullness. These moods and phases vary not only from hour to hour and from day to day, but also from one life period to another. "He's going through a difficult phase." "I can't do a thing with him while he's in this mood." "I got out of the wrong side of the bed this morning." "Today I feel on top of the world." All these and numerous similar phrases, used every day countless times by countless people, describe the influence of the instinctive center on the conscious life.

Generally speaking, the instinctive brain is best left to itself to perform its functions by the light of its own wisdom, which is wordless, primeval and quite extraordinary. There is, however, a shadowy area of awareness in which instinctive and consciously controlled activities overlap. This area was first clearly defined by W. B. Cannon in his classical study, *The Wisdom of the Body*.[72] Cannon's work deals mainly with physical and chemical reactions that happen automatically and very swiftly when the organism is confronted with danger. They are generally termed "fight-or-flight reactions" and they are governed by a part of the nervous system (the autonomic) that is not under control of the conscious will.

For the student of Creative Psychology it is important to acquire an understanding of these reactions. There are several reasons for this. First, they often occur needlessly and create in the general awareness a sense of anxiety by upsetting the inner harmony of the body. Second, they offer insight into the working of a region of the brain that is ordinarily out of reach. Man is, to some extent, a victim of this part of his brain which evolved in days when danger was a major component of everyday life. In the state of physical security in which he now spends most of his life, this primitive mechanism tends to be needlessly active and often does more harm than good.

The physiology of fight-or-flight reactions can be readily learned from any textbook on this subject. Briefly, the process starts with the receipt of an impression (the sight of a snake, the threat of collision on the highway, a menacing sound, the smell of smoke in a room). With incredible swiftness the roof brain classifies the impression, labels it "threatening" and presses the alarm. At once the instinctive brain takes over and a whole series of adjustments are made to prepare the body for fight or flight. In Cannon's words:

> Respiration deepens; the heart beats more rapidly; the arterial pressure rises; the blood is shifted away from the stomach and intestines to the heart and central nervous system and the muscles; the processes in the alimentary canal cease; sugar is freed from the reserves in the liver; the spleen contracts and discharges its content of concentrated corpuscles, and adrenalin is excreted from the adrenal medulla. The key to these marvellous transformations in the body is found in relating them to the natural accompaniments of fear and rage—running away in order to escape from danger, and attacking in order to be dominant. Whichever the action, a life-or-death struggle may ensue.[72]

The trouble with this reaction in contemporary man is that it tends to prepare the body for a "life-or-death" struggle when no such struggle is toward. This is especially true of high ectomorphs with their corresponding cerebrotonic temperaments. Their autonomic systems are so finely set and so overresponsive that it takes no more than the rustle of a mouse under the floorboards to set their hearts pounding as if they had been confronted by a tiger.

Similarly, the incessant noise and bustle in city streets, the endless flow of distracting impressions produce in such people a chronic state of overactivity in the autonomic system which results in their exhaustion. In other types, high mesomorphs especially, this overstimulation has a different effect. It activates the vagus nerve leading to the stomach and generally overstimulates that organ. The "executive ulcer" is a common consequence of this overstimulation.

An important part of the practice of Creative Psychology involves the attainment of control over these fight-or-flight reactions which occur so swiftly and are governed by a part of the brain that operates almost independantly of the conscious will. This control is gained only when much knowledge has been accumulated, knowledge based on direct observation and not on textbook learning. There is, to begin with, a split-second interval during which the impression is registered, classified as dangerous and the alarm sounded. This is an operation of the "conscious mind," but the consequences depend largely on the level of consciousness in which a person happens to be at that moment. In the state of waking sleep the reaction proceeds mechanically. There is no control of any kind. The initial impression is often incorrectly classified and the alarm button pressed for no reason whatever. A person mistakes a rope for a snake, a flapping sheet for a ghost, a harmless beetle for a scorpion. He takes innocuous remarks for insults, "sees red" when there is nothing red to see. So the whole fight-flight machinery is set in motion for no reason.

A person closer to the fourth state of consciousness is less liable to make such errors. When there is a watchman at the gate, impressions can be caught and examined. There is no reduction in caution or in alertness—on the contrary both are considerably enhanced—but there occurs a more deliberate classifying of impressions. The rope that looks like a snake is looked at again, more carefully. Even if an actual snake happens to cross the path, it is looked at calmly. Snake? Yes. Dangerous? No. Of if the answer to the last question happens to be yes—so what? There is room enough in this world for both of us. Go in peace, brother. Though

you may be poisonous, you are not one-millionth part as dangerous as *Homo sapiens.*

But suppose the danger is real. Suppose, on a crowded highway, an error of judgment has been made and a collision appears
likely. Here the "adrenalin reaction" is perhaps desirable (we say
"perhaps" because it is by no means clear in what way the reaction helps someone in this situation). In any case, it will almost
certainly occur, helpful or not. Under such conditions once again
the course of events depends on the level of consciousness. In
sleeping man, the general alarm may provoke not intelligent action but an overall panic, in which centers hopelessly interfere
with one another and so many conflicting orders are given to the
muscles that there results a general paralysis. Colloquially this is
called "losing one's head." A man less deeply asleep feels the
adrenalin reaction but, instead of being reduced to a state of helpless panic, is able to harness the energy it makes available and
take appropriate action to avoid disaster.

Observations at moments of crisis, if accumulated, will gradually acquaint the student with his own autonomic mechanisms.
He will actually learn the "feel" of the adrenalin reaction and,
having learned it, will also learn to use it in such a way that it
does not harm his organism. There are many variants of the reaction involving not only adrenalin but also the related substance,
noradrenalin. Fear reactions, concerning which it is said "he
turned pale with fright," are accompanied by constriction of the
small blood vessels, especially in the face. But the flush of anger or
of shame is under the control of a different neurohormone (acetylcholine) and this, too, must be recognized by its "feel." [73]

In addition to direct fear and direct anger, immediately generated by some threat or provocation, there are reactions of a less
obvious nature in which the flight-or-fight machinery plays a role.
Anxiety, apprehension, suppressed anger are all accompanied by
a chronic activation of these systems. There may be a real cause
for anxiety—a difficult interview, an examination, an appearance
in court, an entry into combat. There may be no cause at all.
There is simply "free-floating anxiety," a sense of impending

doom, an awful fear that is all the more demoralizing because it lacks a cause. The "existential anxiety" so dear to the hearts of one school of psychoanalysts belongs in this category.

The student of Creative Psychology does not attempt to eliminate anxiety of this kind. He simply observes, striving as far as possible, to separate his sense of "I" from the physical sensations he is studying. After a while, he makes a very curious discovery. The effort to observe and, at the same time, not to identify with the sensations he is studying little by little changes those sensations. Without directly trying to do so (how can one "try" not to feel anxiety?), he has learned how to control the reaction. For the fact is (as the student can confirm for himself) that observation, which means bringing a sensation into the focus of awareness, alters the process itself. It brings about a definite change in the nervous pathways that are operating to produce the anxiety. It switches the energy into a different channel. So one who sets out with a firm intention: "I am going to observe carefully the physical sensations of this thing I call anxiety," discovers to his surprise that there is no anxiety left to observe. He has, by his effort, brought about in himself a change in his level of consciousness, has passed from the third room to the threshold of the fourth. In the fourth room, anxiety of this kind cannot exist.

There are other aspects of the work of the instinctive brain that the student both can and should observe. Observation of fluctuating energy levels gives an insight into the working of the great glandular orchestra, whose harmonies vary from hour to hour and from day to day. Biochemical knowledge may be helpful in that it gives names to the members of the orchestra. We can speak of the thyroid acting like the damper in a stove, regulating the rate of metabolism. We can think of the cortex of the adrenal glands pouring out its varied products that govern a host of processes from mineral retention to reaction to stress. We can recall that the gonads (sex glands) secrete hormones which not only have a direct influence on sexual appetite but also affect the metabolism of protein, the distribution of fat, various secondary sexual characteristics. We can remember that the pituitary, at the base of the brain, functions as the conductor of the glandular orchestra, activating one gland or another by means of its special "trophic" hormones. We can also remember that the pituitary is under direct control of the instinctive brain, to a part of which, the hypothalamus, it is directly attached.

All this textbook knowledge is secondary. The important thing is direct observation of the energy levels, aimed at bringing them more under the control of the conscious will. A man has at his disposal far more energy than he ordinarily realizes or makes use of.[74] Gurdjieff, who used the analogy of an accumulator, stated that each center has two accumulators from which it draws its energy but that, in addition, there exists a big accumulator to which it can be directly connected *if efforts of sufficient intensity are made*.

Those familiar with the literature of hatha yoga will have come across several exercises that involve exertions of a kind that might be considered heroic or even impossible by one accustomed to our comfortable style of living. Consider, for instance, the extraordinary exertion demanded of one who would master the art of *tummo* (the generation of psychic heat), which involves being able to dry towels on one's naked body in the arctic temperatures of the Tibetan winter.[75]

The fact that such feats are possible amply proves that energies are available to man that he does not ordinarily use. In the course of reeducating his instinctive center, the student learns how to liberate these energies. He learns to recognize the processes by which they are generated and stored. He must discover how, by the exertion of his conscious will, discords in the performance of the glandular orchestra can be remedied. Periods of *intentional stress* are used by some teachers to enable the student to gauge his hidden potentials and his limitations. These periods are designed to bring the student to a realization of some psychophysical facts concerning his organism and its capacities. The period generally culminates in a ceremony that may take the form of an "initiation," but actually it is the student who initiates himself. The teacher merely provides conditions, teaches the methods and watches over the student to see that he does not harm himself.

This type of "heroic exertion" is not and cannot be a permanent way of life. It is a means of attaining what A. H. Maslow calls "peak moments" and of attaining them deliberately, by intentional effort. The student should not expect to remain on the peak any more than Sir Edmund Hillary, having successfully made the ascent, could remain permanently on the top of Mount Everest. He has to come down, to return to a less demanding level of existence. But the efforts he made in the course of the ascent will have taught him how much power he is able to generate in his own organism by the maximum exertion of his will and what kind of exertions are involved in this operation.

Generally, in our well-upholstered culture man does not exert himself enough. The lack of physical stress results in a deterioration of the adrenocortical machinery and a certain irreversible degeneracy is the result. The student of Creative Psychology, whose aim it is to ascend the peaks and not vegetate in the valleys, cannot tolerate such degeneracy in his own organism. He is compelled to exert himself, to overcome his own inertia, to venture again and again beyond the limit of what he considered to be, for him, physiologically possible. At the same time he has to learn, by careful observation, to recognize the warning signals, the red lights in the body. For there are such warning signals, and nothing is gained by ignoring them. There are times when the body needs rest, when accumulators, for some reason, have failed to recharge, when exertion, far from generating energy, actually depletes it.

There are limits to the usefulness of "super efforts" even under the best of conditions. One who goes beyond these limits may permanently damage his organism. Soldiers who, during the invasion of Normandy in World War II, went without proper sleep for as long as a week and were constantly in danger did not attain, as a result of this stress, any sort of "peak experience." They were merely totally depleted and emerged from the ordeal as nervous wrecks, with an impairment which was often irreparable. Not all stress is useful, and *intentional stress* has always to be built up gradually, under proper supervision, with proper respect for the warning signals given by the body when the safe limits have been overstepped. Peak experiences are earned by prolonged and steadily increasing exertions always held within the limits imposed by the physical type of the person concerned. To know these limits a man must understand the idiosyncracies of his own instinctive center.

The instinctive brain must also be educated to control food intake. Toxic conditions, due to excessive intake of animal protein, are common among the steak-guzzling carnivores which make up most of the human population of the U.S.A. Without going into the moral aspects of eating meat, we can say that he who overloads himself with animal protein out of all proportion to his needs is likely to brew in his gut a fine array of toxic by-products and thus more or less chronically poison himself. The symptoms of such self-poisoning are easily detected and equally easily remedied. A short fast followed by careful attention to the voice of the appestat will teach the observer how to balance intake and output.

Fasting is no cure-all. Undereating can be as disastrous as overeating. Esoteric diets such as the "Zen diet" [76] have been adopted eagerly by certain people. One such enthusiast in New Jersey actually died of malnutrition as a result of a stubborn adherence to a diet of brown rice, kasha and tea. The presumptuous claims made in G. Ohsawa's book (e.g., "Nothing is more simple and easy to cure than cancer, and such other diseases, by returning to the most elementary natural eating and drinking") ought to be quite sufficient to warn the student of the danger of these procedures. As was mentioned before, there is no such thing as a perfect diet, because the needs of the organism change from day to day and food intake must be adjusted to balance these needs.

An important part of the study of the instinctive center has to do with sex. This function, so deeply embedded in the machinery of life, has been described by some investigators as a center in its own right. We can, if we choose, speak of a sex center or a "sexual brain" located predominantly in the hypothalamus but with many ramifications both cortical and subcortical and with a hormonal feedback mechanism linking it both to the pituitary and to the gonads. Or we can think of the sexual function as a part of the instinctive center which, in man at least, is no longer really instinctive but dominated by the "higher brain," hedged in by all manner of artificial taboos.

This interference of the roof brain with the sexual function is peculiar to man and a source, as Freud never wearied of proclaiming, of much of what passes for "mental" illness. It seems to be characteristic of the human animal that it cannot accept its sexual function in the same uncritical way as it accepts its need for food and air. Both the intellectual and the emotional centers interfere with this function, and their interference, in many cases, is disastrous in its effects. Indeed, some of the most horrendous doings in the history of the "bloodstained hominid" (the witch hysteria of the sixteenth and seventeenth centuries, for example) were the direct outcome of the interference of these centers with the sexual function.

The student of Creative Psychology, raised in a culture which still tends to put sex in a big black box and hide it under the bed, is liable to encounter difficulties when he approaches a study of this function. His confusion is apt to be increased by the pontifications of various so-called authorities, especially those affiliated with the Judeo-Christian Guilt Cult, who declare that celibacy is a condition of the "higher life" and that there is some special virtue in continence. The view is not confined to the Christian tradition; it occurs in Buddhist and Hindu teachings, also.

Actually, there is no evidence to suggest that abstaining from sexual experience enhances a person's capacity for attaining either the fourth or the fifth state of consciousness. Indeed, there is much evidence to the contrary. The "struggle with the flesh" that engaged such a large proportion of the energies of hermits, monks and "holy men" produced, in many cases, mere cripples and neurotics or devil-obsessed psychopaths whose ingrown lusts, transformed into cruelty and religious intolerance, compelled them to project their deformed fantasies onto the minds of their fellowmen, whom they then proceeded to burn alive for such fancied offences as having sexual intercourse with devils. These people would have been healthier, happier, better adjusted and more filled with the milk of human kindness if they had accepted Eros instead of denying him.[77]

The Christian tradition has long tried to put love into two compartments, one labeled "sacred" and the other, "profane." This has no biological justification. The sexual function can be used as a means of experiencing higher states of consciousness, a fact well known to the ancient world, from which orgiastic rites had not been banished. However, such an experience is possible only when the sexual function has been trained to operate without interference from the intellectual brain. In our culture sex has become more and more cerebral. We think about it, write about it, talk about it, cold-eyed sexologists gather statistics about it, so that the whole sexual mechanism becomes permeated with verbalizing. This, plus the residue of guilt and shame that, despite more enlightened attitudes, continues to haunt us, puts pure sexual experience out of the reach of many people. They simply cannot let the sex center alone and allow themselves to be carried along on the flood of direct erotic awareness, a powerful primeval force and one which is essentially benign.

If left to itself, the sexual center can teach us much. It is wise, profound, ancient and very powerful. It can operate at different levels of consciousness. In the second state, the Room of Dreams, it can conjure up the entire sexual act, providing a dream partner and inducing, in the male at least, both erection of the penis and seminal discharge. Its operation, in the third state of consciousness, may range from a mere transient relief of tension to a profound, insight-giving experience which, by its orgiastic power can force even scattered disharmonized human beings to become aware, if only for a moment, of its wordless wisdom and its primordial magic. Operating in the fourth state of consciousness, it puts a man or woman directly into contact with the enormous generative force working all through nature once worshipped in the form of Eros and Aphrodite. In this state sex can reveal to a man or a woman certain secrets concerning the energies of the body that are difficult to attain by other means.

Some of these secrets are hinted at in various *Tantras*,[78] in which the use of *maithuna* is described. These practices appeared most improper to the authorities during the days of the British *raj* and the view became widespread that there was something very obscene and wicked about the *Tantras* in general. Actually, all talk of morality in this connection is irrelevant. There is an aspect of physiological yoga in which sexual energy is utilized to awaken certain powers within the body. There is nothing particularly perilous about the practice, but it involves mastery over nervous pathways which, in both male and female, are associated with the generation of the orgasm. Attainment of this mastery involves a training in sexual awareness, conscious control of processes that are normally autonomic. Intentional placing of awareness picks up and amplifies certain faint signals from within the depths of the organism. The practitioner is brought into contact with deep biological levels of his own being and with the being of his opposite, his *shakti*, the female element. What he learns is beyond the reach of words. He cannot describe it. If he tries to do so, he merely spoils the experience. The symbols of the intellectual brain can never express the quality of Dionysian experience.

Education of Movement

The "moving brain," which controls all the voluntary muscles in the body, plays a far larger part in "psychology" than is generally realized. The "psyche" is often regarded as a function dependent on intellect or emotion to which muscular movement contributes little or nothing. Actually the muscles contribute a great deal. The sensation of self, as William James pointed out, is largely made up of muscular sensations concentrated in the facial region, especially the area of the lips. Furthermore, a whole host of symptoms, to which that vague label "neurotic" is commonly applied, are dependent upon or reinforced by muscular tension and can be relieved by the induction of relaxation. Both E. Jacobson and J. Wolpe[59,58] have realized this and the latter's system of psychotherapy is constructed on a foundation of relaxation techniques.

There is an obvious reason why the state of the voluntary muscles contributes so much to the sensation of self. For thousands of years, his muscles were man's sole means of gaining a livelihood. In hunting, fishing, fighting, food-gathering, he was dependent on the skill and coordination of these vital machines. When they failed, he failed. Now, with a host of man-made machines to do the work for him, man depends totally on his muscles only in those communities upon which technology has not showered its questionable blessings. But the habits acquired during millenia are not shaken off in a few decades. So even a "civilized" man whose greatest muscular exertion during a working day is to heave his own bulk out of an office chair still locates the self largely in his musculature.

The same age-old dependence on the muscles accounts for the "hunger for movement" that constitutes one of the basic appetites of man. The hunger is real, healthy, normal and necessary, but it is opposed by an equally real inertia, that appetite for *dolce far niente,* which tends to engulf a man in torpor, like the sombreroed Mexican so popular with cartoonists stretched out in an interminable siesta in the midday warmth. As labor-saving devices, one after another, take over from men's muscles the tasks with which they once busied themselves, as both the back-breaking toil of the laborer and the skilled movements of the craftsman are mechanized and automated, the appetite for movement becomes increasingly blunted by inertia. What hunger remains is satisfied in fashions which become steadily more absurd. A profusion of ridiculous gadgets appears on the market designed solely to set the body in motion. Sweating operators pedal bicycles that go nowhere, row boats that are not in the water, or submit to being stretched, twisted, pummeled by mechanisms that seem like variegated caricatures of Frankenstein's monster designed to extinguish in their victims the last lingering impulses toward self-expression through the moving brain.

The student of Creative Psychology will avoid these absurd devices. Working directly on his own moving center, he will discover an extraordinary abundance of material and a new and deeper means of "knowing." Like the instinctive brain, the moving brain is wise with a primordial, wordless wisdom acquired through the ages. Animals show this wisdom more vividly than humans. The grace of a cat, agility of a squirrel, the poise of a bird soaring on the updrafts of air, the rhythmic hoofbeats of a galloping horse all speak with an eloquence beyond words of the moving-center intelligence. Nor is its wisdom confined to the simpler routines of running, flying, climbing or jumping. All those patterns of behavior which are loosely called "instinctive," which involve creating structures of varying complexities—the nests of birds, the waxen combs of bees, the dams of beavers—are all carried in the moving brain and passed on from generation to generation as an integral part of the genetic code.

Because contemporary man, in the U.S.A. at least, is so gadget-ridden, much of the wisdom of the moving center is undeveloped and the joys and insights it affords are lost. The center tends to be partly atrophied and requires extensive reeducation before it will function effectively. This reeducation and special training of the moving center played a very large part in the methods used by G. Gurdjieff in his Institute for the Harmonious Development of Man. The methods proved very fruitful. By drawing the energy away from the "noise machine" and directing it into the muscles, by channeling the attention and evoking double awareness, these exercises can bring the sensations of the fourth state of consciousness more readily than any other technique with which this writer is familiar.

Such special exercises are not sufficient in themselves to familiarize the student with all aspects of the moving brain. Many and varied activities are necessary, involving the manipulations of materials of one sort or another. Different types of physical skill, various arts, crafts and simple muscular activities offer the careful observer a wealth of material. Rhythmic activities such as sawing logs for the fire, spading the garden, scything, and hoeing offer examples of pure moving center work, which, if it is not spoiled by wandering attention, can be profoundly satisfying, putting the worker in contact with primordial rhythms that are now, for the most part, taken over by some noisy machine.

As moving-center activities grow more complex, the element of skill becomes increasingly important. Movements become finer, more difficult, more carefully integrated as simple manual work grades into craftsmanship. The ancient rhythms are still there but they are more complex. The flow of clay under the fingers of a potter, of wool through the fingers of a spinner, weaver or carpet-maker, the shaping of wood by a carpenter, of iron by a black-smith, all demonstrate the wisdom of the moving brain in relation to various materials. In this area of experience, the student can learn much about the materials themselves, for the moving center brings man into contact with material in a particularly intimate way, be it stone, wood, clay, wool or metal.

As movements become increasingly complex, we pass out of the realm of the "pure" moving brain and enter one in which more than one brain participates. Thus, the purely moving-center skill of a master craftsman will not enable a surgeon to perform an op-eration because no two operations are ever alike, because unex-pected complications may arise, because pathological conditions may be discovered on the operating table that call for quite differ-ent procedures from those originally planned. So a surgeon, be-sides his purely manipulative skills, must be constantly drawing on the wisdom of his intellectual brain. He can never rely on his moving center alone. In the same way, the research scientist, though skilled in a variety of manipulations directed by the mov-ing brain, can never carry out his research with that brain alone. He must constantly be devising new approaches to his problem, developing new techniques, building new apparatuses. For the ability to do this he must rely on the intellectual center. The difference between a good scientist and a technician is that the former employs two centers and the latter need use only one.

Similarly, in the realm of the arts, though the moving brain plays an important role, it will not by itself confer artistic ability. Technique alone does not make an artist. There is a difference between a stone mason and a sculptor, between a sign painter and a portrait painter. This difference involves a certain emotional ele-ment that enters into the activity and makes the difference be-tween the routine and the unique. Admittedly this element is extremely elusive and often consists only of that phoney attempt to seem clever previously mentioned in connection with the influence of the false ego. There can, however, be no doubt about its existence. It is the subtle something that makes the difference between art and craft.

All moving-center activity involves the simultaneous contraction and relaxation of pairs of muscles. It is the balance between tension and relaxation that makes the difference between graceful, harmonious movement and awkward movement. An untrained, unskilled moving brain constantly frustrates its own efforts. It activates muscles that are not involved in the task (facial muscles especially). It misdirects the application of effort. It tries to substitute force for skill and, when results are not obtained, activates the emotional center and arouses anger and impatience, which, of course, merely make matters worse.

An intimate association exists between the moving brain and the emotional brain because emotion is expressed in muscular movement, particularly by the muscles of the face. This muscular expression is so much a part of the "feel" of the emotion that the two are sometimes thought of as inseparable. However, as every competent actor well knows, the expression of an emotion can be "put on" at will by intentional contraction of facial muscles. This arranging of the face does not provoke the actual emotion it portrays. If it did, actors involved in harrowing roles would swiftly act themselves into nervous breakdowns. The opposite process— stopping the muscular expression of an emotion—may modify that emotion very considerably and prevent a destructive, unpleasant emotion from using up great stores of psychic energy in unprofitable manifestations.

The key to the control of the emotional center lies in the moving center. Control of this kind is learned slowly. It becomes possible only when the student has discovered how to separate the sensation of "I" from the sensation of his own muscles. This double awareness is characteristic of the fourth state of consciousness, and it is only in this state that a man really has mastery over the two connected centers, moving and emotional. To learn this control it is necessary first of all to learn how muscular tensions and emotional states are connected. This study must begin with the face, the musculature of which is complex, delicate and highly mobile. The student learns to contract and relax these muscles at will. He then learns to extend this control to other muscles of the body, discovers how to induce total muscular relaxation, to contract single muscles and even single muscle fibers.[79]

All this involves a great deal of effort and observation but, as has been repeatedly mentioned, Creative Psychology is the highest form of creativity and the efforts demanded are proportional to the rewards obtained. Some may object that all this work on musculature puts too much emphasis on the physical body, is not "spiritual" enough, that the body should be ignored or even despised and all effort be directed to ill-defined activities called "prayer," "meditation," "contemplation," etc. Those who think in this way have fallen into the old fool-trap which deludes its victims into thinking that there are two entities, a body and a soul, and that what may be good for one is bad for the other. This illusion has long been the curse of the Judeo-Christian tradition, has led to the elimination of all practices designed to give mastery over moving and instinctive functions, has evoked a flock of unwholesome perversions ranging from celibacy to self-starvation, has banished the dancing, orgiastic, Dionysian element from religion and made man more than ever a stranger to himself. It can be confidently prophesied that only when these elements are reintroduced, only when it is clearly understood that soul and body are one and what is good for one is good for the other, will this tired old religion receive a new lease of life and lead men toward instead of away from the higher goal.

Education of Emotion

Of all the four brains, the emotional brain is most difficult to study. It overlaps and interacts so much with other centers, the instinctive on the one hand, the moving and intellectual on the other, that the purely emotional element is hard to disentangle from all the "side effects" involved in the expression of emotion. Indeed, some have argued that there is no such thing as an emotional brain but merely, on the one hand, a set of instinctive behavior patterns, the flight-or-fight reactions, and, on the other, a set of muscular reactions which cause us to feel what we call "joy," "pleasure," "grief," "irritation," "anxiety" and all the other varieties of emotional experience. But neurophysiology supports the view that there really is an emotional brain apart from centers involved in the *expression* of the emotion. This emotional brain is located within the depths of the "old brain," in the thalamus and hypothalamus, with complex ramifications to the temporal lobe and other cortical regions. So we can and do experience emotions we do not express both in the third state of consciousness and in the second (the state of dreams). For it is a common experience that extraordinarily rich positive emotions can be experienced in dreams as well as extremely negative ones, indeed the "nightmare" has long been regarded as one of the most acute forms of unpleasant emotions, so much so that the adjective "nightmarish" has come to be used routinely by journalists who wish to describe a terrifying episode.

In man the emotional brain is the great motivator. The choice of aims, of goals, of "games worth playing" is made in this brain. It alone electrifies a project with that activist glow that makes the difference between a dream and a reality. All the five "wills"—the will to pleasure, the will to power, the will to meaning, the will to self-transcendence, the will to death—are generated here. It is here that man experiences the "Taste of the Infinite." It is here that the Seeker is generated and the Magnetic Center develops. Certainly both these components of the *persona* can evolve primarily in the intellectual brain, but if they do they will not be effectual. They will lead their possessor only into the dusty wastes of scholasticism, to bookish browsings, to pathetic accumulations of verbal formulae (Catch #1, Table V). Only when the emotional center supplies the motive power will anything real be achieved, for this emotional involvement makes the difference between the word and the deed, the theory and the action.

It was the emotional brain that drove Prince Siddartha from his comfortable palace, sustained him in his fearful asceticisms and in his struggle with Mara and led him to ultimate liberation and

Buddhahood. It was the emotional brain that led Jesus to Jerusalem to confront agony and death. It was the emotional brain that drove on Paul of Tarsus, "in perils of waters, in perils by my countrymen, in perils by the heathen . . . in weariness and painfulness, in watchings often, in hunger and thirst, in fastings often, in cold and nakedness." It was the emotional brain that compelled every *avatar* (an incarnation of deity, as Christ, Buddha), every genuine saint, every true teacher and benefactor of mankind to transform their dreams into realities, to struggle and triumph over their own inertia.

By the same token it was the emotional brain that activated the great conquerors. Alexander, Caesar, Attila, Genghis Khan, Napoleon, Hitler, Stalin, Mao Tse-tung all drew from this center the drive which made them dominant forces in the historical process. The same power, acting through different channels, can make a man an *avatar* or a destroyer, a bringer of life or an agent of death, a blessing to his fellows or a fearful curse. For the emotional center in man, more than any other center, is prone to disorders that make it, under certain conditions, a veritable scourge, a vehicle of Thanatos, a tool of the Destroyer.

The controlling power of the emotional center, as far as behavior is concerned, is dependent in part on an entity which, for lack of a better word, we are forced to call "conscience." Conscience is of two kinds, inward-directed and outward-directed. *Outward-directed conscience* (social conscience) regulates man's dealing with his fellows and the society of which he is part. This conscience, insofar as it incorporates in itself the prohibitions (taboos) of society, corresponds to that part of the psyche which Freud called the "superego." And because society imposes its taboos largely through fear (by threats of punishment, imprisonment, mutilation, death), so the social conscience may also operate through fear, imposing all sorts of restrictions on the psyche, playing the tyrant like a little Jehovah and creating an emotional condition analogous to that which prevails in a state under a tyrannical government, dominated by fear, in constant danger of violent rebellion.

But the social conscience is not constructed entirely out of the individual's acceptance of the taboos his society imposes. There is, it seems, a certain inborn social conscience the simplest expression of which is the Golden Rule: "Do unto others as you would they should do unto you." This conscience represents an extension of the self-sense, a realization of oneness with others, extending, in certain people, beyond the world of men to that of animals, so that they will not willingly destroy even a mosquito. All the great teachers—Jesus, Gautama, Krishna, Lao-tze, and Mahavira, the founder of Jainism—have stressed the importance of developing this function in man. It is the basis of the principle of *ahimsa* (harmlessness) that Gandhi made the keystone of his teaching. Albert Schweitzer embodied it in his doctrine of "Reverence for Life." It is the ultimate and highest expression of Eros (the life giver) as opposed to Thanatos (the death bringer) and is a force in the human psyche which might, if it increased in strength, save this bloodstained hominid from indulging in further orgies of reciprocal destruction.

Inward-directed conscience is the measuring rod whereby the individual measures deviations from his own inner standards. It is the measure of sincerity, of truth, a watchman posted by the essence to guard against the intrusion of the false ego. This is the force which compels the artist to follow his own "inner light" rather than adopt the standards of the world about him and, by employing "slick tricks," become famous and maybe rich. This is likewise the force which protects the creative writer from prostituting his talent and writing what he thinks or hopes will sell rather than saying something he really feels should be said. This is the force which compels the research scientist to resist the temptation of "rushing into print" when he secretly knows that his data does not really support the statements he is so eager to make. It enables him to resist the pressure to publish and compels him to return to the laboratory and repeat his experiments, even though he knows that Dr. X, who is much less scrupulous, is working on the same problem and is likely to publish first.

For the practicing student of Creative Psychology, no other

force in the psyche is more important than this function of the emotional center which is here called "inward-directed conscience." It is the ultimate servomechanism, the only criterion by which he can tell whether he is on course or has deviated from his aim. For it should be clear to the reader by this time that deviations from an inner aim defined in terms of attainment of "higher states of consciousness" can be subtle and difficult to perceive. Laziness, failure to persist in the exercises, talking or thinking about the inner work instead of practicing it (Catch #1, Table V) are deviations which any reasonably sincere student can recognize and struggle to correct. But there are other catches which are far more subtle. Overdependence on the teacher, unthinking acceptance of his every utterance, deification of the teacher (the Starry-eyed Syndrome, Catch #2) are symptoms of a deviation which, for some people, is almost impossible to recognize as such. Similarly, the will to dominate, the urge to teach others what one does not know oneself, the urge to play the savior when one has neither the knowledge nor the being to play that role (the False-Messiah Syndrome, Catch #3) is a deviation to which some people are totally blind. Even more subtle is the Personal-Salvation Syndrome (Catch #4), which causes one to become so identified with his own inner work that his last state is worse than his first.

Catch #5, the Sunday-Go-to-Meeting Syndrome, is the supreme catch among churchgoing Christians who imagine they can keep on the right side of the deity by engaging in a one-day-a-week hymn, psalm and sermon routine in a special building set aside for the purpose. Would-be players of the Master Game are often equally naïve, exerting themselves while in the presence of their teacher, forgetting all about the game when on their own.

Catch #6, the Hunt-the-Guru Syndrome, is a subtle catch because the search for a teacher is an essential part of the Master Game, a test of the seeker's intelligence, perseverance and discrimination. But there are those who make the search interminable by refusing to stay long enough with any teacher really to learn what he has to offer. Such people are always looking for miracle workers and rush here and there in quest of signs and

TABLE V
The Six Catches

Catch #1 Talk-Think Syndrome	Talking or thinking about the Work instead of doing it.
Catch #2 Starry-eyed Syndrome	Fanatical devotion to and belief in a teacher or system to exclusion of all others.
Catch #3 False-Messiah Syndrome	Delusion that I personally am a teacher or savior.
Catch #4 Personal-Salvation Syndrome	Delusion that I personally can be saved, enter "heaven," survive death, etc.
Catch #5 Sunday-Go-to-Meeting Syndrome	Habit of making efforts only when in presence of teacher or with other members of group.
Catch #6 Hunt-the-Guru Syndrome	Habit of wandering from teacher to teacher, without staying long enough to learn anything from any of them.

wonders. They are always full of tales of "higher powers" and "mysterious forces," breathlessly relate how X can read the "Akashic records" and Y can "activate the *chakras*" and Z can foretell the future. One manifestation of Catch #6 is a conviction that some new *avatar* will appear who, by the exertion of his spiritual powers, will "save the world." Often the victims of this catch imagine they have found the long-awaited one and rush around ecstatically proclaiming that a new era of history has begun. But they soon weary of the new *avatar*, and set off again on their search, which will never end because they do not really want it to end. They use the search as a means of evading real inner work.

This brings us into the most difficult area in the field of Creative Psychology. If this sensing device which we call "inward-directed conscience" is defective (and it generally is, one way or another), how can it be corrected? It is a function of the highest level of the emotional center, a sort of spiritual touchstone which enables its possessor to distinguish the true coin from the counterfeit. In terms of "the struggle between the selves," it is the mirror of truth in the hands of the Observer, which enables him to distinguish friend from foe, essence from false ego, faithful servant from scheming flatterer. But if the mirror itself has defects, if its surface distorts and does not give a true image, then what can be done to remove the defects?

Only a tentative answer can be offered to this question. A wise teacher can usually spot the defects in the mirror once he gets to know a student sufficiently well. He can point them out, put the student in situations where he is more or less forced to see them. Unfortunately, man is so constituted that he has certain blind spots in his psyche which obstruct the teacher's effort. Sometimes only a more or less shattering experience will finally bring the student face to face with his inner defect. Thus, Peter had total confidence in his own loyalty to his teacher though the Master had no illusions about his disciple's weakness. ("Before the cock crow thou wilt deny me thrice.") It took the actual experience of making the three denials, hearing the cock crow, remembering the teacher's words to bring Peter to an *emotional* realization of his weakness.

The errors most likely to be encountered in the working of the emotional center can be listed as follows:

1) Accidie or aimlessness.
2) Self-pity.
3) Self-hatred.
4) Overdependence.
5) Will to dominate.

"Accidie" is a word which has gone out of fashion. It used to be described as one of the Seven Deadly Sins and was often regarded as synonymous with "sloth." More properly the word can be applied to *failure in motivation* and the resultant state of listlessness, aimlessness, and boredom. The condition is really malignant and Thomas Szasz is quite justified in attributing to accidie many of the mental illnesses that afflict contemporary man.[1] Accidie represents a failure in gamesmanship and leads to a loss of interest that can be total and devastating. It can strike anybody from a wealthy widow in a Park Avenue apartment to a drifting derelict in a Bowery gutter. Victor Frankl, describing life in Nazi concentration camps, has described how literally lethal accidie could be under those extreme conditions.[56] The prisoners could endure cold, hunger, brutality, degradation as long as they had some sort of aim or some hope to cling to. But when this hope was taken from them, they lay down and died.

The student of Creative Psychology is as prone to accidie as anyone else. He has embarked on a difficult, demanding metagame, the results of which are not outwardly visible, as are the productions of the artist, writer or research scientist. His inner work demands efforts that are not particularly exciting, but which must be repeated hour after hour, day after day. Like Bunyan's Pilgrim, he encounters on his way one obstacle after another or the same obstacle over and over again. Moreover, he plays this inner game in a society that does not value the inner aims he pursues, that gives him no encouragement, no "positive reinforcement," from the members of which he is compelled to conceal his most sacred aspirations lest he be thought "queer" or even mildly insane.

One who has made the decision to play the Master Game inevitably discovers that his emotional force, the wellspring of his inner work, fluctuates in its intensity, may be powerful at one time, fade out completely at another. The fading of the emotional force occurs usually about a year or two years after the student has found his teacher and embarked on the work. In the beginning, the novelty of working under direction, the excitement of new discoveries, the thrill of "belonging" to a group dedicated to a single aim carry the neophyte along and he works with ardor. But when the novelty wears off, when the first impulse weakens, he enters that phase of disenchantment well known to spiritual directors on the religious way and described by them as "periods of dryness." This inward aridity has the same effect on the inner life as has drought on a garden. The flowers of the spirit droop. Zeal vanishes. Ardor fades. The student wonders about his aim. The Master Game loses its magic. To this condition G. Gurdjieff referred in the saying: "In the beginning it is roses, roses. Later it is thorns, thorns."

What is the solution? Is there a solution? If I do not feel an emotion, how can I generate it? For it must be clear to any objective student that man has little control over the emotional center. A good actor can portray the outer form of emotion, can produce real tears and what sounds like genuine laughter. But this is not grief, neither is it joy. These are merely the outward trappings of emotions, their moving-center accompaniments. And what of the will to self-transcendence, the appetite for consciousness, that subtle, hard-to-characterize emotion that stirs only in a few and plays so small a role in contemporary life? How can I awaken that when it dies within me, when the flame on the altar fades, when the peak toward which I was striving disappears in the fog?

This question brings us face to face with one of the peculiarities of the emotional brain. It has, in the third state of consciousness at least, a very bad memory. We can remember an event in our lives, tragic or joyful, but it is difficult to reexperience the emotion that went with it. This applies also to an aim in which there is a strong emotional component. We may remember the aim intellectually but not emotionally. And the intellectual memory, having no fire within it, is a dead, dry remnant. It lacks the sparkle of the original aim.

But just as the moving and instinctive centers can be educated and brought increasingly under conscious control, so the emotional center can be trained not to forget or not to forget so easily. A man does not have direct control over the emotional brain, but he does have control over the moving and intellectual brains and both of these affect the emotional center. Thus, a person who feels totally miserable can smile by an intentional effort. And although the smile may be wooden and contrived, it will, on account of the feedback from the moving to the emotional center, evoke a shadowy memory of happiness. Similarly the appetite for higher consciousness can be faintly reawakened through the intellectual center. Though disenchanted and lacking in zeal, the student can recall his early enthusiasm, saying: "Once this seemed vitally important, the Master Game, the only game worth playing." And from here, still purely intellectually, he can retrace his steps, remembering his old dedication, recalling the processes that led him to his decision, reviewing the alternative life games and sincerely asking what they have to offer as compared with the Master Game. Even though all this is purely intellectual, the effort will, again by feedback from one center to another, evoke a faint taste of the old ardor, a memory of the great enterprise and of all the hope and excitement that went with it.[80]

Self-pity is almost as paralyzing as accidie. It is the emotion of one who falls down in the mud and, instead of getting up again, wallows in it and maybe swallows some just to be able to feel more self-pity. Self-pity, a typical false-ego phenomenon, is utterly false, totally useless. Unfortunately, the prevailing tone of the Judeo-Christian tradition, its emphasis on groveling and the "Lord have mercy on me, miserable sinner" theme, has for centuries encouraged self-pity in its devotees in addition to self-hatred and self-contempt. Indeed, there are subcults in this tradition which convert the rolling-in-the-mud of self-pity and self-abasement into an end in itself. Devotees of this practice draw as much satisfaction from feeling sorry for themselves because they are such tremendous sinners as some people derive from displaying their surgical scars. Needless to say, a good spiritual director has little patience with such nonsense, but, in this tradition, the good directors are outnumbered by the bad, and the latter do not hesitate to encourage the groveling of their "penitents," in fact, will get down in the mud and grovel with them.

How can one correct this bad habit of the emotional brain? Again, it can best be approached through the intellect. Self-pity is an emotion so obviously useless that even a little analysis is enough to reveal its falsity. Why do you pity yourself? What will this pity accomplish? You failed once. Then get up and try again. What benefit can you get by groveling in the mud? This tough, unsentimental line of reasoning puts the false ego in the spotlight and illuminates its absurdities so brightly that no objective observer can take them seriously.

Self-hatred and self-contempt are also examples of the wrong working of the emotional brain but are far more difficult to evaluate and correct than is the obviously useless emotion of self-pity. There is, in the emotion which urges a man to engage in the Master Game, a strong negative element which might be called "self-contempt." Nietzsche's Zarathustra knew this well:

> Alas! There comes the time of the most despicable man, who can no longer despise himself. . . .
> What is the greatest thing you can experience? It is the hour of great contempt. The hour in which your happiness becomes loathsome to you, and so also your reason and virtue.[81]

Insofar as the "hour of great contempt" leads to great endeavors, great efforts to emerge from that sorry puppet-like state of semihypnosis into one of full consciousness, it is salutary. It is not, in this form, a negative emotion at all but a very powerful impulse toward true health and full development, a negative reaction that engenders a positive response. Unfortunately, the positive response does not always follow the negative reaction. Confronted for the hundredth time with some unpleasant manifestation, the student groans inwardly: "I hate myself," He then proceeds to wallow in the emotion, indulging in a masochistic orgy of self-condemnation, deliberately recalling all the stupidest, most degrading things he has done, performing a psychological self-flagellation, and getting the same perverse satisfaction from it that real self-flagellation affords those who practice this art. In this way self-contempt, which might be useful, degenerates into mere wallowing and groveling. It is perfectly clear, from the popularity of such wallowings, in the guise of penetential practices, that they offer such satisfaction that those who indulge in them will go to extraordinary extremes, not excluding physical self-torture.

This wrong working of the emotional brain can be corrected by the practice described in an earlier chapter. Self-hatred and self-contempt are both based on an illusion, the great fallacy that man has one "I" whole and indivisible. Actually he has no such permanent "I" but only a constantly changing pattern of selves. The emotion loosely described as self-contempt becomes positive and of value only when this fact is understood. There is a certain separation between "I" (in the sense of the Observer, who is the seed of the permanent "I") and the various dwarfs, cripples, morons and fools who also happen to be in the House of the Selves and whose antics, when they happen to get control, can be very embarrassing or actually dangerous. As the Observer learns to know these characters, he ceases to call them "I." They are simply mechanical dolls which he is compelled to carry around with him. It is just as silly to hate them as it is to hate a rake which hits one on the head because one left it lying with the teeth up and then trod on it. One can logically *fear* these dolls because they are dangerous but the fear will be useful only if it engenders watchfulness, for only by watchfulness can they be prevented from getting control.

Overdependence, the fourth example of the wrong work of the emotional brain, occurs in certain people, usually high in viscerotonia or somatotonia, when they have "found their faith" or "consolidated their belief." This generally means that they have become members of some cult or settled themselves at the feet of some teacher to whom they listen in starry-eyed rapture, accepting as "gospel" any information he chooses to offer them. The phenomenon is very common in India, where *guru* worship (along with cow worship) constitutes a national vice. It is also common in the West, for the Christian tradition, with its emphasis on the Good Shepherd, on sheepishness and on the "believe and ask no questions" attitude has always encouraged this form of emotional overdependence.

The Starry-eyed Syndrome represents one of the most frequented and most favored cul-de-sacs on the Way. Its popularity is understandable enough. It results from a human craving for certainty, for consolation, for guidance and for obedience. Despite all their big talk about freedom, men still wish to be slaves. They want to be told what to do, what to wear, what to think, what to believe. This saves them from the effort and suffering involved in thinking for themselves. Once they have hung about their necks the label stating their "faith," they protect that label with a passionate intensity and will gladly kill anybody who dares to question the truth of any of the statements on the label.

The Starry-eyed Syndrome is a form of the wrong function of the emotional brain that is very hard to correct. The ancient assertion: "If you believe what I tell you, you will be saved. If you don't you will be damned," has been used for centuries by priests of various religions for their own profit. It is an integral part of the world's oldest confidence trick. It is still played today and is still profitable, though the sophisticated members of a science-based society might be expected to know better than to fall for such a trick.

A tough teacher who has no use for starry-eyed students will naturally try to discourage the overdependence that such students display. "Have faith in nothing. Believe nothing. Test everything." With such exhortations he may attempt to cultivate that sturdy spirit of self-reliance so well characterized in Emerson's great essay[82] and to reduce the level of credulity and suggestibility that, coupled with his ferocity, combine to make man the most dangerous of herd animals. But those who suffer from this particular defect of the emotional brain will commonly go on believing despite these exhortations. If a tough teacher refuses to let them indulge in this weakness, they will leave him and seek one more accommodating who will tell them just what to think, to do, to feel in every situation, what they may eat, drink, when they may copulate and whether or not, when so doing, they may use a contraceptive. They will follow him as meekly as sheep in the happy assurance that this is the path to salvation and, if anyone questions their assumptions, they will gladly boil him in oil for daring to attempt to "shake their faith."

The will to dominate, fifth type of wrong work of the emotional brain, is the exact opposite of the Starry-eyed Syndrome just described. This is the basis of the False-Messiah Syndrome, and those in whom it occurs are responsible for vast amounts of human misery. This error occurs in people who naturally possess some special power. They are less scattered, less divided, less lacking in unity and in will than the average man. They are able to apply themselves to a single aim and to pursue that aim with an emotional intensity of which their more tepid fellowmen are incapable.

Many of the characteristics of the False-Messiah Syndrome have already been described in the chapter on types. It results from an error in the function of the emotional brain which causes displacement of the powerful emotion that should lead to self-transcendence. The victim of such an error, instead of becoming liberated from the self, is more tightly bound to it. He uses the power he has attained by inner discipline to further the aims of the self, these being often identified with some organization which is, in fact, the self amplified. If he is politically-minded, he projects the self into his party; if religious, he projects it into his church. Or he simply uses his powers to serve his own ends, setting himself up as leader, an infallible authority, demanding absolute obedience (and getting it) from the members of his "flock."

The condition, once it has developed, is hard to correct. That aspect of the emotional center called "inward-directed conscience" has, when it functions correctly, the power to warn its possessor. It can tell him the difference between fool's gold and real gold. It can tell him when he has attained that level of being which will enable him safely to teach others. But if the inner conscience fails to operate, there is no other function in a man that can take its place. The victim of the False-Messiah Syndrome may be told by others that he is making a mistake, but their voices do not carry the same force as does the voice of the inner conscience and can always be ignored. "They are jealous, they are blind, they do not have the insight to appreciate my power, they do not hear my inner voices." By these means and countless others, the victim of this malfunction will justify his actions. He is blocked from any sort of corrective action by his tragic conviction that he *must be right*. If he ever loses this conviction, the result may be so shattering that he falls apart completely, deprived of the grand illusion from which he drew his strength.

The above examples all deal with errors in the working of the emotional brain and with steps that can be taken to overcome them. But there is another aspect of the education of the emotional center that is much more controversial. A person can struggle not to express negative emotions, but can he, by any kind of intentional effort, educate his emotional brain to generate positive emotions?

Undoubtedly there are people whose emotional brains function in such a way that the dominant emotional tone is positive, nor does this mean that they are too stupid or insensitive to be aware of the fact that the world of man contains much that is evil and abominable. Walt Whitman (to whom William James devotes much attention in his chapter, "The Religion of Healthy Mindedness") was far from being a facile optimist. Grief, wounds, war, death all have their places in *Leaves of Grass*. But the man himself, as his disciple, Dr. R. M. Bucke, described him, seemed almost totally positive in his emotional expression, as the following statement shows:

> Perhaps, indeed, no man who ever lived liked so many things and disliked so few as Walt Whitman. All natural objects seemed to have a charm for him. All sights and sounds seemed to please him. He appeared to like (and I believe he did like) all the men, women and children he saw (though I never knew him to say that he liked anyone), but each who knew him felt he liked him or her, and that he liked others also. I never knew him to argue or dispute, and he never spoke about money. He always justified, sometimes playfully, sometimes quite seriously, those who spoke harshly of himself or his writings, and I often thought he even took pleasure in the opposition of enemies. When I first knew [him], I used to think that he watched himself, and would not allow his tongue to give expression to fretfulness, antipathy, complaint, and remonstrance. It did not occur to me as possible that these mental states could be absent in him. After long observation,

however, I satisfied myself that such absence or unconsciousness was entirely real. He never spoke deprecatingly of any nationality or class of man, or time in the world's history, or against any trades or occupations—not even against any animals, insects, or inanimate things, nor any of the laws of nature, nor any of the results of those laws, such as illness, deformity, and death. He never complained or grumbled either at the weather, pain, illness, or anything else. He never swore. He could not very well, since he never spoke in anger and apparently never was angry. He never exhibited fear, and I do not believe he ever felt it.[83]

Whitman, it appears, was equipped with an emotional brain so harmonized and balanced that it simply did not generate those poisons which spoil the lives of others not so gifted. One might justifiably call him a "natural saint." The question is whether, by any means at all, the emotional brain of one less gifted can be trained to function in a similar way. Following Paul of Tarsus, we may accept the idea that love is the highest of all positive emotions and admit that we are merely sounding brass without it even though we do speak with the tongues of men and of angels. But can a man learn to love? Can the emotional center be educated to generate this high emotion? Can this function (the genesis of love) ever be brought under the control of the conscious will?

Obviously the founder of Christianity thought that it could. "A new commandment give I you, that ye love one another." Would he have given such a command if its fulfillment had been physically impossible?

Alas, the history of the Christian Church gives us little reassurance. We read of crusades, massacres, burnings, torturings, a hideous catalog of cruelty compiled by Inquisitors and fanatics. These "servants of the God of Love" not only failed to learn to love each other, but also used their religion as an excuse for hating and performed, in the name of the loving Savior, actions that would have made a Yahoo blush. If the cruelty of man has become less in recent times, it is certainly not on account of the influence of the Christian Church.

Love, hope and faith are not emotions that can be learned.

This is the conclusion to which we are forced by all the evidence available. It is easy to teach men to hate. The efficacy of wartime propaganda makes this clear. It may be possible, though not easy, to teach them not to hate, to recognize hatred as an evil emotion, one not worthy of civilized beings. But to teach them positively to love in an objective, universal way is not possible.

Centers, the emotional center in particular, work differently in different states of consciousness. Man in the third state of consciousness, identified with his petty personal ego, is quite incapable of the impartial love of the saint or Bodhisattva. The closer he approaches to the fourth or fifth states of consciousness, the more capable of genuine love does he become. The new commandment which Jesus gave to his disciples could be obeyed only by fully awakened beings. This is equally true of the other positive emotions mentioned by Paul, namely faith and hope. Both are affected by the level of consciousness of the individual. Hope in sleeping man (that is, man in the third state of consciousness) is mere wishful thinking as a burglar *hopes* he will not be caught by the police or a hostess *hopes* the weather will be fine for her garden party. *Faith* in sleeping man is mere self-delusion, a naïve belief in miracles, in dogmas, in the infallibility of his teacher or the head of his church. Only when a man attains the fourth state of consciousness do faith and hope become really effective emotions.

It is true to say, as far as the education of the emotional brain is concerned, that this brain *can* be taught not to generate certain harmful emotions such as accidie, self-pity, self-hatred and various forms of anxiety. It *cannot* be trained to feel the great positive emotions—love, faith and hope—but will generate these as the level of consciousness changes and self-transcendence replaces identification. Man's ability to resist the powerful forces that are drawing him closer and closer to the ultimate orgy of destruction, depends on the reeducation of the emotional brain. Unfortunately, it is exactly this education which is most sadly neglected in contemporary society. The child can scarcely toddle before it is subjected to displays of violence and manifestations of every negative emotion of which man is capable. Effects of early training are further strengthened by various hate campaigns against non-conformists of one sort or another. All this creates in the emotional center so many erroneous patterns of behavior that the re-education of this center becomes very difficult.

Education of Intellect

The intellectual brain is generally the only one to which any attention is devoted by the exponents of what passes for education in contemporary society. Certainly this brain is important. It stands at the gate which links the inner and outer worlds of man. It has given man all the advantages he now enjoys in the form of increased control over his environment. It has enabled him to supplement the strength of his own muscles with that of a host of machines, to develop the most advanced form of agriculture ever known, to control most of the great plagues that once decimated his numbers, to command those energy sources from which the stars draw their heat, to reach into space and into matter, to understand his own position in the universe and his own minuteness in relation to its immensity.

But although the intellectual brain is a powerful instrument and has given man most of the blessings he now enjoys, it is prone to forms of malfunction that make it at times more of a curse than a blessing. It may be said, without exaggeration, that man has too much brain for his own good; he has more brain than he knows what to do with. The huge cerebral cortex, operating at the low level of efficiency characteristic of the third state of consciousness, instead of bringing man closer to reality creates a whole jungle of illusions that merely serve to complicate man's existence and often, by their hypnotizing effect, prove acutely dangerous. Because intellectual and emotional centers continuously interact, the defects of the intellectual brain tend to amplify wrong working of the emotional brain. This sets up a reverberating circuit, a damaging oscillation, like the vibration set up in a building by certain frequencies of sound which, if they become strong enough, can shake the structure to pieces. These circuits are not only the basis

of disturbed behavior of individuals but also underly those outbursts of destructive activity—riots, revolutions and wars—that
devastate human communities and cause the death or mutilation
of millions. For this reason, it may be asserted that the most dangerous mechanism on earth is the human brain.

Both the emotional and the intellectual brains function differently at different levels of consciousness. Man in the state of waking sleep, deeply identified, immersed in dreams, is at the mercy
of a system of illusions generated by the defective working of his
intellectual brain. His brain creates these illusions because he uses
for his "thinking" a part of the intellectual brain that is not really
capable of thinking at all. This part of the brain consists of a labeling or coding instrument that stores information in the form of
words. Words are certainly handy devices; without them the in-
ventive capacity of the brain would be severly curtailed. Moreover, the accumulation of knowledge and its handing on from
generation to generation would not be possible without words.

So the labeling device is very important and its products, the
written word and the spoken word, make possible all those flexible
interactions that distinguish human societies from the rigid in-
stinct-dominated aggregations of social insects. But the labeling
device is a very poor thinker. It is not really capable of thought at
all. Man in the third state of consciousness does not know this and
constantly tries to think with the labeling device. As a result he
becomes tangled in a web of unreality, an elaborate tissue of illusions. He mistakes the word for the thing, the map for the land it
represents. He thinks he knows the truth when in fact he is merely
juggling with verbal symbols.

The role played by linguistic defects in human society was emphasized by Alfred Korzybski[84] and more fully described by Theo-
dore Longabaugh in his *General Semantics*.[85] Longabaugh recognizes that the development of human society was dependent on
the evolution of speech but states that "the articulate way of life
was a tricky and hazardous device." The device would not be hazardous if the brain that uses it operated at a higher level of consciousness. When seen in a very dim light, all sorts of quite harm-

less objects may appear sinister and threatening, especially to one whose emotions are as prone to defective working as his intellect. The level of consciousness is equivalent to the intensity of light. Improve the light and the seeming threat disappears.

In the Gurdjieffian system, the labeling part of the intellectual brain was called the "formatory center," concerning which P. D. Ouspensky frequently stated that "it could only count up to two." This is the chief characteristic of that form of defective mentation called "formatory thinking." Formatory thinking has played, now plays and is likely to play in the future a large and disastrous role in the life of mankind. This form of "thinking in absolutes" generates human conflicts because it creates opposing systems and represents one as totally good, the other as totally evil. The current pair of opposites, "Capitalist *versus* Communist," is as good an example of this division as was the equally disastrous duad, "Catholic *versus* Protestant," that so preoccupied our ancestors and lured them into one of the most disastrous conflicts of all times (the Thirty Years War).

The emotion-loaded words of the present age—"Communist," "Imperialist," "saboteur," "Fascist," "Marxist"—carry political overtones. Those which haunted our ancestors—"heretic," "witch," "the Devil," "Papist," "unbeliever"—carried religious ones. Both have justified hideous doings, the record of which is sufficient to convince any impartial student that something is terribly amiss in the psyche of man. Only a "fallen being" or a very badly constructed one could allow itself to be so deluded by shadows of its own creating.

It was formatory thinking, thinking in absolutes, in terms of black and white with no shades in between, that generated the great disasters of the twentieth century. The supreme mistake, the arch error from which flowed an almost unlimited stream of evil consequences, was the insane prolongation of World War I, the absolute refusal to negotiate, the resolute pursuit of a phantom called "absolute victory." This resulted in the collapse of Russia, the triumph of Communism, the rise of Nazism, a second disastrous world war, in which was repeated the arch error of the first.

All this prepared the way for a splitting of earth's human community into two armed camps, each with its own label and set of political beliefs, each armed to the teeth and firmly convinced of the absolute rightness of its own views and the absolute wrongness of the opinions of "the enemy."

The student of Creative Psychology will have no difficulty, once he becomes familiar with its workings, in observing the operations of the formatory center in world affairs. It shows best in the glib pronouncements of politicians, the grotesque oversimplifications that, in the field of foreign policy especially, conceal issues of all kinds, in the pronouncements of fanatics, political or religious, in absolutist or totalitarian statements of every kind. True democratic procedure is dominated by a wise distrust of this terrible mechanism and tries to limit its working by allowing both sides of a case to be presented. But democratic procedure all too easily breaks down. The hypnotic power of labels, the craving for simplification, the passion for a "black and white" dyad becomes dominant even though this form of thinking may lead men to the loss of everything they hold most dear.

If men could learn to think with the appropriate part of the intellectual brain, the tragic misunderstandings that now jeopardize their survival would disappear. This cannot happen without an overall change in the level of consciousness, for it is the level of man's consciousness that governs the working of his intellectual brain. The misshapen outgrowths of the formatory center flourish like fungi in the darkness of the third state of consciousness. Where there is total identification, total immersion in self, there is also a tendency to think in terms of the crudest possible pairs of opposites. I am right, therefore you are wrong. I am good, therefore you are evil. I am saved, therefore you are damned.

As man ascends toward the fourth state of consciousness, his thinking undergoes a change. He begins to understand the limits imposed by labels, by absolutes, by names and forms. He seeks, almost without knowing what he is looking for, for means of thinking in other categories. He begins to distrust words and verbal definitions. They appear to him as clumsy artifacts which conceal more than they reveal, which impose a veil between him and reality.

One who has reached this point is ready to undertake the re-education of his intellectual brain, a reeducation which will enable him to emerge from the fogs of verbalism. The essence of the new form of thinking is a direct awareness of processes, a face-to-face encounter with actual events. Meditation is its basis, but meditation does not necessarily involve sitting cross-legged with ones eyes half-closed in a sort of stupor. Meditation is possible anywhere. It is a state in which the student permits the outer world to tell him about itself. He does not "think" about it. The whole process is nonverbal.

This mode of awareness introduces elements that do not normally enter into our perception of the world. There is a change in awareness of dimensions, forms are seen not as fixed, but as "time-shaped." Verbal accounts of "time shape" are very wooden and do not convey the essence of this form of awareness. A rosy apple in a food store is seen in all its stages, bud, blossom, green, red, on the tree, off the tree, in the store, etc. But this verbal account is all too slow. The direct perception is quite different. It involves awareness of time as a shaping dimension, time as a component of form. We know this theoretically. It is a principle of physics. But the direct perception of "time shape" is a very different matter.

The same is true of materiality. A ripe apple has a different materiality from an unripe one and from the wood of the apple tree on which it grew. It can undergo different transformations, is potential food for another organism. The materiality of a statue is different from that of a lump of stone even though stone and statue are chemically identical. The materiality of a painting is different from that of pigments, etc., from which it is composed. This may seem like a misuse of the word "materiality" but, as already mentioned, words do not convey the essence of these new perceptions. They are mere approximations.

The perception both of "time shape" and materiality involves also an awareness of process. Process involves an awareness of triads and octaves. In *most* processes, if not in all, there are three elements which can loosely be called "active force," "passive force" and "neutralizing force." Man in the third state of consciousness sees the first two, but generally is blind to the third. Yet the third force, operating as a catalyst, determines the nature of the result.

It is characteristic of man in waking sleep that he tries to produce a desired result by using the wrong triad. He is passive when he should be active, active when he should be passive, uses a sledgehammer when he should use a feather, tries to obtain results by brute force that can only be produced by patience and skill. The skill of Prince Hui's wonderful cook illustrates what it means to understand the nature of the third force as it relates to skill and "point of application" of force:

> A good cook changes his chopper once a year—because he cuts. An ordinary cook once a month because he hacks.
> But I have had this chopper nineteen years, and although I have cut up many thousands of bullocks, its edge is as if fresh from the whetstone.[49]

Here the difference among nonskill, average skill and superior skill is related, as Chuang-tze relates everything, to being in harmony with *Tao*. He who is thus in harmony intuitively understands the nature of triads. By establishing a correct relationship between the three forces, he invariably obtains the desired result.

Triads can be creative or destructive, according to the way in which the forces are related. The triad involved in building a house is different from that involved in wrecking a house. One requires much skill, the other very little. The development of a series of triads is governed by a law loosely known as the "law of octaves" or "the law of unequal development of vibrations." There has been a great deal of speculation about this law, the name of which derives from the seven-tone scale in music, in which there occur two "intervals" or missing semitones, one between *mi* and *fa* and one between *si* and *do* (the first note of the next octave). Those interested in the theory of the law will find it described at some length in works by Ouspensky and Gurdjieff.

The law is not universal. There are no discontinuities in the development of electromagnetic vibrations, the huge spectrum of which extends from waves longer than the diameter of the earth to ultrashort cosmic radiations with wavelengths measured in fractions of an Angstrom unit. On the whole, however, the concept of "octaves of development" is a useful framework within which to meditate on the theme of triads, *provided one does not become rigid in one's thinking*. Daily life, the affairs of men both on a large and on a small scale, offer examples of the working of the law. Enterprises started with enthusiasm lose their initial impetus, slow down and die out or change their direction. The working of the law is tragically illustrated by the history of Christianity, which began as a religion of love, humility and poverty, deteriorated into a rich, proud, corrupt organization, punishing with torture and death any who dared to question its authority. Marxian Communism provides a no less tragic example, starting as a dream of a classless society in which the state would "wither away," ending as a bureaucratic tyranny in which the rights of the individual are sacrificed and a drab uniformity imposed in the name of "the dictatorship of the proletariat."

When the intellectual center is reeducated, it looks, to use Jakob Boehme's phrase, directly at the "signature of things." It provides its possessor with much knowledge that is hidden from others by the veil of verbal illusions. It offers, among other things, the "gift of prophecy," a power, within certain limits, to foretell the future. It brings, step by step, an awareness of the cosmic process in all its vast complexity. Finally, there occurs a face-to-face confrontation between the microcosm and the macrocosm such as that decribed in the *Bhagavad Gita* when Arjuna asks Krishna to reveal his "Isvara-form." One who penetrates the veil without preparation may experience the cosmic dance with feelings of terror. This is why, in the occult tradition, so many references are made to "guardians of the threshold," mechanisms in man's brain that prevent him from seeing or knowing more than he is able to tolerate. In the course of the normal practice of Creative Psychology, there is no danger of going too far or seeing too much. Inner strength gradually increases and the organism is trained to handle the powerful forces liberated within. But when shortcuts are attempted, particularly those involving drugs, the normal safety devices are bypassed and damage may result.

In addition to meditation on forms, centering on the play of the phenomenal world, the student must practice "meditation without forms" or contemplation. There is no definite point at which meditation ends and contemplation begins. One blends with the other. Stages in the approach to contemplation are given in the *Sutra of the Setting up of Mindfulness:*

> Aloof from sensuous appetites, aloof from evil ideas he enters into and abides in the first *jhana* wherein there is cogitation and deliberation, which is born of solitude and is full of joy and ease.
>
> Suppressing cogitation and deliberation, he enters into and abides in the second *jhana*, which is self-evoked, born of concentration, full of joy and ease, in that, set free from cogitation and deliberation, the mind grows calm and sure, dwelling on high.
>
> Further, disenchanted with joy, he abides calmly contemplative while, mindful and self-possessed, he feels in his body that ease whereof Aryans declare: "He that is calmly contemplative and aware, he dwelleth at ease." So does he enter into and abide in the third *jhana.*
>
> Further, by putting aside ease and by putting aside malaise, by the passing away of the happiness and of the melancholy he used to feel, he enters into and abides in the fourth *jhana*, rapture of utter purity of mindfulness and equanimity, wherein neither ease is felt nor any ill. This is what is called right rapture.[48a]

In the Zen schools and in some of the Tibetan ones, the approach to contemplation involves offering to the student a problem that is insoluble or a statement that makes no sense, such as the *koan* "What is the sound of one hand?" The problem has no verbal solution, thus forces the student to go beyond verbal limits. The struggle to break through the verbal barrier is the greatest challenge that the Zen monk confronts. His learned questions are replied to by the Master with answers which seem like arrant nonsense, reinforced as often as not with a whack with the *hossu.*

Finally, when the breakthrough occurs, there is a sudden shift in focus and the monk experiences *satori*.

In the Christian tradition, one of the best accounts of the nature of the contemplative process occurs in the writings of Jakob Boehme:

> When you stand still from the thinking of self and the willing of self, when both your intellect and will are quiet, and passive to the expressions of the Eternal Word and Spirit; and when your soul is winged up and above that which is temporal, the outer senses and the imagination being locked up by holy abstraction, then the Eternal Hearing, Seeing and Speaking will be revealed in you, and so God hears and sees through you, being now the organ of his spirit and so God speaks in you and whispers to your spirit and your spirit hears his voice. You are blessed, therefore, if you can stand still from self-thinking and self-willing and can stop the wheel of your imagination and senses . . . since it is nothing but your own hearing and willing that hinders you.[86]

Such are the practices involved in the reeducation of the psychic centers. The objection may be made that the procedure involves altogether too much effort and that "there ought to be some easier way." Unfortunately there is none. An athlete training to compete in the Olympic games, a dancer training to become a prima ballerina, a singer aspiring to become a prima donna, a scientist hoping to solve some fundamental problem all take it for granted that prolonged effort and much self-discipline are required if the goal they dream of is to be attained. To emerge from the third state of consciousness and attain the fourth or fifth involves exertion of will and intelligence, a constant struggle against inner obstacles, inertia, credulity and various illusions. To imagine that it can be accomplished easily is merely to indulge in one more form of self-deception.

VIII. Creative
Psychology and
Mental Illness

The Vital Balance

A QUESTION MAY BE ASKED: Is Creative Psychology a form of psychotherapy and, if so, should it not be included in the training given to psychotherapists? Before we can discuss this subject, we need clearer definitions. What is psychotherapy? What is "mental illness"? Do the psychiatrists who attempt to "minister to the mind diseased" with shocks, comas, convulsions, leucotomies, pills and couches really know what they are doing? [87, 88] What truths, if any, are concealed in that jungle of verbiage they have cultivated about their specialty? And does Creative Psychology, the meta-game of metagames, have a place in this discipline?

To answer this question, we turn to a recent book by Karl Menninger, Martin Mayman and Paul Pruyser entitled *The Vital Balance*.[51] This book "fills a long-felt need," as critics are fond of saying. It rescues the discipline of psychiatry from the jungle of its own verbiage, takes it out of the realm of mythology and places it on a firm biological footing. It provides a framework for thought similar to that provided by Sheldon's typology, into which all the practices collectively known as Creative Psychology can be conveniently fitted and linked to those of psychotherapy, insofar as the latter practices *really are therapeutic.* (Some of them are not. Shock treatments, insulin comas and above all lobotomies fall into the category of "heroic treatments," which have been the curse of medicine since the days of Hippocrates.)

First, it must be realized that there is no such thing as "mental illness." The term is a thoroughly bad one and serves to perpetuate the old dualistic fallacy that there is something called "mind" and another thing called "body" and that the "mind" has illnesses peculiar to itself. In fact, body and mind are inseparable and health is a form of inner harmony or "vital balance" involving every organ in the body from the highest level of the brain to the humblest viscera. Disharmony, disorder or imbalance can be produced either by influences coming from outside (cold, germs, radiation) or by influences from within (failures on the part of various balancing or detoxifying mechanisms). There is no such thing as absolute health or illness. There is rather a continuous spectrum of health ranging from the extreme infrared (conditions that seem incurable and hopeless) to a glowing ultraviolet state that might be called "super health" (being "weller than well" is what Menninger et al. call it), in which all the latent potentialities of a man are developed and in which he attains to the fourth or fifth state of consciousness. Between these extremes there are various degrees of dis-ease (which is simply a way of saying "absence of ease" in two syllables), some of which affect behavior in a more or less disruptive way. These types of disease which affect behavior are the subject matter of psychiatry.

When one uses this idea of the health spectrum one can link the science of Creative Psychology to that of psychotherapy. Creative Psychology teaches the art of super health, the means whereby man attains the fullest possible development, the maximum realization of his latent resources. It proposes that even a man who appears to be in good health (in the sense of being free from obvious disease) is not really so "well" as he might be, because, by failing to develop his full potentialities, he is living at a level of being which is suboptimal. It challenges man to transcend himself, to emerge from the third room, the state of waking sleep, and strive to enter the fourth or even the fifth. It teaches him how to do this, how to channel his energies and prevent their useless dissipation, how to reeducate his psychic centers, how to strengthen his various functions and bring them increasingly under the control of the will, how to cope with the illusions created by a false sense of self, how to create a unity from a multiplicity, a genuine, permanent "I" from a mosaic of conflicting selves.

Orders of Dysorganization

In many of these aspects Creative Psychology blends directly with psychotherapy. The various upsets of the vital balance, which Menninger defines as five "orders of dysorganization," are all explicable in the terms of wrong work of centers, conflicts between essence and *persona*, depletion of vital energy-substances, failures of gamesmanship, etc. Traces of almost every disorder that the psychiatrist describes can be found by an observant student of Creative Psychology *within the labyrinth of his own psyche*. They are all there, the potential breakdowns, the latent madnesses. Let this or that malfunction go a little too far or continue a little too long, let this or that illusion attain a little too much power, and presto! we have stepped over the shadowy line that separates health from illness. Moreover, surprising though this may seem to some who hold a different theory concerning "salvation," there is no place of absolute security on the Way. Even at very high levels the traveler may slip, lose or misuse everything he has gained. A slight miscalculation, a small misunderstanding, a trifling accident can wipe out everything that a man has won by decades of intensive effort.

This should be borne in mind by every practicing student of Creative Psychology. An old temptation dogs the steps of such a one, the pride of the Pharisee, "God, I thank thee that I am not as other men." How easily he and his fellows fall into the habit of smugly regarding themselves as a spiritual aristocracy who, by right of conquest, occupy the high places while the rest of mankind slosh in the mud down below, chasing false aims and wasting their lives on fooleries. Sooner or later the *Curse of the Cult* blights every group that sets out to attain the heights. They close the circle, form a tight little mutual-admiration society, deify their leader (especially after the leader is dead), despise nonmembers as uninitiated barbarians, flatter themselves that they alone hold "the keys of the kingdom," and turn into spiritual fossils while deluding themselves into thinking that they are High Initiates.

All such would do well to remember some words of William James: "Nothing I possess can defend me from that fate if the hour should strike for me as it struck for him." These words were evoked by the sight of an epileptic patient in an asylum, "a black-haired youth with greenish skin, entirely idiotic, who used to sit all day on one of the benches or rather shelves against the wall, with his knees drawn up against his chin and the coarse grey undershirt, which was his only garment, drawn over them enclosing his entire figure." The spectacle induced so profound a horror that for months the great philosopher-physician was "unable to go out into the dark alone." William James finally transcended his illness to become "weller than well" and make his immense contribution to the mainstream of human thought, but he never forgot his glimpse into the pit. It left him with a salutary humility, a profound insight into the troubles of the sick soul.

Here is the reason that every serious student of Creative Psychology should familiarize himself with those conditions which are loosely called "mental illness" for which Menninger et al. substitute the term "orders of dysorganization." Not only must he learn to recognize the seeds of such dysorganization in himself, but also he must, if he becomes a teacher, be able to see them in his students. The tough Eastern tradition holds the student responsible for his own decision to enter the Way (the lama who reproached Madame David-Neel for her sentimentality regarding his devil-deluded pupil made it clear that the pupil himself was responsible for having dared to undertake the "Short Path"), but our Christian ethic and Hippocratic tradition place more responsibility on the teacher. Just as a wise physician takes into account a patient's weaknesses when prescribing a regimen (he would hardly advise a victim of coronary thrombosis to make a practice of climbing in the Sierra), so a wise teacher of Creative Psychology will look for those weaknesses in a student which might, under conditions of increased stress, dangerously upset the vital balance.

This does not mean that every teacher of Creative Psychology must be a full-fledged psychiatrist.[89] It means that he must be familiar with the principal orders of dysorganization and be able to "sense" (for this perception is a sort of intuition) the essence weaknesses that may bring his students (or himself) into a state of serious imbalance. This study is mainly an extension of the methods already described in connection with essence weaknesses, with the formation of the *persona* and the false ego and with the wrong work of centers. It also involves knowledge of certain phenomena not previously mentioned.

The vital balance is the essence of the life process. Every organism, from the simplest to the most complex, has certain needs which must be satisfied if it is to continue to exist. As long as these needs are satisfied, the organism is in balance. When one of the needs is not satisfied, the organism is out of balance and, if the imbalance continues, may be in serious danger of disintegrating altogether. It is a fundamental property of living things that they will strive most vigorously to restore the balance by satisfying the need.

Most of the needs of the body are taken care of by the instinctive brain and do not enter a person's consciousness. There is, for example, a host of hormones, ranging from the complex hormones of the pituitary to such simpler entities as adrenaline or acetylcholine, that must daily be generated in varying amounts and, having been generated, must be destroyed or inactivated. (So far as the vital balance is concerned, too much of a hormone can be just as upsetting as too little.) Such needs as these, and a multitude of others, are not even noticed by the conscious mind, which has no mechanism for measuring these inner chemical processes, though it knows, by a general feeling of malaise, when something is amiss.

Needs which cannot be satisfied by the instinctive mind alone bring into play the moving brain, the emotional brain and the intellectual brain. Basically, these needs are concerned with the obtaining of food, shelter, a mate, care and protection of the young and escape from various natural enemies. But civilized man is not limited to this simple catalogue. His needs are associated with both primitive and higher urges, with the will to pleasure, to power, to meaning, to self-transcendence. Moreover, his more primitive needs cannot be immediately satisfied. He may not grab and copulate with every girl who takes his fancy. He may not attack every man who arouses his ire. He is enmeshed in a code of behavior imposed upon him in the name of civilization. For a certain order and security, he is expected to pay a certain price, to forego easy satisfactions, to restrain powerful impulses. This subjects him to a certain tension, a certain strain, a strain which becomes so great at times that Freud, writing in *Civilization and Its Discontents*,[12] seriously inquired whether the advantages offered by civilization were worth the cost.

When the personal "I want" encounters society's "Thou shalt not" (whether or not the latter is backed by a deified father-substitute called "God"), the ensuing struggle upsets the vital balance. The upset may be very trifling or very serious, depending on how intense is the struggle involved. Restoration of balance is the function of that portion of the organism which Menninger, following Freud, calls the "ego." This, in the third state of consciousness, is a somewhat unstable entity, changing from day to day, from hour to hour, depending on the level of identification, the surroundings, the state of health, and so on. Even in the third state of consciousness, the ego can handle ordinary everyday stresses, work out some compromise between the organism's needs and the social taboos which will restore the vital balance.

There are circumstances, however, which impose more stress than the ego can handle. Such circumstances are seen in their most obvious form when man indulges in one of his nastier pastimes, the process of organized reciprocal destruction which he calls "war." This activity, being totally unnatural, is also very stressful. It compels man to break all the taboos he has been taught to revere. He has been told never to kill another man. Now he must kill as often as possible. He has been taught not to destroy other people's possessions. Now he is expected to destroy whole cities, devastate whole countries. Moreover, in order to engage in these nefarious activities, he is forced to abandon every life game that he loves, to spend hours, days, years in boring routines punctuated by episodes of danger and horror, to submit to domination by a group of professional butchers who take organized manslaughter for granted, regarding it as a perfectly natural and even heroic activity (the Moloch Game).

Under these circumstances it is surprising that any man remains sane. The fact that he does is due to the buffering mechanism, the enormous capacity for self-deception, the lack of inner consistency and real integrity that characterizes man in the third state of consciousness. But there are times during war when the combination of danger, bad conscience, lack of sleep, grief over the loss of a comrade, so totally overwhelms the vital balance that the ego becomes powerless to restore equilibrium. There results the condition called "shell shock" during World War I, "battle fatigue" in World War II. This is a more or less incapacitating condition due, biochemically speaking, to an almost total depletion of certain of the body's vital substances, resulting in virtual paralysis of the capacity to make decisions or take action.[90]

Ordinary life does not normally impose such stresses, but reactions similar to battle fatigue nonetheless occur. The ego endeavors to restore the vital balance at the cost of some sacrifice, perhaps a partial withdrawal from the game of life, the institution of some habit that drains off tension, partial retreat into fantasy, violent acting out of agressive impulses, total withdrawal to the point of catatonia, in which all movement is inhibited and interaction with the environment is reduced to a minimum.

These various levels of dysorganization result from a failure of the ego to restore vital balance by draining off tension with the various "coping devices" ordinarily available. Such devices (nineteen are listed by Menninger) include laughter, crying or cursing, talking, thinking through, working off, dreaming and reassurances of touch, rhythm, sound or speech. The mechanism chosen will depend on type. Cerebrotonics seek solitude, viscerotonics seek company, somatotonics seek action. When the coping devices fail, there may occur a first-order dysorganization, a slight departure from the normal commonly described as "nervousness." Then comes second-order dysorganization, involving various "neuroses" which, though painful both for the individual and those about him, still permit work to proceed and a livelihood to be earned. Next comes third-order dysorganization, involving outbursts, attacks, assaults, sexual offenses which bring their perpetrator into conflict with the law, land him in jail or a mental hospital. Fourth-order dysorganization involves partial withdrawal, abandonment of "reality loyalty," disruption of thought, demoralization and confusion. The fifth and final order of dysorganization involves total withdrawal, abandonment of the will to recover and the will to live.

Of the five orders of dysorganization, the first two leave a person able to earn his living, though his efficiency may be impaired and his happiness marred. The third produces serious trouble but does not constitute "insanity" as generally understood. *The Mask of Sanity* (to use Cleckley's phrase) is maintained in these conditions, which include paranoia and the "psychopathic personality" and often culminate in explosive episodes of violence.[91] The fourth state gives rise to the condition once called "lunacy," later called "dementia praecox," now referred to as "schizophrenia," "the schizophrenias" or "the schizophrenic reaction." In this state, contact with reality is severely impaired and custodial care may become necessary, at least for a time. The fifth state is a more advanced stage of the fourth, in which the patient has lost all will to recovery and seems therefore beyond the reach of therapy.

All these conditions result from stress which upsets the vital balance to such an extent that the ego is unable to restore it without making some more or less severe sacrifice. If these stresses were all *external*, like those which a soldier confronts in combat, both the theory and practice of psychiatry would be a lot simpler than it is. It would merely be necessary to remove the patient to a less stressful environment (as a soldier is removed from combat) and the *vis mediatrix naturae* would restore the balance by itself. Unfortunately, this is not the situation. Some states of dysorganization, particularly certain forms of depression and schizophrenia, are of *endogenous* origin, which means they have no apparent external cause and are presumably produced by forces at work within the body. Every psychiatrist is familiar with such sudden inexplicable "nervous breakdowns" and has shared the astonishment which Dr. Howard Fabing expressed in relation to endogenous depression (melancholia):

> I have never gotten used to this disorder. I am just as amazed at a case I saw last week as those I saw as a student. Why or how can a normal, hard-working, God-loving man or woman suddenly be thrown into a state of disturbed sleep and disordered mood which is completely disabling? I have seen this happen between a Tuesday and a Thursday. These people suddenly lose their power to concentrate their minds on the simplest activity such as reading the evening newspaper, they find all social intercourse painful and give up their friends, they believe that they are burdens on their loved ones, they develop the most illogical feelings of guilt and sin, and they quit eating. Unless something is done about them suicide occurs all too frequently.[92]

Schizophrenia can develop just as suddenly as melancholia, also without any apparent external cause. The victim of the illness is assailed by strange voices, the visible world assumes an awful brightness as if illuminated by the harsh glare of cosmic floodlights, food tastes strange, the time sense becomes distorted, thoughts refuse to obey the will and logical thinking becomes difficult or impossible. Irrational, nameless overwhelming fear and an awful sense of inner tension commonly accompany these symptoms. All this can convert a normal man or woman into a frightened, babbling lunatic or a withdrawn, waxlike figure, mute and immobile, within the space of a few days.[93] The transformation is shocking and terrifying for those who witness it and serves to explain why our ancestors clung so fondly to their concept of demonic possessions. For, in the absence of any assignable external cause, how else could they explain the change? Ignorant as they were of chemistry and obsessed as they were by demonology, they concluded that an alien malignant spirit had taken charge. With such arguments as these, our forebears justified their abominable treatment of the mad by arguing that by chaining or flogging the physical body they might drive out the demon.

These endogenous upsets of the vital balance, produced not by external stress but by forces coming from within, enormously complicate the task of the psychiatrist. He cannot restore the balance simply by manipulating the environment, by removing stress, by advocating a "change of air" or a change of scene. He is confronting the result of an error that has occurred deep within the body, an error in its chemistry which has resulted either in the production of a poison having an action similar to that of LSD or in lack of production of some vital component, a hormone perhaps or an enzyme without which normal function cannot be maintained. We are able to state with certainty that such deficiencies occur. They are *inborn errors in metabolism*[94] and include such conditions as inability to metabolize phenylalanine (phenylketonuria), to generate sufficient insulin (diabetes), to eliminate uric acid (gout). It is logical, therefore, to regard recurring schizophrenic episodes as having chemical causes and therefore as requiring chemical treatment.

Four Lost Souls

If we accept the idea that there is no way of separating mind from matter and that all mental phenomena, even the most lofty, have a chemical basis, it will follow that the depletion or erroneous metabolism of certain materials in the body will produce defects in behavior. This is as obvious as the fact that wine can turn to vinegar if exposed to air or milk, unsterilized, will turn sour. But what, if anything, can be done about it? If people have these essence defects, does this render them incapable of playing the Master Game? Does the inner work become actually harmful rather than beneficial to a psyche already teetering on the edge of dysorganization?

A few examples will illustrate this problem. Consider the case of Joe. He has a natural aptitude for music, could, if he really tried, be a fine musician. He also has a weakness for dabbling in the occult, has read whole libraries full of books on yoga, occultism, theosophy, magic, the Tarot. He has a history of drifting never holds a job longer than two months. His sex life consists entirely of liaisons with women old enough to be his mother, with whom he establishes a parasitic relationship. He regularly gets drunk, and when drunk, regularly becomes offensive. Has driven his car into the ditch, emerged unscathed and unrepentant, putting the blame on the road. Now he wishes to become a candidate for the higher life. He has applied to a teacher. Is he worthy to receive guidance and instruction?

Or here is Sue. She, too, loves the occult, religiously attends seminars at which mystical teachers of various kinds offer their recipes for the higher life. She drifts from one to another, tries a technique, tires of it, turns to another. She drinks too much, takes LSD whenever she can lay hands on it, smokes "pot" (as does everyone else in her circle), was recently arrested for possession of the weed and had to spend much money on lawyers to stay out of jail. She, too, now decides she needs a teacher, is eager to accept discipline and direction.

Or here is Willy. Willy is poetic, bearded, unwashed and dreamy. He has drifted around various college campuses seeking enlightenment but decided that none had anything to offer him. He writes poetry of the "fried shoe" variety, practices *asanas,* now and then adopts the lotus posture and squats like a yogi at the gate of his favorite campus. Often he waves placards inscribed with words like "shit" and "fuck" to show that he is a rebel, but no one, including Willy, understands what he is protesting against. He eats peyote, smokes "pot," tried heroin but did not become addicted. Now he, too, after a disappointing affair with a "chick" and a bad bout of Asian influenza, has decided that this will not do. He wants more structure in his life; he wants more discipline. He wants a teacher.

Or here is Sandra. One glance at her evokes Cythera and the "pale lost lillies" or drowning Ophelia and her trailing flowers. She is pale, underweight, her contact with reality tenuous at best. She cultivates the type of arty *persona* that involves long, loose hair and feet shod in sandals or not at all. She dispenses both with panties and brassieres and wears sacklike muumuus reaching to her ankles. She plays the samisen and even the sitar, all other musical instruments being either too obvious or too noisy. She composes *haiku*, paints *sumi*-style pictures, has a boy friend as otherworldly as herself who dreams of entering a Zen monastry. She shares these dreams, influenced by the prevalent glorification of Nippon, which depicts Japan as a haven from Western worldliness, full of cherry blossom, flower arrangements and tea ceremonies where, under sighing pines, smiling Zen masters politely guide their pupils toward *satori*. Neither she nor her boy friend has money enough to get to Japan so they are reluctantly forced to seek a "Master" in the West.

Any genuine teacher will immediately detect the essence weaknesses which have made these aspirants failures from the ordinary life standpoint. Joe shows the characteristics of the psychopathic personality. Such types are the despair of wives, parents, guardians, law-enforcement officers. They seem totally lacking in social conscience and in the capacity to learn from experience. However often they are rescued from the results of their own stupidity, they always seem to make the same mistake again and land once more in the same sort of trouble. They leave behind them a trail of ruin but are themselves unaffected, for their lack of conscience makes them immune to remorse and incapable of real repentance. They suffer from dysorganization of the third order.

Sue, with her habit of drifting from cult to cult, her weakness for psychedelics, her troubles with the law (which she seems to invite by a sort of deliberate recklessness as if to punish herself for hidden guilt) also shows third-order dysorganization, though she is less psychopathic than Joe. She explores everything, persists in nothing. Her whole life is strewn with unfinished enterprises. She is hounded by guilt. Her wild escapades are part of a desperate effort to escape the harpies that pursue her.

What of Willy, the long-haired protester? Is he simply a phoney or a hopeless misfit? He has no skills, no knowledge, has entirely failed to equip himself for life's battles, justifying his failure with the statement that the battle offers no prizes for which he considers it worth fighting. Is this the truth or is he fooling himself? Can such a one ever impose on himself the discipline demanded of a man who aspires to ascend from the third room to the fourth?

Finally what of Sandra, whose whole appearance cries out "latent schizophrenia" to anyone even vaguely familiar with the illness? How can this frail nymph, whose hold on reality is so tenuous, who lives in fantasy and neglects her physical body, find that inner force required for self-transcendence? Would she not do better to continue to dream of her nonexistent Zen master in a prettified and equally nonexistent Japan? How can she face the harsh realities of Creative Psychology, an unsentimental discipline which insists that two and two can never add up to five, that only by prolonged effort guided by right knowledge can any permanent change be produced in a person's level of being?

A teacher trained in the "tough" tradition would chase all four applicants out of his presence after sharply reproaching them for their rashness in coming to him at all. Such teachers insist that the methods of Creative Psychology can be used only by those who are already in good health and already successful in whatever life game they have chosen. They will declare that the Way is not for weaklings nor for dabblers, nor is it for misfits or "neurotics" (whatever this word means). They insist on stern practicality, absence of sentimentality, ability on the part of the aspirant to estimate correctly his inner resources. "If you have not the strength to climb some trivial hill, how can you hope to ascend a lofty mountain? Go back! Stop fooling yourself! This is presumption and stupidity as if a cripple were to set out to run the four-minute mile."

Such warnings as this are given by many of the Masters. That tough old Stoic Epictetus was especially fond of this line of talk.[95] Jesus, despite cosy assurances that those who "labor and are heavy laden" could cast their yoke upon him and lean on him, repeatedly emphasized to his disciples the importance of not overestimating their own resources: "Which of you, intending to build a tower, does not sit down first, and count the cost, and consider whether he have sufficient to finish it?"

Other teachers make no attempt to warn ill-prepared applicants that they are undertaking something far beyond their strength. They accept the pupil with all his defects, with all his weaknesses, in a spirit of experimentation to see what will happen. They are willing to take chances, to accept the risk that a borderline schizophrenic, for example, may disintegrate completely under the additional stress imposed by the inner work. They know they will be blamed for this, if it occurs. (Relatives and friends of schizophrenics always try to *blame* someone when the illness manifests itself in its more alarming forms.) They simply take the attitude that the applicant is a responsible being, is entitled to take a risk, just as a mountaineer is entitled to risk breaking his neck or a scuba diver to risk drowning. They know only too well that there is little chance that the weak, the sick, the "neurotic" will persist in their efforts. As soon as the "roses, roses" phase comes to an end and the "thorns, thorns" begins, they will leave the teacher, probably declaring that he is not really a "Master" and was not worthy to be their *guru* in any case. It is a curious fact that the weaker the aspirant, the higher the demands he makes of his spiritual guide.

Teachers trained in the "mild" tradition do what they can to protect the pupil from the effects of his own weakness, patiently picking him up when he falls, forgiving his failures, endeavoring, as far as possible, to do for him the work he cannot or will not do for himself. Such teachers, needless to say, are frequently regarded as saints. But adherents of the tough tradition reproach them with being altogether too sentimental, with a failure to provide the student with proper challenges, with misunderstanding that principle of Creative Psychology which states that one can no more do another's inner work for him than one can digest his lunch for him. By trying to make the Way easy, they declare, one merely encourages self-deception and laziness.

Probably the ideal teacher is one who can be both tough and mild as the occasion demands, who knows that the student must make efforts in order to progress, but who never pushes him beyond the breaking point. Such a one can be trusted to take the balanced view. He knows there is much truth in the principle: "He who is weak in life will be weak in the Work." But he also knows that there are exceptions to this rule. Some who appear to be weak, who might be classed as misfits, drifters or failures, are so because, in a money-obsessed, gadget-intoxicated society, they have not been able to find a game worth playing. Once they do find a worthwhile game, they may display great energy, pursuing their new aim with vigor that contrasts surprisingly with their previous lethargy. Others, who are obviously prone to one or another degree of dysorganization are able, after a descent into the depths, to pull themselves out of the mud and to go on ascending until they have attained very high levels of being. Several examples of this phenomenon are given in the last chapter of *The Vital Balance*. For this reason, a wise teacher is likely to be cautious in passing judgment. That which may seem, on the face of it, like a crippling essence defect may mask a hidden creative force in need of some drastic shock to set it in motion.

IX. The Creative Community

The Way of the Recluse

FOR THOSE WISHING to devote their whole energies to the quest for higher consciousness three possibilities exist. They can withdraw from active life; they can become part of a special community in which the work of inner creation is combined with other creative activities both artistic and scientific; or they can continue to live as before but with special rules of inner work.

One who withdraws from life enters the way of the recluse. He may attain great heights by singleminded application to the disciplines he is using. He is, however, living in what one might call an "impoverished environment." If he reduces external stimulation to a minimum, as do the hermits of Tibet who actually allow themselves to be walled up in their caves and live in semidarkness for years, he is likely to suffer from hallucinations, the results of sensory deprivation that the subjects of both John C. Lilly's and Donald O. Hebb's experiments[44] reported. Indeed we find in one of Alexandra David-Neel's books[60] a clear account of just such hallucinations. These fairy-like displays may offer amusement and entertainment to the solitary hermit, but it is questionable whether they do much to advance his inner development.

This Tibetan practice is, of course, an extreme and perhaps pathological form of the way of the recluse. In a less extreme form (e.g., Thoreau's retreat into solitude at Walden), the practice may be valuable in that it frees a man of many entanglements, forces him to rely on himself, to assess realistically his own inner resources. For some people, especially hypersensitive, overreactive cerebrotonics, the way of the recluse may be the only practical way. Participation in any sort of social life drains them of their energies to such an extent that inner work becomes impossible. Such people are more or less forced, by the limitations imposed on them by their essence, to seek solitude and quietness, to live alone in the desert or mountains. Others, for whom the need for solitude is strong but not imperative, may strike some sort of balance between the need to participate and the need to retreat, taking an active part in affairs for awhile and then withdrawing from them to recharge their exhausted batteries. These alternating periods of participation and nonparticipation have characterized the careers of many people who have played major historical roles. In fact, the practice has been elevated to the level of a principle by Arnold Toynbee and called by him "Withdrawal and Return."

Followers of the way of recluse, in order to escape from what the religious call "temptation," simplify their life games to the point at which they have almost no game left. The walled-in Tibetan recluse represents the extreme form of nonparticipation, but the cloistered monastic also places himself in a very impoverished environment. One can take as an example of the way of recluse the life of the monks in one of the monasteries on Mount Athos in Greece. Day after day life proceeds along almost exactly the same lines. Sensory input is reduced to a minimum. With the exception, perhaps, of a single icon, the cell is bare of ornaments. Food is simple and sparse. Normal sexual activities are totally prohibited. Prayers with bowing occupy most of the night, hard physical work, most of the day.

Such a discipline may, when persisted in long enough, engender a certain inner serenity, but that serenity is purchased at a very high price. Under these cloistered conditions, the full development of an individual's potentialities cannot take place. He is in a very real sense a deprived individual and the fact that the deprivation is self-imposed does not make it any less mutilating. The flash and sparkle of life, its challenges, triumphs, sorrows, temptations, obstacles, pass by the cloistered monk, leaving him untouched. He is sterile, having deliberately refused to perform the reproductive function, and his sexual sterility is often accompanied by spiritual sterility. He may attain great development in one part of his being, but that development, because of his restricted environment and experience, is bound to be lopsided, unless he entered the monastery *after* he had had a full taste of life's variety.[96]

The Ordered Community

If the life of a cloistered monk, whether Buddhist or Christian, is too limiting, the life of full participation is often too distracting. So, for one who seriously wishes to engage in the Master Game the problem of finding the right environment becomes acute. Ideally, he should become a member of a creative community which would offer him some of the advantages which the monastery offers the monk without depriving him of that large segment of experience which the monastic discipline places out of reach of those who submit to it.

Do such communities exist? If they do not, is it possible to create them? Theoretically, yes. The megaculture in the United States imposes many restrictions on its members but has not so far enforced total uniformity. Microcultures *can* be created if people want to create them and are prepared to make the necessary efforts, make the needed sacrifices. (The *kibbutzim* of Israel show what can be done by resolute men and women who have no need of commissars to drive them.) It must, however, be realized that in every community, both micro and macro, there are forces that tend to pull them apart and disrupt the whole structure. The stability of the community depends on the balance between forces that tend to unite and forces tending to disrupt.

The simplest form of microcommunity is the school or *ashram* which develops around a teacher. Such microcultures are "teacher-dominated" and those who belong to the group are bound to obey the teacher even when his demands seem harsh or unreasonable. Very often they are both. In the tough tradition of the Orient one reads many examples of incredible demands made by teachers. Marpa, the teacher of Milarepa, compromised his pupil's health and almost drove him to suicide by insisting that he build unaided a series of houses of different shapes. No sooner had Milarepa finished one than he had to pull it down and rebuild it somewhere else. Marpa justified the harshness by insisting that Milarepa had acquired evil *karma* by engaging in black magic. But this same teacher was just as rough with another disciple who had not been a black magician, forcing him, after the latter had brought him all his cattle as an offering, to return home (a journey lasting several days) for one old goat left behind because it was lame.

In the West, by the religious way, stability has also traditionally been obtained through unquestioning obedience. Such obedience was taken to its extreme limit by Ignatius Loyola. "I ought," he is reported to have said,

> to desire that my Superior should oblige me to give up my own judgement, and conquer my own mind. . . . In the hands of my Superior, I must be soft as wax, a thing, from which he is to require whatever pleases him, be it to write or receive letters, to speak or not to speak to such a person, or the like; and I must put all my fervor into executing zealously and exactly what I am ordered. I must consider myself as a corpse which has neither intelligence nor will, be like a mass of matter which without resistance lets itself be placed wherever it may please anyone; like a stick in the hands of an old man, who uses it according to his needs and places it where it suits him. So must I be under the hands of the Order, to serve it in the way it judges most useful.[97]

Teacher-dominated communities tend to attract pupils who suffer from the Starry-eyed Syndrome, a state of infatuation in which the teacher can do no wrong, in which everything he says is accepted without question. For many people it is very easy to adopt this attitude, especially when the teacher is a powerful father-figure and possesses that peculiar hypnotic power which is a part of the make-up of the Magus type. The flight from freedom is just as real a phenomenon as the struggle for freedom, is, in fact, a much more popular game, for the retreat toward dependence and infantilism liberates a man from one of his heaviest burdens, the fearful task of making choices for himself.[98] Such a retreat can be made to justify any number of ugly doings, as the trials of the Nazi war criminals clearly showed. Their defense, "I was only obeying orders," justified in their own minds all their atrocities. If we accept the idea that man has a right to abandon personal responsibility in the name of obedience to a superior, then we must admit that their defense was logical.

There is absolutely no guarantee that the teacher in a teacher-dominated school will not make mistakes. There is also no guarantee that he will stay clear of the False-Messiah Syndrome. Even when a teacher *starts* on the right path, he may lose his way later, misuse his powers and lead his obedient flock into some very strange places.

A typical example of this was the Swedenborgian group founded by Thomas Lake Harris and called by him the "Brotherhood of the New Life." Harris was a fine example of the Magus type and his power was such that even highly educated people such as Sir Laurence Oliphant and his wife gave up everything to join his Brotherhood. Laurence Oliphant had been a member of Parliament, Commissioner of Indian Affairs, a diplomat in Japan and China, the author of several books, was a favorite of Queen Victoria and Lord Salisbury. Yet this highly educated and sophisticated Englishman laid everything at the feet of the Prophet. Only after the gift of a hundred thousand dollars and the rest of their property, including Lady Oliphant's rings, brooches and court jewelry, were they allowed, after long probation, to enter the community.

All this was entirely in keeping with the tough tradition, it being accepted that he who would purchase the pearl of great price must be willing to pay for it with all that he possesses. The trust which the Oliphants placed in Harris enabled Laurence without complaint to rise at four in the morning in zero weather, to milk the cows, board trains with baskets of milk and sandwiches, while his wife scrubbed the kitchen floor, her rings given to Mrs. Waring, the grand lady and manager of the Utopia. All the faithful abjectly worshipped Harris, who was "Father" or "Faithful," whose power was absolute and from whose decisions there was no appeal.

Harris finally moved his "Cosmos" for the regeneration of mankind from Lake Keuka, New York, to Fountain Grove near Santa Rosa, California, where he poured forth in a cataract of words the new sacred doctrine, a mélange of the Vedanta, the Cabala, Swedenborg and the Hermetical philosophers, which Arai, the Japanese devotee who ran the printing press, dutifully recorded in thousands of folio pages. (This enormous output of words seems characteristic of the Magus type. The works of Swedenborg and Blake's *Prophetic Books* belong to this type of literature. Not, however, Blake's *Marriage of Heaven and Hell*, which, for brevity, rivals some of the writings of the Zen masters.)

If Harris ever had any real understanding of the principles of Creative Psychology, it is clear that he soon lost it. The creative octave underwent several disastrous changes in direction. The final decay of the enterprise is well described by Idwal Jones:

> The disciples at Fountain Grove complained that life in the Heaven was Spartan, that favors went to the inner group about Harris, who basked in luxury, and that Miss Waring, dressed like a Turkish princess, and smoking a hookah, had to be waited upon by "pivotals" reduced to slavery. Madame was eternally ringing the bell—for tea and muffins, the carriage at five, or for any whim that seized her. Harris's young daughter poisoned herself. Rumors and black charges were in the headlines. Disciples left and brought actions to court. That counterpartal business was good for newspaper stories a page long. Schism split the Heaven in two, and Harris, under pressure of these "low and sinister influences," hastily left for Europe, after a marriage to Miss Waring, and returned to California no more.[99]

This story is offered here to illustrate the dangers that threaten teacher-dominated groups where the teacher himself has not transcended the limits imposed by his personal ego. It is a part of the "curse of the cult" that those who fall under the influence of such a teacher go through a very difficult time when they can no longer blind themselves to his defects. The task of seeing these defects is made for them doubly difficult by the use which some teachers make of the techniques of Outer Theater. The pupils can never feel sure about the Master's manifestations.[100] Is he behaving like this because he cannot help it or is he playing a role to test their reactions? Again and again they give the teacher the benefit of the doubt, compelled by feelings of loyalty and devotion, by the investment both financial and emotional they have made in the community and by their reluctance to pass judgment on one whose level of being they assume to be far higher than their own. For it is stated as a principle that the lower cannot understand the higher, that a man can only take the measure of his own equals.

The real creative community can be constructed only by a teacher who has thoroughly understood certain basic principles. The first of these, "He who would be greatest let him be as a servant among you," protects the leaders of the community from misusing their power. The second, "Believe nothing, test everything," saves those with a tendency to suffer from the Starry-eyed Syndrome from falling into this fool-trap. The third, "Enter the silence as often as possible and remain there as long as possible," saves the intellectual with his overactive roof brain from becoming hooked on the Talk-Think Syndrome, which causes one suffering from it to substitute dreaming about the inner work for the actual struggle with wandering thoughts and identification. The fourth principle, "Establish a link between inward and outer creativity," prevents *external aims* from monopolizing the energies of members of the community and bringing to a halt the inner creative process.

Aims Subjective and Objective

The creative community must have external aims.[101] These may range from the growing of food to the building of a meeting-house, the running of a hospital, the creation of works of art, the pursuit of scientific research, the manufacture of some characteristic product, carpets, pottery, silverware, etc. All these external aims give to the members of the community opportunities for self-study, for observation of the working of centers, for studying the interplay of triads and octaves, for gaining insights into the nature of materiality. Every task, even the simplest, offers its own lesson, can be performed "in harmony with *Tao*," with double awareness and in inner silence. But the outer tasks, especially the more complex ones, invariably tend to take on a life of their own. The inner work is forgotten and the outer aims become all important. When this occurs, the "inner octave" of development comes to a halt and only the outer work continues. This cessation of the inner octave tends to occur repeatedly and demands from the leader of the community much watchfulness and insight, for his task is to apply the needed shock that will restart the inner octave. If he fails to supply it, the whole community becomes outer-directed, its energies entirely devoted to its external affairs. The community may continue to function on this level as a sort of cooperative, offering its members a livelihood, a congenial environment and a certain degree of security,[102] but its inner light will have gone out.

If we wish to find examples of stable microcommunities in the United States, we need look no further than Pennsylvania, in which the Amish and the Mennonites live by their own standards and pursue their own inner aims and have been doing so for the past 250 years. These are "land and Bible"-based communities which have a good deal in common with the monastic way but have not made the error of imposing on themselves that unnecessary sterility which is the curse of the monk. The high rate of increase characteristic of these sturdy folk demonstrates their respect for the text, "Increase and multiply, replenish the earth." They have their feet firmly planted on the breast of Mother Earth and next to their God they love their soil, the rich, deep soil of Lancaster County, a land truly flowing with milk and honey.

When we say that their way of life has much in common with the way of monk, we refer to the intentional "doing without," the resolute simplification of existence that members of these groups have imposed on their lives. They seek neither ease nor convenience nor do they endanger their inner peace with a thousand imbecile distractions purveyed by radios, televisions, phonographs and other mechanical devices. The devout Amish will not even own a tractor, for he places the emphasis more on inner work than on ease. "A tractor gets the work done more quickly but a horse and the love of hard work keep us nearer to God," said an Amish bishop in a recent interview.[103] They have freed themselves totally from the curse of legalized murder, refusing to bear arms, taking literally the great commandment: "Resist not evil: but whosoever shall smite thee on they right cheek, turn to him the other also." Their distrust of the military is absolute. They will not even wear buttons on their jackets because it reminds them of the glittering brass of uniforms. The men wear beards but shave off their moustaches because the "military moustache" is for them still a symbol of a butcher of men.

The Amish and Mennonites have purchased their stability at a price. Their beliefs are fixed. Their communities are closed or nearly closed. They do not seek converts or willingly accept them. Their lives pass on a simple, humble level, for them richly satisfying but not necessarily so for others. One admires them for the same reason that Tolstoy admired the Russian peasants, because they are essence-dominated, almost completely free of the artifices of the *persona* and because, in a drifting, strife-ridden culture with confused moral standards, they represent solid ground, value systems as firmly established as the fruitful farms from which they draw their sustenance. But their communities can hardly provide a blueprint for intellectually more adventurous spirits who are not prepared to confine themselves within a framework of fixed beliefs.

A few words must be said about these more "adventurous intellectuals." When it comes to creating a stable community, they have a hard time. The "intellectual" is poor material from which to construct a stable community. His weakness for theorizing, his fondness for argument, his habit of losing himself in the jungle of

X. Conclusion

THE GREAT ARC OF LIFE, stretching from conception to death, can be divided into four sections, each having its own characteristics. Section one is short and hectic, a furious orgy of proliferation and construction in the course of which one microscopic egg develops into a baby. This phase lasts nine months. Section two lasts from birth to puberty, a preparatory phase, a period of growing and learning. Section three lasts from puberty until approximately the fiftieth year, a phase normally devoted to the raising of a family. Section four lasts from the fiftieth year until death which, in one who has properly guarded his inner resources, should not occur before the hundredth year of life. This final phase, which may last as long as the first three phases put together, is the second life. It should be, and in a developed man is, wholly devoted to the "making of the soul," or the perfection of the body of consciousness. In religious language, it is devoted to the attainment of union with God, which involves entering into and abiding in the fourth state of consciousness and striving toward the fifth.

He who has chosen to play the Master Game enters this last

phase of life with eagerness and pleasure. He is now in a position to devote all his energies to the great game. His life can be simplified, reduced to the bare essentials. His children are grown up and gone, his biological urges are simplified, his needs are few. He now can give his time to the guidance of his spiritual children, not in order to inflate his false ego by strutting around in the mantle of a saint or sage, but because it is a law of the Work that he who gets must give and from one to whom much has been given much shall be required. Happy that man who enters on the second life with such an abundance of inner wealth that he can gather about him his own students and function as a guide, not as a parrot mechanically repeating the instructions he has received but as a genuine inner-directed teacher whose level of being is proportional to his knowledge. A real teacher is no mere echo of his own teacher; he sounds a new note characteristically his own. Hence the Tibetan saying: "Every lake has its own fish, every lama has his own doctrine."

Alas, how rarely it happens in a land cut off from its spiritual traditions that a man enters the last stage of life with a clear understanding of the opportunities it offers. Left uninstructed from childhood in the rules of the Master Game, exposed only to the stale dogmas and hoary superstitions of a moribund religion, harassed by the insane demands of conspicuous consumption, hypnotized by the hucksters, misled by pseudo scientists, muddled by pseudo philosophers, he enters the final phase in a state of inward bankruptcy. Can one wonder that the poor thing finds little pleasure in the freedom given by retirement? Though cushioned from want by pensions, savings and Social Security, he can find no joy in the last years. He is at a loss for a game to play. Pathetically he spends his time, like an overgrown child, knocking about a little white ball on a golf course, running around the world on pointless cruises, making cumbrous efforts to dance the Twist, or chasing a blonde young enough to be his daughter. Meanwhile, his elderly wife spends her time in the beauty parlor struggling to recapture, through the use of massage and pomades or with help from the plastic surgeon, the smooth skin and slender figure of youth.

He has never learned how to live; he does not know how to die. For it has truly been said: *"Only he who has striven to create in himself a soul is a candidate for a honorable death. He who has not has lived like a fool and will die like a dog."*

How different is the history of one who, by a blend of intelligence, good luck and strenuous effort, has become a member of a truly creative community and played the Master Game within the matrix it offers. In such a community, every stage of life except the first is planned to give the greatest possible opportunity for inner growth. The child is protected from the barbarizing effects of a materially rich but spiritually impoverished culture; he is shielded from influences which glorify violence, aggravate greed for possessions, inflate the false ego, clutter the mind with vast stores of more or less useless information, but fail to train the possessor of that mind in the art of using his functions in the most effective manner.

In a creative community, the young adults are relieved of narrow preoccupations with their personal affairs and the excessive devotion to object games that our culture encourages in the name of "success." They strive to follow the advice of the Sage of the Garden: "Live unknown. Make your wants few." Fame is a delusion, grandeur a pitiful rag, wealth a mirage, security a will-o'-the-wisp. He alone is rich who has transcended his personal ego, is no longer deluded by ideas of "I" and "mine." He alone is secure who has created within himself an island which no flood can engulf.

In this creative community, these young adults in the third stage of life and the full flow of biological vigor are encouraged to be active. It is through activity that man comes to know himself, to understand the working of centers, the nature of materials, the interplay of triads and octaves. A purely contemplative life is neither desirable nor profitable for Western man and probably not for Eastern man, either. As overactivity is the curse of the West, so underactivity tends to be the curse of the East. In a creative community, a balance is sought. Build, create, grow things and make things, but learn the secret of the separation of self from your own activity. Learn the lesson of Prince Hui's wonderful cook. Learn to act in harmony with *Tao,* to harness the octave of inner creation to that of outer creation. Then you will not need to fear the fate that constantly threatens overbusy Western man, the danger of being spiritually strangled in the web of his own activity.

In the creative community, those who have reached the last stage of life receive instructions in the difficult art of dying. This does not mean that these elders of the community withdraw from the communal life. Far from it. On their shoulders rests the greatest burden, the heaviest responsibility. From them comes the guiding impulse, the necessary reminder to the younger people that object games, including love games and parenthood, must be subsidiary to the Master Game, that outward aims must take second place to inner aims. But despite this burden of responsibility, these elders of the community have time to prepare for death, and learn to regard this process not as a fearful event to be anticipated with dread but as the final, most difficult of many tests, a test of will power, of fortitude and of inner strength.

Few things demonstrate more vividly the spiritual bankruptcy of this "Great Society" than the prevailing attitude of its members toward death. How can any man in his right senses fail to deplore this mixture of sickly sentimentality and bad art, the shameless lobbying of ghoulish funeral directors eager to line their pockets from the estates of the dead, the spineless submission to this lobby by legislators who have now made it almost impossible for a man to die simply and be buried in a place of his own choice, the participation by so-called Christian priests in a degrading "cult of the casket," and last but not least, the well-intentioned but hopelessly muddled interference by members of the medical profession who, with oxygen tents, intravenous drips and bevies of nurses deprive the patient of his chance of dying with dignity and awareness? The whole subject of death has become befogged as a result of total failure to understand its significance. It has now become the focal point of a semi-imbecilic brand of humor in which the crazier aspects of the "cult of the casket" are blended with a mixture of sex and embalming fluid to give a product silly enough to make angels weep and misanthropes cackle.

No one, neither priest nor scientist, seems willing to affirm that dying can be an achievement, that the art of dying is as difficult as the art of living, and he who would master the first must also be master of the second. That a person can know when to die and can die at will, intentionally, with full awareness of what he is doing, is a concept so alien to our culture that one scarcely dares mention it without an apology. One who presents this concept is accused of being "morbid," of suffering from an excess of the Freudian death wish, even of openly advocating suicide. But intentional dying has nothing to do with such flamboyant acts of self-destruction as setting fire to oneself or jumping off the Golden Gate bridge, or even with such quiet exits as can be obtained from an overdose of barbiturates. Intentional dying is possible only for one who has attained a high degree of mastery over his physical functions, who knows how to project the principle of consciousness out of the physical body, who is able to tell, by certain inner signs, when his time has come, and who is able with full awareness and without artificial aids to *let the life process come to a halt* so far as this particular body is concerned.

This process, though alien to Western thought, has long been understood in the East. W. Y. Evans-Wentz, commenting in *Tibetan Yogan and Secret Doctrines*[19] on two aspects of Tibetan yoga called "The Yoga of the After-Death State" and "The Doctrine of Consciousness-Transference," has this to say:

> No master of *yoga* ever dies in the normal manner, unless, perchance, he be killed suddenly and unexpectedly; he merely relinquishes the physical form which he has come to recognize as no more than a garment to be put on or off as desired, in full consciousness while immersed in the ecstatic condition of mind wherein the Clear Light ever shines. . . . It is through mastery of *Pho-wa* that the Great *Yogin* transcends normal processes by voluntarily relinquishing his old, outworn body and taking a new body, without suffering any break in the continuity of his consciousness. In the esoteric sense implied by the Christian initiate St. Paul, the grave thus loses its sting and death its victory; the Great *Yogin* becomes truly the Conqueror both of Death and of Life.

Needless to say, such an achievement is made possible only by years of intensive inner work. The great capacity for one-pointedness, for concentration of awareness, for indifference to pain and fearless confrontation of the unknown is not something to be acquired in a few weeks or a few months. In a truly creative community, the elder member approaching death would have both the knowledge and the power to face this final test with courage, regarding dying as a feat to be achieved rather than a fate to be passively suffered.

It is impossible for any student of Creative Psychology to *prove* that the process of dying can be accomplished without loss of consciousness, as is indicated in *The Tibetan Book of the Dead*. Nor can we prove that the attainment of a higher level of consciousness produces an entity capable of existing after death. The whole question of survival after death is cluttered with theories, befogged with wishful thinking and complicated with "evidence" obtained from mediums, much of it fraudulent. A skeptical biologist is liable to dismiss the idea of survival as another pathetic example of man's capacity for self-delusion. What, he will ask, is there to survive? The organism is a biochemical process, taking in and transforming materials. One side-effect (and quite a minor one) of this process is, in man, a sense of "I." But when the living process ceases, the sense of "I" must also cease. One does not even have to die for it to cease. It ceases every time man enters the first room and becomes, in deepest sleep, totally unaware of his existence. If anything survives death, it must have some form, be associated with matter or with energy, a cloud of electrons or even neutrinos. Vague talk about "souls" and "spirits" merely puts us back in the world of superstition which so muddled our ancestors and led them to so many disastrously incorrect conclusions.

The biologist's skepticism is justified. Not a shred of really sound evidence can be offered to suggest that there is any *personal* survival after death. So why bother about death at all? Why not take it simply as a termination of a process, the essence of which is an expression of potentials initially contained in the genetic code of the fertilized egg? This expression in man can be rich, diverse and complex, but it is programmed to terminate after approximately one hundred years and generally terminates before this time. To dream of something continuing independently of the complex physical machinery that formed the body is to indulge in wishful thinking, a pathetic dressing of the ego in a mantle of spurious immortality.

If we take this view, does it mean that the whole panorama of dying described in such detail in *The Tibetan Book of the Dead* is also a tissue of delusions? Not necessarily. The process of death may indeed involve all sorts of visions; the evidence obtained from those who have almost died supports this idea. But the "art of intentional dying" has nothing to do with *personal* survival after death. It involves rather a reblending of the separate consciousness with a larger, more generalized state that may be thought of as all-pervading. In the language of Tantric Buddhism, this state is called the *dharma-kaya,* and reentry into the *dharma-kaya* through the condition known as the Clear Light is what the master of yoga achieves at death.

Man in the third state of consciousness can no more understand this condition than a blind man can understand the nature of color or visual form. To understand what this means, a man must enter the fourth room and at least have glimpses of the contents of the fifth. For the *dharma-kaya* resembles that state of "being-nonbeing" which is beyond name and form, beyond the pairs of opposites and described in the *Upanishads* as the *atman.* He who wants a description of this state can hardly do better than read the message of Yama, Lord of the Dead, as it is written in the *Katha Upanishad:*

> THAT is not born, neither does it die; it sprang from nothing, nothing sprang from it. Unborn, eternal, everlasting, ancient, THAT is not killed though the body is killed.
>
> If the slayer thinks he slays, if the slain thinks he is slain, both are deluded; THAT slays not nor is it slain.
>
> Smaller than small, greater than great, in the heart of all creatures THAT resides, seen only by one who is free from desires and from grief.

Sitting still he walks far; lying down he goes everywhere; bodiless within bodies, unchanging among changes.

How can one who is not tranquil or subdued, whose mind is not at rest, understand THAT through mere knowledge?

How shall an ordinary man conceive THAT being, for whom both priest and warrior are as food, and death a condiment?

NOTES AND
BIBLIOGRAPHY

1. Szasz, T. S., *The Myth of Mental Illness* (New York: Hoeber-Harper, 1961).

2. "You're free. Choose. That is, invent." Sartre, J. P., *Existentialism and Human Emotions* (New York: Philosophical Library, 1957).

3. Berne, Eric, *Games People Play* (New York: Grove Press, 1964).

4. Von Neumann, J., and Morgenstein, O., *Theory of Games and Economic Behavior* (Princeton, N. J.: Princeton University Press, 1947); Wiener, Norbert, *The Human Use of Human Beings* (Garden City, N. Y.: Doubleday, 1954).

5. Hesse, Hermann, *Steppenwolf* (New York: Holt, Rinehart and Winston, Inc., 1963).

6. ———, *Magister Ludi* (New York: Frederick Ungar Publishing Co., 1957).

7. See section on "matrices and codes" in Koestler, Arthur, *The Act of Creation* (London: Hutchinson, 1964; New York: Dell, 1967).

8. Shakespeare, W., *The Tempest* (New York: Dell, 1961). This is the most esoteric of all Shakespeare's plays. Its central theme is the alchemical *Magnum Opus*, the forces which further this work and those which hinder it. For a modern variation on this theme, the reader

should consult Fowles, J., *The Magus* (Boston: Little, Brown, 1965).

9. Carthy, J. D., and Ebling, F. J., editors, *The Natural History of Aggression* (New York: Academic Press, 1965).

10. Some of the war poets (World War I vintage) had bitter things to say about this phrase:

> "If you could hear, at every jolt, the blood
> Come gargling from the froth-corrupted lungs,
> Bitter as the cud
> Of vile, incurable sores on innocent tongues,
> My friend, you would not tell with such high zest
> To children ardent for some desperate glory,
> The old Lie: Dulce et decorum est
> Pro patria mori."

(Wilfred Owen, *Poems* [New York: The Viking Press, 1931].)

11. "Creative thought, creative art or creative poetry are all excuses to expose the world to aberrations born in the sullied minds of the so-called intellectual élite of the West. The true creative artist never cries his creativeness to the skies. The true intellectual never claims to be one. It is the unfulfilled, the unsuccessful, the lazy and the foolish who weld together old bicycles and claim to be creative. They are surrounded by their kind who shower the rubbish with praises so that, in their turn, they may be the recipients of praise." (Shiekh Abdul Muhi in Rafael Lefort's *The Teachers of Gurdjieff* [London: V. Gollancz, 1966], p. 115).

12. Freud, Sigmund, *Civilization and Its Discontents.* (New York: Doubleday, 1958).

13. Jung's writings on alchemy are at times as obscure as the texts they interpret. The shortest and most lucid of his commentaries on this subject will be found in the chapter "The Work" in his *Memories, Dreams, Reflections* (New York: Pantheon Books, 1961).

14. This term, "waking sleep," is one of several technical terms used in the system of G. Gurdjieff, as intrepreted by P. D. Ouspensky. See Ouspensky's *In Search of the Miraculous* (New York: Harcourt, Brace & World).

15. For an account of the possible evolutionary origin of these obstacles, see de Ropp, Robert S., *Science and Salvation* (New York: St. Martin's Press, 1962).

16. An attempt to outlaw use of peyote by members of the Native American Church was made by the legislature of the State of California but was ruled unconstitutional by the State Supreme Court.

17. It must be admitted that Patanjali, the great Hindu commentator on yoga, describes "simples" (*ausadhi*) along with *samadhi* (roughly, a state of meditation) among the means of attaining the *siddhis* (yogic powers) but ". . . hemp and similar drugs produced *ecstasy* and not the yogic *samadhi*." See Mircea Eliade's book in note 19. According to the latter authority the use of hemp, opium or other narcotics belongs properly to shamanism, and to decadent shamanism at that.

18. "Verily there are many hard and almost unsurmountable obstacles in Yoga, yet the Yogi should go on with his practice at all hazards; even were his life to come to the throat." *Siva Samhita,* translated by Vasu, R.B.S.C. (Lahore, 1888; reprinted in Allahabad, 1914).

19. Creative Psychology, a modern synthesis, combines physiology and psychology, eliminates the artificial barrier created between them by dualistic theories separating mind and matter. There is no single formulation of the teaching. It cannot be learned from books, but only by practice under the guidance of a teacher. The author learned much that was of value to him from his own teachers, P. D. Ouspensky, G. Gurdjieff and others. See Ouspensky's *In Search of the Miraculous, op. cit.;* and his *A New Model of the Universe* (London: Kegan Paul, 1938); Gurdjieff, G., *All and Everything* (New York: Harcourt, Brace & Co., 1958); Gurdjieff, G., *Meetings with Remarkable Men* (New York: E. P. Dutton, 1964).

References will be made in this book to the "Gurdjieffian System," but the term is used only for convenience. The studies of Rafael Lefort in *The Teachers of Gurdjieff* (London: V. Gollancz, 1966) suggest that the special methods taught by Gurdjieff were relevant only for a certain time and are no longer valid at the moment. The reader must decide for himself to what extent the criticism is warranted.

Although it must be repeatedly emphasized that little can be learned from books, reading may be of some value in preparing the student and helping him to define what he needs to know. The student, however, should beware of substituting mere reading for actual practice and guard against losing himself in the jungles of terminology and the deserts of mere scholasticism. The following books may prove useful:

Bernard, Theos, *Hatha Yoga* (London: Rider and Co., 1950).

Eliade, Mircea, *Yoga: Immortality and Freedom* (New York: Pantheon Books, 1958).

Evans-Wentz, W. Y., editor, *The Tibetan Book of the Dead* (London, Oxford University Press, 1935).

————, *Tibetan Yoga and Secret Doctrines* (London: Oxford University Press, 1935).

Frankl, V. E., *Man's Search for Meaning* (New York: Washington Square Press, 1963).

Idries Shah, *The Sufis* (New York: Doubleday and Company, 1964).

Jacobs, H., *Western Psychotherapy and Hindu Sadhana* (London: Allen and Unwin, 1961).

James, William, *On Vital Reserves: The Energies of Men* (New York: Holt, 1939).

————, *The Varieties of Religious Experience* (London: Longmans, Green and Co., 1929).

Maslow, A. H., *Toward a Psychology of Being* (New York: Van Nostrand, 1962).

Mishra, R. W., *The Textbook of Yoga Psychology* (New York: The Julian Press, 1963).

Watts, Alan, *Psychotherapy East and West* (New York: Pantheon Books, 1961).

————, *The Way of Zen* (New York: Pantheon Books, 1957).

20. Madame Alexandra David-Neel has described in some detail the trials and tribulations of would-be initiates in Tibet during their search for a teacher. Admission to the Way is never made easy. Overcoming the obstacles deliberately put in the path demands heroic efforts on the part of the student. See David-Neel, Alexandra, *Magic and Mystery in Tibet* (New Hyde Park, N.Y.: University Books), Chapter V.

21. Leary, T., Metzner, R., and Alpert, R., *The Psychedelic Experience* (New Hyde Park, N.Y.: University Books, 1964).

22. Baudelaire, P. C., *Les Paradis artificiels* (Paris: Poulet-Malassis, 1860).

23. See de Ropp, R. S., *Drugs and the Mind* (New York: St. Martin's Press, 1951). Also Ebin, D., *The Drug Experience* (New York: The Orion Press, 1961).

24. An account of Daumal's experience was published in *Psychedelic Review* No. 5, 1965.

25. Cohen, Sidney, *The Beyond Within* (New York: Atheneum Press, 1965).

26. For the method of preparation, see "Chromatographic Separation of the Phenolic Compounds of *Cannabis sativa,*" *Journal of the American Pharmaceutical Association*, Scientific Edition, Vol. 49 (1960), p. 756.

27. Ludlow, Fitz Hugh, *The Hasheesh Eater* (New York: Harper Bros., 1857).

28. People vary enormously in their reactions to psychedelic drugs. For some, both peyote and its chief alkaloid, mescaline, are quite poisonous. Even a modest dose of 300 mg. causes chills, vomiting, general malaise. LSD can also be quite toxic for hypersensitive individuals at the usual dose level (150 micrograms). Seeds of morning glory and the scarlet caps of the fly agaric (*Amanita muscaria*) are even more dangerous and unpredictable.

29. Huxley, Aldous, *The Doors of Perception* (New York: Harper and Bros., 1954).

30. Watts, Alan, *The Joyous Cosmology* (New York: Pantheon Books, 1962).

31. Another variant of the myth is the Sufi fable of the Islanders. See Shah, I., *The Sufis* (New York: Doubleday, 1964).

32. Luce, G. G., *Current Research on Sleep and Dreams* (Washington, D.C.: U. S. Public Health Service Publication No. 1389, 1966). This admirable report should be carefully studied by students of Creative Psychology. It is available from the Superintendent of Documents, U. S. Government Printing Office, Washington, D.C., 20402, for 65 cents.

33. Kleitman, N., *Sleep and Wakefulness* (Chicago: University of Chicago Press, 1963).

34. Dill, S., *Roman Society from Nero to Marcus Aurelius* (New York: Meridian Books, 1956).

35. Leadbeater, C. W., *The Astral Plane: Its Scenery, Inhabitants and Phenomena* (London: Theosophical Publishing Society, 1898).

36. *Toward a Psychology of Being, op. cit.* (note 19).

37. Bucke, R. M., *Cosmic Consciousness* (Philadelphia, 1901).

38. Sinh, Pancham, translator, *Hatha Yoga Pradipika* (Allahabad: The Panini Office, 1932).

39. Bernard, Theos, *op. cit.* (note 19).

40. Vittoz, R., *Treatment of Neurasthenia by Teaching of Brain Control*, H. B. Brooke, translator (London: Longmans, Green and Co., 1911).

41. *The Conferences of John Cassian*, Part I, in *Nicene and Post-Nicene Fathers*, Vol. XI, E. C. S. Gibson, translator (London and New York: The Christian Literature Co., 1884).

42. *Bhagavad Gita*, Annie Besant and Bhagavan Das, translators

(Adyar: Theosophical Publishing House, 1940), Discourse Six, v. 34.

43. Suzuki, D. T., *Manual of Zen Buddhism* (Kyoto: Eastern Buddhist Society, 1935).

44. Reported in Heron, W., Doane, R. K., and Scott, T. H., "Visual Disturbances after Prolonged Perceptual Isolation," *Canadian Journal of Psychology,* 10 (1956): 13-18.

45. "By rousing himself, by earnestness, by restraint and control, the wise man makes for himself an island which no flood can immerse." *The Dhammapada,* Irving Babbitt, translator (New York and London: Oxford University Press, 1936).

46. The Stoic Epictetus clearly understood this aspect of Creative Psychology. "A man's only freedom is his freedom to deal with his impressions, to accept one, to reject another. All human history is shaped by this. Had Paris reacted differently to his impression of Helen, the Trojan War would not have happened and a great city and its people would not have been destroyed. See how much may depend upon reactions to impressions. Watchfulness therefore is the vital need, for he who does not watch is soon overwhelmed. The steersman need only sleep a moment and the vessel is lost." See *The Stoic and Epicurean Philosophers,* P. E. Matheson, translator (New York: Random House, 1940).

47. See *In Search of the Miraculous, op. cit.* (note 14), pp. 184–187.

48. This use of the words "carbon," "oxygen," "nitrogen" and "hydrogen" to describe matter in a certain state of excitation is an extension of the alchemical form of nomenclature. Alchemy was, on the one hand, a very inexact form of chemistry directed toward such material aims as the transmutation of base metals into gold and, on the other, a veil used by those interested in the practice of Creative Psychology at a time when the tyranny of the Church made any open admission of such interest dangerous. So the "gold" referred to by these alchemists described not the yellow metal, but a certain type of energy substances in the body on the level of which the attainment of higher consciousness was thought to rest. Thus, there were two different forms of alchemy. Esoteric alchemy was concerned entirely with processes taking place within the body.

48a. *The Maha Satipatthana Suttanta,* in Davies, T. W. Rhys, editor, *Sacred Books of the Buddhists* (London: Oxford University Press, 1921).

49. Giles, H. A., *Chuang-tze, Mystic, Moralist, and Social Reformer* (London: Quaritch, 1889).

50. Watts, Alan, *The Way of Zen, op. cit.* (note 19).

51. Menninger, K., Mayman, M., and Pruyser, P., *The Vital Balance* (New York: Viking Press, 1963).

52. French, R. M., *The Way of a Pilgrim* and *Pilgrim Continues His Way* (two volumes in one; New York: Seabury, 1952).

53. The preoccupation of C. G. Jung with *mandalas* has led to widespread misunderstanding of these *yantras* in the West. "Jung has introduced the term *mandalas* by mistake as it signifies in the East something entirely different from what it conveys to him: insofar as *mandalas* do occur in Indian or Tibetan spiritual practices, they are instruments for concentrating the mind, which has to pass beyond them." Hans Jacobs, *op cit.* (note 19).

54. *Bhagavad Gita, op. cit.* (note 42).

55. Ardrey, Robert, *The Territorial Imperative* (New York: Atheneum, 1966).

56. For a clear definition of the "will to meaning," see Frankl, V. E., *op. cit.* (note 19).

57. The entity is called "deputy steward" in Ouspensky's *In Search of the Miraculous* (*op. cit.*). The psyche of sleeping man is compared to a house full of disorderly servants. "The only chance of salvation is for a group of the more sensible servants to meet together and elect a *temporary* steward, that is a *deputy steward*. This deputy steward can then put the other servants in their places." The analogy seems a little farfetched. The Observer is the embryo of the Master, who represents that altered sense of self attained in the fourth state of consciousness.

58. Wolpe, J., "The Systematic Desensitization Treatment of Neurosis," *Journal of Nervous and Mental Disease,* 132 (1961): 198–203.

59. Jacobson, E., *Progressive Relaxation* (Chicago: University of Chicago Press, 1938). See also Schultz, J. H., and Luthe, W., *Autogenic Training: A Psychophysiological Approach in Psychotherapy* (New York: Grune and Stratton, 1959).

60. David-Neel, Alexandra, *op. cit.* (note 20).

61. Von Holst, Erich, and von St. Paul, Ursula, "Electrically Controlled Behavior," *Scientific American,* March 1962, p. 50.

62. Sheldon, W. H., *The Varieties of Temperament* (New York: Harper Bros., 1942).

63. Eysenck, H. J., *The Scientific Study of Personality* (London: Routledge, Kegan Paul, 1952).

64. Hoelzel, Frederick, "Use of Non-nutritive Materials to Satisfy

Hunger," *The American Journal of Digestive Disease,* 14 (1947); 401–404.

65. Carlson, A. J., and Hoelzel, F., "Apparent Prolongation of the Life-Span of Rats by Intermittent Fasting," *Journal of Nutrition,* 31 (1946): 363–375.

66. For a full account of these and other muscular exercises with appropriate illustrations, see Bernard, Theos, *op. cit.* (note 19).

67. See note on Kwanzan Kokushi's Admonition in *Manual of Zen Buddhism, op. cit.* (note 43), p. 180.

68. Evans-Wentz, W. Y., *Tibet's Great Yogi Milarepa* (London: Oxford University Press, 1928).

69. Goethe, J. W., *Faust* (Leipzig: Insel-Verlag).

70. Rumi, Jalaluddin, *The Mathnawi,* R. A. Nicholson, translator. (London: Cambridge University Press, 1926).

71. Williams, R. J., *Biochemical Individuality* (New York: John Wiley and Sons, 1956).

72. Cannon, W. B., *The Wisdom of the Body* (New York: Norton and Co., 1932).

73. For more information on neurohormones and their effects, see *Drugs and the Mind, op. cit.* (note 23).

74. For examples, see James, William, *On Vital Reserves, op. cit.* (note 19).

75. The physiological mechanisms underlying *tummo* are understood instinctively by many animals which inhabit cold environments. The process involves shunting the blood away from the extremities, the temperature of which is allowed to sink to a level close to the freezing point. This occurs in animals as diverse as the dog (husky), caribou, seagull, seal and polar bear. See Irving, Laurence, "Adaptations to Cold," *Scientific American,* January 1966, p. 94.) Evidently man does not know how to do this by instinct but can learn how to do it by attaining direct control over certain aspects of the working of the instinctive brain. (See David-Neel, Alexandra, *op. cit.* [note 20], p. 227.) Members of the Sir Edmund Hillary expedition to the Himalayas were amazed by the endurance of a Nepalese pilgrim who walked barefoot in the snow and wore only light cotton garments. They subjected him to "scientific" tests and published a paper on his reactions (Pugh, L.G.C.E., "Tolerance of Extreme Cold at Altitude in a Nepalese Pilgrim," *Journal of Applied Physiology,* 18 [1963]: 1234).

76. Ohsawa, G., *Zen Macrobiotics: The Art of Longevity and Rejuvenation* (New York: Ohsawa Foundation).

77. For a fuller account of the lamentable results of this misuse of the sex center, see Young, Wayland, *Eros Denied* (New York: Grove Press, 1964); and Taylor, G. R., *Sex in History* (New York: Vanguard Press, 1954).

78. The role of sex in the *Tantras* is discussed by Mircea Eliade in a section entitled "Mystical Erotism" in *Yoga: Immortality and Freedom, op. cit.* (note 19), p. 254. (The *Tantras* are a collection of about 64 Hindu books compiled in the 6–7th centuries and regarded as sacred texts.)

79. For more details concerning muscular control, see Basmajian, J. V., *Muscles Alive: The Functions Revealed by Electromyography* (Baltimore, Md.: Williams and Wilkins, 1962).

80. The process of the loss of inner aim and its slow and painful rediscovery is beautifully described in Hermann Hesse's allegorical novel, *Journey to the East* (New York: Noonday Press).

81. Nietzsche, F., *Thus Spake Zarathustra* (New York: Modern Library, Random House).

82. Emerson, R. W., "Self-Reliance," in *Essays* (New Haven, Conn.: Yale University Press, 1950).

83. Bucke, R. M., *op. cit.* (note 37).

84. Korzybski, A., *Science and Sanity* (Lancaster, Pa.: Internation Non-Aristotelean Library Publishing Co., 1933).

85. Longabaugh, T., *General Semantics* (New York: Vantage Press, 1957).

86. Boehme, Jakob, *Dialogues on the Supersensual Life* (New York: Frederick Ungar).

87. See, for example, Grinker, R. R., "Psychiatry Rides Madly in All Directions," *Archives of General Psychiatry*, 10 (1964): 228.

88. Eysenck, H. J., *The Uses and Misuses of Psychology* (Baltimore, Md.: Penguin Books, 1953).

89. This fact is recognized by the authors of *The Vital Balance* as regards psychiatry. "Psychiatry continues to expand. It is no longer the private esoteric wisdom of a few traditions. [Psychiatry] is a discipline served by doctors, psychologists, lawyers, judges, clergymen, and welfare workers; indeed by all social scientists theoretical and practical" (p. 7).

90. Bartemeier, L. H., et al., "Combat Exhaustion," *Journal of Nervous and Mental Diseases*, 104 (1946): 358–389.

91. Cleckley, H., *The Mask of Sanity* (St. Louis, Mo.: C. V. Mosby Co., 1955).

92. Fabing, H. D., "The New Pharmacologic Attack in Psychiatry," *Drug and Cosmetic Industry*, 78 (1956): 32.

93. For a detailed account of the *feeling* of schizophrenia, see Stefan, Gregory, *In Search of Sanity* (New York: University Books, Inc., 1966). The author emphasizes the futility of treating what is actually a biochemical disorder with the probings and questionings of psychoanalysis. According to some psychiatrists, there are two forms of schizophrenia—"process schizophrenia," which proceeds slowly but inexorably to a more or less incurable condition; and "reaction schizophrenia," brought on by stress with acute onset and favorable prognosis. For a simple account of the symptoms of this disorder, see *What You Should Know about Schizophrenia*, put out by the American Schizophrenia Foundation, P.O. Box 1000, Princeton, N.J.

94. Hsia, D. Y., *Inborn Errors of Metabolism* (Chicago: The Year Book Publishers, Inc., 1959).

95. "I wish to win at the Olympic Games.
"So do I, by the gods, for it is a fine thing.
"Yes, but consider the first steps to it and what follows: and then, if it is to your advantage, lay your hand to the work. You must be under discipline, eat to order, touch no sweets, train under compulsion, at a fixed hour, in heat and cold, drink no cold water, nor wine, except to order; you must hand yourself over completely to your trainer as you would to a physician. . . . Man, consider first, what it is you are undertaking: then consider your own powers and what you can bear. . . . Do you suppose that you can be a philosopher if you do as you do now, and indulge your anger and displeasure just as before?" (*Discourses of Epictetus*, Book III, Chapter 15, in Oats, Whitney J., editor, *The Stoic and Epicurean Philosophers* [New York: Random House, 1940].)

96. The powerful figure of Father Zossima, the elder, a figure drawn by Dostoevsky from life, stands out from among the other monks in *The Brothers Karamazov*. He is a product of monastic discipline which *followed* a full and sometimes violent life. He has thus a maturity and power which the other monks lack.

97. Bartoli, D., *History of the Life and Institute of St. Ignatius de Loyola* (New York: P. J. Kenedy, 1894).

98. Fromm, Erich, *Escape from Freedom* (New York: Farrar and Rinehart, 1941).

99. Jones, Idwal, *Vines in the Sun* (New York: William Morrow and Co., 1949).

100. Ouspensky's decision to break away from Gurdjieff and set up his own group (described in *In Search of the Miraculous,* see note 14) was made difficult by this uncertainty. Gurdjieff made much use of Outer Theater and the question whether he was playing a role or manifesting mechanically often troubled his followers.

101. The building of the Gothic cathedrals provides an example of the blending of inner work with the realization of an external aim.

102. The Oneida Community in New York State was founded in 1848 by John Humphrey Noyes and has endured to this day. Its continuation was assured not so much by psychological techniques as by its success in the production of distinctive silverware.

103. Gehman, Richard, "Amish Folk," *National Geographic,* August, 1965.

104. Skinner, B. F., *Walden Two* (New York: Macmillan, 1962).

105. Huxley, Aldous, *Island* (New York: Harper Bros., 1962).

106. For an up-to-date account of current efforts to form creative communities, the reader should consult *The Modern Utopian,* published bimonthly by Richard I. Fairfield, Tufts University, P. O. Box 44, Medford, Mass. 02153.

Muscular control: These exercises involve the practice of sensing and the practice of feeling. Sensing is *passive* awareness of a fully relaxed muscle or set of muscles. Feeling is *active* awareness of a muscle system produced by contracting both the muscle and its antagonist or contracting against a resistance (isometric contraction). Sensing and feeling exercises must begin with the facial muscles, which give man a key to the regulation of his "self-sense." They progress downward through the muscles of the neck and throat, the shoulders and arms, back, abdomen, upper and lower leg. First the muscle or muscle system is passively sensed, then actively felt. The exercise involves no outward perceptible movement so can be practiced anywhere. It is especially useful when tension is beginning to build up and control is becoming lost. The effort of focusing attention on the muscles, especially those of the face and diaphragm, will halt the build up of tension.

Asanas and *mudras:* These exercises involve the placing of the body in certain postures and holding it in those postures for a period of time, the length of which depends on the strength of the practitioner. Time is measured by number of breaths. Positions involving strong

Figure I

1. Headstand I	5. Supine Thunderbolt	3. Peacock Stand	13. Drawn Bow
2. Headstand II	6. Locust	10. Vajroli Mudra	14. Shoulder Stand
3. Headstand III	7. Cobra	11. Pascimottanasana	16. *Plough II
4. Thunderbolt	8. Bow	12. Reversed Bow	17. Half Spine Twist

*15. Plough I is the same as Plough II but with the legs fully extended.

muscular contraction are followed by relaxing postures. The sequence is as shown in Figure I.

Note: HEADSTAND. This posture as illustrated in texts on yoga shows the practitioner supporting himself with forearms on the floor, hands behind head. The posture here shown (fists on the floor) is less elegant but gives better control of balance.

SUPINE THUNDERBOLT. Upright position should be regained without bending at hips.

UDDIYANA and NAULI. These important exercises for the abdominal muscles are not shown here. For a full description with illustrations, see *Hatha Yoga* by Theos Bernard.[19] These exercises can be conveniently performed either standing or kneeling after position (3).

The standard exercises described in *Autogenic Training* by J. H. Schultz and W. Luthe can be used to induce the state of passive awareness needed for the proper practice of Inner Theater. The six exercises can be practiced in the posture of meditation (*siddhasana*) once the student has acquired the ability to hold this posture comfortably. The prostrate position recommended in *Autogenic Training* may be tried but is apt to induce drowsiness or actual sleep. Briefly, the six standard exercises are as follows:

I. HEAVINESS: "My right arm is heavy" (or left if the person is left-handed). The sense of heaviness corresponds to muscular relaxation of the limb in question. This sense of heaviness can be evoked in the arms, legs or any chosen region of the body.

II. WARMTH: "My right arm is warm" (or left arm or legs or other body region). Passive awareness of warmth in a given region induces a widening of the blood vessels in that area. This practice when fully mastered gives a measure of conscious control over the peripheral circulation of the blood. The technique is a part of hatha yoga and underlies the mastery of that art called by the Tibetans *"Tummo"* or the Generation of Psychic Heat (see Chapter VII).

III. CARDIAC REGULATION: "Heart beat calm and regular." This exercise helps the student to "discover" his own heart and take steps to regulate and steady its action. Again, this involves bringing a process which is normally autonomic partially under the control of the conscious will. The aim of the exercise is not to enable the student to "play tricks" with his heart. Its aim rather is to reinforce the self-regulating function of the heart, a vitally important property on which the welfare of the whole body depends.

IV. RESPIRATION: "It breathes me." The formula helps to induce completely relaxed, natural breathing. This is the exact opposite of *pranayama,* which involves the conscious control of breathing, including suspension of breath. From the physiological standpoint, the emphasis placed on breath control and especially on breath retention (*kevala*) in hatha yoga is puzzling. Theos Bernard has described[19] his own struggles with this technique. He acquired the power to suspend breathing for five minutes but states "this is far from the standard required by the texts for attaining the supernatural powers described in all Yogic literature. To acquire such powers it is necessary to hold the breath for an hour or more." It is hard to see how the anoxia (lack of oxygen in the blood) produced by such a practice could fail to inflict damage on the brain, which, of all organs of the body, is most sensitive to a lack of oxygen. However, among aquatic mammals, breath retention of 40 minutes (seal) or two hours (sperm whale) is possible. Presumably man can learn, by long and intense effort, to do what a seal does instinctively. The practice is certainly dangerous and its value questionable.

V. ABDOMINAL WARMTH: "My solar plexus is warm." The exercise is reputed to have a calming effect on central nervous activity. There is evidence that passive concentration on warmth in the upper region of the abdomen influences mechanisms in the liver and pancreas that regulate carbohydrate metabolism.

VI. COOLING OF THE FOREHEAD: "My forehead is cool." This exercise, like II, involves extension of voluntary control into an area usually out of the reach of the will. The cooling of the forehead is usually considered a calming and agreeable sensation, one that is effective in inducing drowsiness and sedation.

The "Meditative Exercises," with the exception of number four (VISUALIZATION OF ABSTRACT OBJECTS) can be useful to one who is beginning to practice the techniques of Inner Theater. The first and second of these exercises (EXPERIENCE OF COLORS) should convince those who have seen color visions when under the influence of mescaline that all these luminous colors can be generated once the student learns what inner mechanisms to activate. The "wonder worlds" of mescaline and LSD are all present in the mind and can be evoked at will without the drugs. The serious student will soon conclude that such performances are hardly worth the trouble of evoking, though they may provide some entertainment for those who enjoy this sort of inward display.

(*Autogenic Training: A Psychophysiological Approach in Psychotherapy,* by Schultz, J. H. and Luthe, W. [New York: Grune and Stratton, 1959].)

"You know that our breathing is the inhaling and exhaling of air. The organ which serves for this is the lungs which lie round the heart, so that the air passing through them thereby envelops the heart. And so, having collected your mind within you, lead it into the channel of breathing through which air reaches the heart and, together with this inhaled air, force your mind to descend into the heart and to remain there. Accustom it, brother, not to come out of the heart too soon, for at first it feels very lonely in that inner seclusion and imprisonment. But when it gets accustomed to it, it begins on the contrary to dislike its aimless circling outside, for it is no longer unpleasant and wearisome for it to be within. Just as a man who has been away from home, when he returns is beside himself with joy at seeing again his children and wife, embraces them and cannot talk to them enough, so the mind, when it unites with the heart, is filled with unspeakable joy and delight. Then a man sees that the kingdom of heaven is truly within us; and seeing it now in himself, he strives with pure prayer to keep it and strengthen it there, and regards everything external as not worthy of attention and wholly unattractive.

"When you thus enter into the place of the heart, as I have shown you, give thanks to God and, praising his mercy, keep always to this doing, and it will teach you things which in no other way will you ever learn. Moreover you should know that when your mind becomes firmly established in the heart, it must not remain there silent and idle, but it should constantly repeat the prayer: 'Lord, Jesus Christ, Son of God, have mercy upon me!' and never cease. For this practice, keeping the mind from dreams, renders it elusive and impenetrable to enemy suggestions and every day leads it more and more to love and longing for God." (E. Kadloubovsky and G. E. H. Palmer, Translators. *Writings from the Philokalia on Prayer of the Heart.* [London: Faber and Faber, 1951], p. 33.)

APPENDIX D:
BUILDING THE
SPIRITUAL EDIFICE

QUESTION: What is the good of having learned what is best if it cannot be attained even when known? The mind, which every moment wanders off vaguely, whenever it is brought back to spiritual contemplation, before it is established in it darts off and strays. When we have discovered that it has wandered and want to recall it to the meditation from which it has strayed, to bind it fast with the firmest purpose of heart as if with chains, even while we make the attempt it slips away like an eel out of the hand. Wherefore we, being inflamed by daily exercises of this kind, and yet not seeming to gain from them any strength or stability, are, in despair, driven to this opinion: that it is from no fault of our own but from a fault in our nature that these wanderings of the mind are found in mankind.

ABBOT SERENUS: It is dangerous to jump to a conclusion without sufficient evidence. Nor should you, looking only at your own weakness, pronounce judgment on the value of the practice itself. This is as if one who was ignorant of swimming came to the conclusion, because he himself could not hold himself up in the water, that this is the state of bodies generally. They cannot swim.

By its nature our mind cannot remain idle. Therefore unless it has in itself subjects prudently provided beforehand with which it can exercise its movements and be constantly engaged, it is inevitable that the mind, by reason of its mobility, should run here and there and fly everywhere until, through long exercise and constant practice (what you call useless labor), it learns by experience what materials it has to prepare in its memory, so that the mind can turn round them in its ceaseless flights, and through continually persevering in this work acquire the power to repulse suggestions of the enemy opposed to them, which formerly distracted the mind, and thus firmly remain in the desired state [of imperturbability and inner calm]. You see that it is in our power to place in our hearts either ascent, that is thoughts reaching to God, or descent, that is thoughts reaching downwards toward things earthly and carnal.

The activity of our mind can well be compared to a millstone which revolves rapidly with the rapid flow of water; but it lies in the power of the overseer to grind wheat, barley or cockle. In the same way our mind, in the course of the present life, being incessantly brought into movement by the streams of impressions rushing at it from everywhere, cannot be free from the tumult of thought. But it depends on our will and on our discretion which of those thoughts we accept and adopt.

The image of the perfect mind [ruling over its thoughts] is very well represented in the person of the centurion of the Gospels. In the story about him the moral power—giving the possibility of not being carried away by every incoming thought, but instead, by one's own judgment, of accepting the good thoughts and driving away without difficulty the adverse ones—is described in the following words, if taken figuratively: "For I am a man with authority, having soldiers under me, and I say unto one: Go, and he goes, and to another: Come, and he comes, and to my servant: Do this, and he does it."

If we, fighting valiantly against disorderly inner movements and passions, took the strength to subjugate them to our power and our reasoning, to extinguish the contending lusts of our body, to keep the disorderly crowd of our thoughts under the power of the yoke of reason, for such triumphs and victories we should be raised to the rank of centurion in its spiritual meaning. And in this way, having risen to the height of this dignity, we should have the same governing strength as he had and not be carried away by thoughts we do not desire, but would acquire the possibility of remaining in the thoughts which give us spiritual joy and would cleave to them, authoritatively commanding evil suggestions: Go away, and they will go, and inviting good thoughts: Come, and they will come.

But how can this be attained? It will come by itself when we unite with God with such utmost sincerity that he will act in us. Nothing that we may undertake with the object of conquering our thoughts can succeed unless God himself begins to act, having united with us. Then even our feeble means will become powerful and all-conquering. They will demolish the enemy's strongholds and will strike down and banish all thoughts.

Naturally this requires constant effort and work, but without this no success is possible in any undertaking. And still less can this be expected in such an important matter. No virtue can be perfected without labor and no one can subdue thoughts without strenuous work. The following words of Our Lord refer directly to this: "The Kingdom of Heaven suffereth violence and the violent take it by force."

Therefore all our attention must always be directed toward one thing, to recall our thoughts to a vivid remembrance of God from their wanderings and their moving in a circle. Just so one who, wishing to erect correctly and bring together the vaulting of a cupola, continually passes a chord from the center round the building and in this way gives an equal direction to its curvature everywhere. Whoever attempts to perform this task without this means, however great his craft, cannot keep the curvature faultlessly exact and cannot define by eye alone how much he has deviated from it. In the same way, unless our spirit, having fixed in itself as some immovable center the loving memory of God, bases itself upon it and verifies with it at every moment all his deeds and works, using it as a standard to determine the quality of thoughts and actions in order to accept some and repulse others, and at the same time, unless he uses this memory as a compass for giving the right direction to every thing he does he will fail to build the spiritual edifice as it should be built.

(Abridged from *Conferences of the Fathers in the Desert of Sketis,* by John Cassian, 360–435 A.D., in *Nicene and Post-Nicene Fathers, op. cit.*)

Index